Hide and Seek

THE ARCHAEOLOGY OF CHILDHOOD

Hide and Seek

THE ARCHAEOLOGY OF CHILDHOOD

JULIE WILEMAN

TEMPUS

This book is dedicated to
Douglas Wileman (1920-2003) the best father a child could have,
and all past and present members of Surrey Young Archaeologists Club

First published 2005

Tempus Publishing Limited
The Mill, Brimscombe Port,
Stroud, Gloucestershire, GL5 2QG
www.tempus-publishing.com

British Library Cataloguing in Publication Data.
A catalogue record for this book is available from the British Library.

ISBN 0 7524 3462 4
Typesetting and origination by Tempus Publishing Limited
Printed in Great Britain

CONTENTS

ACKNOWLEDGEMENTS

I should like to express my thanks to those who have helped and supported me during the writing of this book, particularly the following: Caroline Jones for her research and contributions; Judie English for her encouragement and editorial assistance; Paul Hill for his readiness to discuss and support the work; Steve Dyer and Dave Potts for their help with pictures and computer glitches; and Irene Luna and Hilary Underwood for picture research. I should also like to thank all those friends and students I have pestered over the last year on the subject.

Thank you to all the members of the Surrey Young Archaeologists Club whose enthusiasm, hard work and sense of fun have inspired me to write this book. This club's future is currently endangered because of financial difficulties. If there is any one cause that all archaeologists, professional or volunteer, should embrace and support, it is the encouragement and training of young people to secure the future of our past. Go and see what you can do to help your local branch of the YACs now!

INTRODUCTION

Over a number of years now I have worked on several archaeological excavations and surveys which have enjoyed the participation of members of the local Surrey Young Archaeologists Clubs, and great fun this has been. I have been vastly impressed by the hard work, dedication, intelligence and enthusiasm these children have shown in their desire to learn about the past and the practice of archaeology. It is a fact that we would have found it hard, if not impossible at times, to carry on without the skill and determination the children have shown. On a number of occasions and in many ways, we have relied on them and given them our trust, and they have never let us down. We are desperately proud of them. If children make such good archaeologists, then, why are children so rarely seen in the archaeological record?

This lack has been noticed by several other writers, notably Joanna Sofaer[1] Deverenski (1994) and Kathryn A. Kamp (2001). Kamp has considered one suggestion about why archaeology has failed to pay much attention to children. 'Perhaps the material traces children leave are minor and hard to interpret or are too difficult to untangle from those of adults'.[2] However, neither writer believes this to be true and both press for the inclusion of a study of the archaeology of children in the mainstream research of the discipline.

This book sets out to examine the evidence for children in the past, and to try to encourage others to bear in mind, when they are writing research designs for archaeological investigations or interpreting the material evidence for ancient cultures, that every society had children, that children would have been present at almost every site and that the roles of those children in their societies would have been significant in a number of ways.

Twenty-five years ago, Margaret Ehrenberg tried to explain why the role of women in the past had been undervalued and under-investigated. She discussed patriarchal attitudes, historical bias in gender valuation and the forms of evidence available for identifying women and their lives in the archaeological record. She noted the contributions made by anthropological studies, studies of other animals, documentary sources and archaeological studies of burial customs, paleopathology, craft and subsistence activities, settlement sites and art.[3] She concluded by saying: '...in the past many archaeologists have written accounts of prehistoric men in Europe, ignoring, albeit unconsciously, the prehistoric women with whom they must have shared their lives. But women did exist in prehistory, and can be made visible....'

Precisely the same argument is made in the present volume about children. It is possible that children have been largely ignored in archaeology for the same reasons that women, for so long, went unrecognised. Nineteenth- and earlier twentieth-century academics were part of a strongly male-dominated society, for whom women and children were adjuncts to their professional life rather than foci of it. Emphasis on materialist or, in the mid-twentieth century, Marxist concerns with industrial and cultural processes and production seemed necessarily to exclude women and children, who, if considered separately at all, were largely regarded as passive consumers rather than actors in the pattern of past societies. Various excuses have been made – children's bones do not survive as readily in the soil as those of adults, children's activities are too generic and ephemeral to leave much physical trace – and there seems to be a general subconscious assumption that what happened to children was not particularly interesting or culture-specific enough to be researched. 'Backwards inference from our own culturally specific concepts of childhood, as a prolonged period of dependence on the parent or an age of innocence, leads to an assumption that it is adults (i.e. fertile and sexually mature individuals) who have political and social control over the production of material culture and social ideologies'.[4]

All these excuses are patently untrue, as will be seen. Physical traces of children's lives and bodies are found for all periods and in just about every location where archaeological research has taken place. It is equally clear that the way children have acted and been regarded in their societies has differed enormously, both in comparisons to be made between cultures and time periods and in the different forms and levels of wealth, status, ethnicity or religion within any one society at any one time.

The arguments that have been made for the importance of recognising the position of women in ancient societies are concerned with the investigation of cultural attitudes, gender roles and economic contributions; it is important to understand the role of women, because without that it is not possible to understand the society as a whole. No society can be comprehended if only 50 per cent of it is known or considered. Equally, every society must produce children in order to survive. Every society will have been concerned with the upbringing of children – their care and nurture, education and training, their control and future. How these things were done must surely tell us a great deal about each society. Some societies held different values about male and female children, or healthy and disabled children, or rich and poor children. Some societies care for all children and dedicate themselves to their protection, whilst in others, children have been regularly abused or exploited. Children represent the future of a society and the ways in which they are brought up underline and perpetuate the beliefs and mores of their communities.

It follows, therefore, that the role of children should be an important area for archaeological research. In addition, the assumption that children are merely passive receptors of their society's attitudes and activities must be dismissed. Children are, and always have been, significant in economic and subsistence activities, both as workers and as supporters and influencers of their parents' work. They have often been extremely significant in religious and ritual beliefs and ceremonies, because of their perceived innocence and purity, their liminality (standing as they do between the normal, adult, everyday world and the mysterious realms before and beyond life from which they have come), and sometimes, because they were expendable and easily replaced. The nurture, education and entertainment of children have also been areas for adult employment and activity at least since classical times, with whole industries being dedicated to the production of the necessary equipment, clothing and toys for the young.

There are difficulties in tracing children in the archaeological record, it must be admitted. Many of these problems relate to the constructs of childhood that people make in their minds. In the modern world, we have a fairly clear idea of what we mean by the notion of childhood; it is by no means clear that past societies shared this clarity of concept. In different societies, the age at which a child is regarded as firstly human and secondly a full member of the community can vary greatly. We do not always know what counted as 'child', 'person', or 'adult' or indeed, as 'family'. Children in our modern western societies are quite clearly separated from other groups (for example, the elderly, or workers); they are restricted in their activities and roles by legal and social constraints and are accorded specific protections, services and supervision. This is not always the case in other parts of today's world, however, where children enter the workforce much earlier, and are often expected to care for themselves to a much greater extent. Children in the Third World as, we can assume, in many past societies, are much more integrated into the society around them.

Children are capable of creating their own societies and artefacts, and should not be regarded as simply passive recipients of adult care or abuse. They are agents of their own lives and can affect and change the world around them. 'Children learn from adults and act as the recipients of culture, but children also learn from other children, innovate, and pass their innovations on to other children and perhaps adults as well'.[5] Having children alters the behaviour of adults, affecting their subsistence activities, the way they react to threats to their own or their children's security, the resources they have available and the choices of lifestyle available to them or preferred by them. Nor are children uniformly innocent or powerless. Children can and do commit crimes, even murder; they can fight in wars and terrorise others. The upbringing of Spartan children, for example, seems very reminiscent of the *Lord of the Flies*, with gangs of boys living wild, stealing their food and struggling for supremacy amongst themselves.

All these issues are surely central to most forms of archaeological understanding and interest; it is all the more surprising, then, that so few conscious efforts have been made to integrate the study of children into research designs and interpretative strategies. It also seems particularly surprising that so few feminist archaeologists have recognised or commented on the neglect of children in archaeological research. There are, of course, important exceptions and more articles have appeared on the topic in recent years, but many of these are highly academic and offer complex and erudite arguments that are perhaps difficult for non-theorists to come to terms with. The present contribution to the subject is intended to bring the topic of children in the past to as wide an audience as possible, in the hope that if more recognition of the presence of children in past societies is achieved, more evidence may be gathered, and the academic community will have more material to work with to explain and understand the lives of our ancestors.

This book is organised into sections which attempt to collate evidence for children in archaeology under some simple headings – care and nurture, education and training, the death and burial of children, children and beliefs, issues to do with the suffering and abuse of children, the role of the child in human evolution, and the progress of the child towards adulthood. Under the first heading, some of the customs regarding childbirth are briefly examined, together with examples of information about clothing and appearance, toys and games and the domestic space the children inhabited. There is some archaeological evidence for the more formal types of education given to children in past societies and their inculcation into the knowledge and skills they will require as adults; evidence for their working lives is harder to establish, but there is some, examples of which are discussed.

The evidence for the death, burial and commemoration of children is more obviously available to archaeological research, although until recent years much of the material was sometimes treated rather cursorily, the real interest of the excavator being the bodies and artefacts of adults. The graves of children, however, are capable of offering us information about the organisation and status of social groups, and deserve closer study. Modern scientific techniques are now able to provide a great deal more information about the lives of the children whose bodies we find and this is a great area for future potential. The role of children in ritual activities has also been rather more studied than other aspects of their lives. Children have been sacrificed or worshipped (sometimes both) in various ways and for different reasons in many societies. Some of these instances are discussed in this volume, in an attempt to understand the processes at work.

The effects of war upon children are often severe, as they are frequently specifically selected as victims or are more susceptible to damage in one way or another than adults; starvation and disease also tend to affect children particularly badly. Much attention has been paid in the past to warriors and battlefields, destruction horizons and weaponry. A study of the children involved in war can only help to add richer dimensions to our understanding of conflict in the past. Studies of slavery also often tend not to consider the child, and yet child slaves are relatively common in iconographic sources. Children have also suffered physical abuse, both at home and in the sphere of labour and many have fallen into crime and prostitution. The lives of these children deserve our recognition, not least for the way in which they illuminate the state of the societies from which they were otherwise excluded.

A few thoughts are offered about the role of children in the evolution of our species; admittedly, these are hardly original and the debt to other, greater, authors is fully acknowledged. It would not, however, seem right to exclude discussion of some of these ideas, as potentially, they offer a fundamental reassessment of the way in which humans gained their advantages over other primates. Finally, consideration is given to the evolution of the child into the adult, via rites of passage of various forms, which allows an opportunity to consider interpretations and symbols of recognition of stages of development in past societies.

The data presented is necessarily very incomplete and, perhaps, simplistic in its analysis. Much reliance is placed on documentary and iconographic material, especially where archaeological research is underdeveloped, or physical evidence is lacking. Partial and faulty though it may be, however, it is hoped that this book will stimulate others to take the research much further, to gather far more material and to create a developed archaeology of childhood in the future.

I

LITTLE DARLINGS –
THE CHERISHED CHILD IN
THE PAST

It is not possible to love the small child, the middling-sized child, or the
older child. It is hard to raise the small infant and it does not permit people
to sleep at night. The middling-sized child wanders out into the street and
must be protected against horses and carts. The older child fights his father
and must be dragged out of the tavern.'
(J. Ulrich, 'La Riote du Monde', *Zeitschrift für Romanische Philosophie* 7 (1884) 282-3)

The love between parents and offspring is considered to be one of the most
important characteristics of upper animals. Many animals display extraordinary
determination and ferocity in their attempts to provide for and to protect their
young, and sometimes we may even be able to see signs of real emotional
attachment that transcends basic needs and instincts, for example among
elephants and some apes. The human species is special in that it possesses extra
abilities, such as speech, laughter, reasoning and the ability to predict future
events, which together add many further dimensions to the natural bond.

Human young are dependent upon their parents for a far longer time than is
the case with other animals. The human child is born less well developed, less
able to survive on its own, and it needs to learn far more before it can function in
our complex societies. It seems, therefore, that Nature has predisposed us to give
children this extended training and protection by providing us with hormonal
and instinctive reactions that ensure our attachment to our children. This, of
course, can be seen in other animals, but for humans, this is supplemented by
additional factors that allow us to maintain this attachment for a much longer
time; indeed, throughout our entire lives. We do not, usually, growl and threaten
our children to encourage them to leave once they are big enough to care for

themselves. We continue to recognise them and to feel particular sentiments towards them even after they have flown the nest and created families of their own. Few other animals demonstrate this extended connection.

So it seems there is more to the relationship between human parents and children than a simple genetic or Darwinian tendency designed to promote the survival of our species. Humans have the ability to love unconditionally, to offer love to children other than their own biological progeny, and even to despise and harm children, both their own and those of others. We are not just creatures of instinct and the products of chemistry; our attitudes to children are conditioned by social experience, learning, prediction and rationality as well as by Nature.

The manner in which children have been regarded and treated in ancient societies highlights the way in which people in those communities experienced childhood as part of a much wider set of social and cultural norms particular to them. The treatment of children reflects notions about the value of human life, about the place in society of people of different classes, occupations, gender, wealth, belief and ethnicity, and about attitudes towards the past and the future. The way children are nurtured and prepared for entry into their adult community illuminates the nature of that community and its attitudes towards itself and its posterity. This makes the study of the archaeology of childhood an important tool in the interpretation of the past of the human species and the ways in which it has developed.

Evidence for the love and care that parents in the past have lavished upon their children may be found in the physical artefacts left behind. These include objects specially designed or modified for the feeding, clothing, housing and care provided for children, the provision of education, socialisation and entertainment, and the tragic memorials raised by loving parents to children who have died. There are also records and descriptions of ceremonies that celebrated the birth of children, and their achievement of stages of growing up and acceptance into the wider adult society of their communities.

In our own society, the equipment and commodities associated with the loving care and upbringing of children form the basis of multi-billion pound industries; parents are, like it or not, drawn into a spiral of competitive buying in order to demonstrate the extent of their love for their children through their provision for them, a spiral that becomes, effectively, social blackmail. Prehistoric parents were, as far as we know, not bombarded with constant advertisements and comparisons at the school gate! But perhaps one can wonder whether the palaeolithic mother who failed to provide her baby with a nicely-cured doeskin matinee jacket was regarded with opprobrium by her peers! The matinee jacket, it has been suggested, actually represents one of the oldest forms of clothing design in the history of humankind, being based upon the most economic and simple use of the belly skin of a fawn – easy to cut and construct yet soft, warm and durable (1). If this is true, it must say something about the importance loving and caring for children has had for the human species since earliest times.

1 The earliest cut pattern? How the baby's matinée jacket may have derived from the skin of a fawn (cutting lines shown solid, sewing lines shown dashed)

INFANT CARE AND NURTURE

Many societies have left written records that offer clues about the way the birth of children was regarded. The physical evidence for infant care is much less obvious as many aspects of this stage in the raising of children are likely to leave little or no archaeological trace. It is the mother who provides protection, food, warmth and care, and there may be little or no need to develop specific artefacts for these purposes. Even if artefacts were created, they are likely to have been made of organic substances that rarely survive archaeologically: cloth, wood, animal skin and tissue, plant materials and so on. Rarely, such artefacts survive, but for the most part the best we can do is make informed guesses about infant care. About other aspects of childhood, however, there are some physical clues and information, derived not only from artefacts, but from pictures and ancient writings.

Childbirth has been met, in various societies, with a variety of attitudes which have ranged from joy and celebration to fear and the implementation of protective rites. In ancient Egypt, the infant was regarded as an embodiment of the god Horus, who is sometimes depicted sitting on the lap of his mother Isis, ranking amongst the earliest examples of Madonna and child iconography.[1] Naming took place during the birth itself; the names chosen reflected either the presence of a deity (for example 'May Amun protect him') or loyal sentiments towards the king (such as 'Sneferu is good') or, most charmingly, the words of the mother welcoming her child (an example being 'The pretty girl has joined us'). The choice was generally, it seems, the mother's; the child would also often be given a nickname, less grandiose but easier to use day to day, which might reflect some physical attribute. Hieroglyphic inscriptions and ancient graffiti provide many examples of these names.

The Aztecs regarded women who were giving birth as brave warriors fighting to produce more warriors, and a woman who died during childbirth was accorded divine status.[2] In this society, the birth of children was regarded as a kind of victory and was celebrated as such, whereas Judaic and Christian traditions have tended to regard the new mother and her child as dangerous and unclean. Classical, Biblical and later written sources illustrate a range of different attitudes. A Jewish mother obeying the rules set out in Leviticus finds herself to be regarded as unclean for seven days after the birth of a male child, until he is circumcised on his eighth day, and still polluting for a further 33 days, unable to touch hallowed objects or enter holy places such as synagogues. If she gives birth to a female child, the periods are longer – 14 days of 'uncleanliness' and 66 days of being polluting.

Medieval Christians inherited the belief that the child was inherently unclean. 'The custom of baptizing an infant several days after birth was inspired by the negative image of childhood. The human infant, having been born in sin as the fruit of sexual intercourse of his parents, which since the original sin has been marked by carnal lust, and as the heir of the sin of Adam and Eve, must be cleansed of the sin of his conception and heritage immediately after his birth'.[3] Augustine of Hippo held that 'It is the weakness of the infant's body which is innocent, not his soul'.[4] Aristotle found the child to be flawed and incomplete, incapable of noble actions, and his attitudes were adopted by a number of early Christian writers. 'St Augustine attempted to initiate a Christian belief that an infant who died without being baptized was condemned to hellfire; this extreme view, however, was never widely adopted and, from the twelfth century onwards, it was thought that although an unbaptised infant could not enter heaven, nor would it be consigned to hellfire, but rather it would go into Limbo'.[5] Pope Innocent III regarded the whole business of childbirth and childhood as disgusting; children were 'conceived with lasciviousness and filth, brought forth with sorrow and pain, nourished with trouble and labour, watched over with anxiety and fear'.[6] Certainly childbirth was a period of fear; mortality rates were high for both mother and child. Care of the mother was generally placed in the hands of a midwife, and many of these women had a great deal of practical experience and common sense, but options were often limited. Early marriages for dynastic purposes frequently put the life of the women at risk. Margaret Beaufort was only 13 when she gave birth to the future Henry VII, and the lasting physical damage she suffered made her reluctant to impose an early marriage on her granddaughter, despite the political benefits to be gained. If a midwife could not cope, the choice lay between miraculous intervention, as in the case of the young lady 'not yet of an age at which she should have become a mother',[7] saved by a relic of Thomas à Beckett or the dubious assistance of a member of the medical profession. 'The arrival of a surgeon during a difficult delivery almost invariably spelt death and dismemberment, the main goal being to remove the child for emergency baptism, should a flicker of life remain, and ensure that the mother, freed of her burden, could be buried in consecrated ground'.[8]

A more popular and less misogynist view of children was based on *Matthew* 18:3-6 which advises believers to 'become as little children' implying notions of innocence, beauty and purity of soul; it is from this that the worship of Christ as a child derives, along with the later medieval veneration of the Madonna. Saints were assigned to the process of childbirth (Antony of Padua, Margaret and Dorothy) and the state of pregnancy became such a fashionable concept that clothing styles for women imitated the condition. Nevertheless, the taboo against new mothers attending church for a period remained – children were usually baptised at the age of one week in their mothers' absence. Anthropological sources have recorded similar fears associated with childbirth. The Kaulong people of New Britain share the notion of childbirth as a time of danger for the rest of the community – a woman at the time of childbirth is forbidden to go near sources of water or to enter gardens lest she leaves behind pollution that will make adult men of the tribe ill.

On the other hand, a notice painted on a wall at Pompeii shows that some Roman parents were proud to announce their new arrivals: 'Our daughter was born early in the evening of Saturday, August 2'.[9] Nevertheless, Romans too regarded the newborn and mother as unclean, possibly even dangerous. Ritual purification of the house took place eight days after the birth of a female child, nine days after a boy was born, and involved, in the richer houses at least, a complex ceremony involving vigils, the challenge of three men armed with an axe, a pestle and a broom, and the use of divination of birds to predict the infant's future. Children were given a bulla or amulet to wear around their necks for protection, which, in the case of a boy, was not removed until he reached the age of manhood. The Emperor Augustus became concerned about the declining birth rate among the Roman aristocracy and introduced legislation to encourage large families, commissioning the poet Horace to write songs to propitiate divine assistance in increasing the birth rate. Augustus also initiated the registration of births publicly in the forum. The Latin word *infantia* means 'unable to speak', and in the Roman world there was a general acceptance that an infant under 40 days old was not fully human, and therefore could be excluded from the law that burial should not take place within a town or settlement. Indeed, there is no Latin word for 'baby'. Infants were buried within or close to houses or even under the eaves of houses.[10] Children born with defects, of the wrong gender, or otherwise regarded as unwanted were often disposed of immediately after birth. Many methods for killing these children are unlikely to be detectable – they could be exposed in the wilderness, drowned, smothered, or simply left neglected and unfed. However, it is clear that not all societies reacted to handicapped children in such a draconian way. In Anglo-Saxon cemeteries, adolescents with birth defects are represented, and in one instance, a specially modified pot designed to be used by a child with a cleft palate has been found.[11] The ancient Greeks regarded twins as abnormal 'because their formation is contrary to the general rule and to what is meant', according to Aristotle. The ancient Romans may have shared this belief, perhaps explaining the exposure of the twins Romulus and Remus before they were found and suckled by the she-wolf.

Medieval children, once they were born, were washed with warm water, milk or wine, or perhaps with salt, rose petals or olive oil. Honey might be rubbed around the baby's mouth to encourage it to feed, and a female doctor, Trotula, practising in Salerno in the twelfth century, recommended washing the tongue with hot water to make sure the child would learn to talk.[12] The baby would then be swaddled and placed in its cradle in a dark place, because it was believed that bright daylight would harm its eyes.

The Maya people of Central America used cradleboards, one type of infant-related artefact that has been found. In Yucatan, mothers washed their new born infants and then strapped them into a cradleboard that pressed the baby's head between two rigid planes:

> The Maya treatment of their infants had the effect of producing a permanent fore-and-aft flattening of the head, which was considered to be a sign of beauty. The parents also visited a Mayan priest to learn the destiny of their infant and the name it was to bear, and there followed a ceremony which bore a strong resemblance to baptism …. Slightly crossed eyes were considered to be attractive or desirable, so parents attempted to maintain or induce the condition in their babies by hanging small beads over their noses.[13]

A number of figurines display these cranial and facial characteristics, and finds of skulls in burials show deformations of the shape of the head reflecting the use of cradleboards in a number of areas of Meso- and South America. The Mayan baptism ritual took place at an auspicious time when sufficient boys and girls aged between three and twelve were available for the ceremony. From this time on, they were regarded as full members of the community and were prepared for their future roles. The Aztecs also had birth rituals signifying the future roles of the children; the umbilical cords of boy children were buried on a battlefield, while those of girls were placed beneath the family hearth or quern stone, and a naming ritual took place in which miniature objects, often made of aramanth

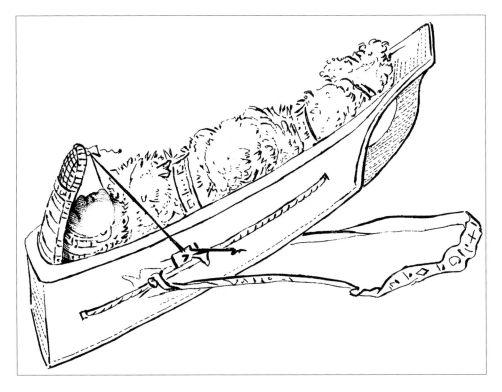

2 Drawing of an American Indian cradle with board for flattening the baby's forehead. *Courtesy of the Wellcome Library, London*

seed dough, were presented to the babies (a shield, bow and arrows for boys and spinning and weaving tools for girls). Water was then poured over the baby's head, and girls were placed in their cradles while boys were publicly lifted four times to the sun.[14] Some of these customs were recorded by the Spanish at the time of their conquest of the region, whilst others remained current for a long time afterwards, especially in more remote districts. The practice of artificially shaping a baby's skull through the use of cradleboards was also performed among indigenous tribes across North America up until the early twentieth century (*2*).

Interestingly, and perhaps confusingly for latter-day investigators, it was reported by the explorers Lewis and Clark in their journey across the heart of America in 1805 that the Flathead Indians were so named because they had normally shaped heads, unlike the cone shape of neighbouring tribes.[15] Deliberate alternation of the shape of a child's skull through the application of boards is recognised in several areas, but it has been argued that it also occurred unwittingly, for example by the Attapakan tribe, through use of cradleboards to free mothers' hands for work tasks.[16]

Among the Inuit of Northern Canada and Greenland, children were seen as part of a continuum of the life of their society. A new baby was given the name of someone who had recently died, receiving not just a name but a 'name spirit' from that person, along with some of their attributes:

> Once a name had been bestowed, it became a compelling factor in the development of a child's character and personality, and a crucial element in his or her relations with other people.[17]

The naming ceremony generally took place about four days after birth; from this time on the child was not just a child, but a known person into which it would develop. Its life course was predetermined by the associations carried within the name, something that even allowed crossing of gender roles, so that if a girl baby acquired the name of a recently deceased hunter, she would be expected to grow up with the skills of her namesake, and not be confined to more traditionally female activities such as cooking and preparing skins. Very young children were recipients of much affection and care; for the first year and a half of their lives they were carried in their mother's hoods, and were the centre of family attention.

Babies, therefore, have been the recipients of a range of differing attitudes by various societies. Most, we must assume, were warmly welcomed, despite the fears associated with the birth process, attitudes perhaps more closely aligned with the way women were regarded than directed at the child itself.

FEEDING AND CLOTHING THE BABY

The normal method of feeding babies is, of course, with breastmilk from the mother, although the employment of wet nurses is known from Pharaonic Egypt (e.g. *Exodus* 2:7) and Biblical Israel (recorded in *Genesis* 35:8; 2 *Kings* 11:2; 2 *Chronicles* 22:11) as well as ancient Greece and Rome, and they continued to be used into the recent past.

The process of weaning the child onto solid food has varied from society to society, particularly with regard to the age at which this occurs, and the form of food offered to the child. At the Palaeolithic site of Wadi Kubbaniya in Upper Egypt, infant faeces have been identified on the grounds of composition and provenance; they contained sand, which crawling infants are more likely to pick up and ingest.[18] The analysis showed that children were weaned on pulped and mashed vegetable foods at the age when they were crawling – grinding stones have been found at the site, and there is a very broad range of plant species indicated from the remains.

Egyptian reliefs depict breastfeeding, including that of Queen Nefertiti feeding one of her daughters that was found at Amarna. There is written evidence of the use of magical incantations to remedy shortage of milk, and some pottery jugs depicting nursing mothers may have been used to hold surplus milk. Hollow clay figures of women which have holes in the nipples may have had a similar purpose or have been used in the rituals of sympathetic magic to encourage lactation. The milk of mothers of male children was regarded as especially potent in curing children's ailments, and little jugs shaped in the form of Isis kneeling with her child Horus at her bosom were used to store it. Incantations accompanied its use:

> Flow out, Daughter of all Colds, who breakest bones, grips the skull and dost
> painfully molest the seven openings of the head! O companion of Re, give
> honour to Thoth! Behold, I bring thee thy medicine, thine own saving potion,
> the milk of a woman who gave birth to a he-child....

It was believed that a sick nursing child could be cured by administering medicine to the mother; it is only in recent times that the effect of drugs passed on in breastmilk has been recognised and utilised in medical treatment. Children were normally breastfed for three years, according to various documentary references. Where a wet nurse was used, she would bring the child into her own home if it was from a poor family, or she would move into the parents' home if they were rich but, in either case, she was subject to a contract which stipulated that parents should be shown the child at regular intervals to ensure it was prospering, to nurse no other children but her own, and to refrain from pregnancy and sexual activity. The parents agreed to take the child back only when weaned, to provide its clothing and oil for its body, and to pay for the milk and the nurse's food. The Egyptian royal children were provided with many other nurses and tutors for their care, and particular wetnurses are remembered by portraits and inscriptions in the tombs of their former charges. Papyrus No. 3027 in the Berlin collection is entitled *Spells for Mother and Child* and includes written precepts and incantations designed to protect infants from a variety of ills. Amulets were another form of protection, and many have been found in children's graves. Various forms of amulet are associated with children, such as the 'eye of Horus', but many consisted of spells written on tiny papyrus rolls, folded into miniature cylindrical boxes made of wood or metal (3).

A Middle Kingdom amulet case in the Petrie Museum is made of gold-covered copper alloy and contained three small balls of copper wire and some traces of an organic substance which may have been papyrus. An example found at Deir el-Medina contains a spell against catching the common cold, and others sought protection from a wide range of evils including bites from poisonous creatures, blindness, leprosy, demonic spite and black magic and mischievous spirits. Much attention was paid to particular diseases such as intestinal problems and skin and eye complaints, very common along the warm and damp banks of the Nile.

Recent studies of carbon and nitrogen isotopes in bone collagen at an Iron Age cemetery at Wetwang in Yorkshire have suggested that although most adults subsisted on a diet rich in animal protein, the bones of the infants seemed to

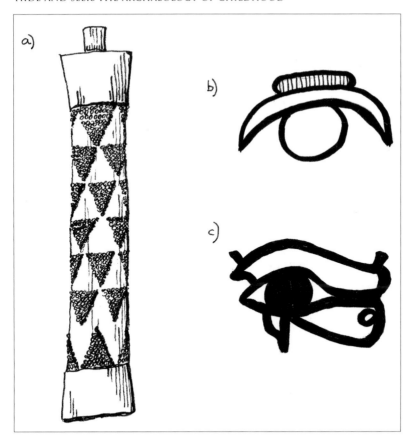

3 Ancient Egyptian measures to protect children from disease or harm:
a) a Twelfth-Dynasty cylindrical child's amulet case. Copper overlain with gold,
approx. 5cm long; b) a rising moon amuletic sign; c) an Eye of Horus protective sign

show that they had been fed on cow's milk at an early stage in their lives. Two
possible explanations for this have been offered: either children were being fed
cow's milk early in order to 'toughen the children up', or during pregnancy
and/or breastfeeding, women became vegan, possibly because of some dietary
taboo. It is suggested that the cow's milk diet may have led to higher levels of
infant mortality.[19] Other explanations are possible; breastfeeding can act as a
form of contraception, so early introduction of other sources of food may have
allowed more frequent pregnancies, desirable if large families are preferred. The
use of cow's milk may have allowed women to undertake work more quickly
after giving birth, perhaps leaving babies with a minder who could thus feed
them in the mother's absence. There may also have been connections between
the introduction of children to cow's milk and the value placed upon cattle as
a symbol of wealth and success in Iron Age society. Unfortunately, Iron Age
skeletal remains in Britain are extremely rare, and the inhumation ritual practised

at Wetwang among people of the Arras culture is not found elsewhere, so we are unlikely to find other contemporary populations with which we can compare these findings and interpretations.

In Anglo-Saxon England, weaning appears to have been achieved around the age of two years; Bede suggests that a couple were supposed to refrain from sexual relations until the child had been weaned, but that some people flouted this rule by employing wet nurses. Apparently cow horns were used as feeding bottles. Young children were given pap (bread or cereal soaked in milk or water), and bread was seen as a general staple of children's diets. Children were exempted from fasting and religious dietary laws, even in monasteries, but they were not allowed wine. Meat and ale were thought desirable for older children to enable them to grow well.

A study of the bone stable isotope evidence from the medieval village of Wharram Percy in North Yorkshire has shown that here, infants were weaned between the ages of one and two. This remained the case through the 600 or so years of the village's life, and represents a rather earlier cessation of breastfeeding than might naturally be the case. One study suggests that any time between two-and-a-half and seven years old might be the 'natural' age.[20] The apparent conformity at Wharram Percy indicates 'that breastfeeding duration was generally constrained by community-wide cultural factors rather than decisions being made freely according to individual circumstances'.[21] In other words, in this community, weaning was a process that had a generally accepted timescale, as is generally the case today. This implies several things – that suitable alternative foods for babies were available, that the activities of mothers (working, caring for other children and the like) encouraged them to make the choice to wean their babies at a certain stage, that mothers were not consciously attempting to use continued lactation as a form of contraception, and perhaps that there was general agreement about the desirability and suitability of a cessation of breastfeeding after a certain period. We cannot know which, if any, of these implications were dominant or even fully recognised by the women of Wharram Percy at the time, but we can see the effects.

Alternative medieval methods, used when the mother was unable to feed her child, included soaking a rag or bread in milk for the child to suckle, or pouring milk into the child's mouth through a horn. A common weaning practice was for the mother or nurse to chew food to a paste and then transfer it to the baby's mouth, which may seem unhygienic, but is common among many animals. Saliva contains enzymes which have antibiotic qualities.

Swaddling of medieval children was designed to keep their limbs straight as they grew, but babies were not kept constantly swaddled and in some societies the practice was not used as all. Giraldus Cambrensis noted that Irish children grew well and straight without ever being swaddled. For the peasant mother, swaddling or tying her child while she worked might be a way of keeping it safe from harm in the fields or farmyard or kitchen. No skeletal evidence has been found which would suggest any deformity resulting from this practice.

The necessities for a late medieval child of means may be inferred from the list given in *The Gentle Craft*, a novel of about 1597, quoted by Nicholas Orme:

> beds, shorts, biggins, waistcoats, headbands, swaddlebands, cross-clothes, bibs, tail-clouts, mantles, hose, shoes, coats, petticoats, cradle and crickets, and beside that a standing-stool and a posnet to make the child pap.

(Biggins were caps and a cross-cloth was a linen cloth worn across the forehead; tail-cloths may have been nappies or wiping cloths; a cricket was a small stool for the mother to sit on beside the cradle, and a standing-stool was a baby walker; a posnet was a kind of ceramic saucepan on legs, perhaps for warming milk or pap.[22])

Poorer medieval children may have been simply clothed – we have very little evidence for babies' costume of the period. A plain shift dress would be easy to wash and put on the child. The custom of dressing small boys and girls identically, which persisted into the Victorian era, was equally practical. Changing the baby is a much simpler proposition if it is wearing skirts rather than the complex tied breeches of the older male.

The way in which children were presented and dressed indicated many things, among which were wealth and status, gender, and stages of development. Changes in hairstyle and costume were important as indicators of the degree of maturity and social integration achieved by the child as it grew.

Ancient Egyptian children are often depicted naked except for a necklace or an amulet. To what extent nakedness is an artistic convention is open to argument. Writers such as Turek have pointed out that 'in the winter at least it is distinctly cold in the early mornings and late evenings [in Egypt]; nor is it confirmed by real garments that have survived'.[23] It may be that while clothing was available for young children, it was only obligatory when they reached puberty. Nakedness in paintings and monuments can be regarded as an artistic emblem for childhood, a kind of symbolic shorthand. There is also evidence to suggest that at different periods there were varying attitudes towards nudity in Egyptian society, sometimes reflecting religious concepts.

Where clothes are shown, they seem to be similar to those of adults. The dry climate of Egypt has preserved some actual examples of ancient children's clothing, including a pleated dress in fine linen, which may make a claim to be the world's oldest surviving garment. It was found in a mastaba tomb at Tarkhen (4) and has been dated to about 2800 BC. 'Creasing, particularly round the armpits and elbows, proves that the dress was worn in life. It had been pulled off over the head, the sleeves with their very narrow wrists following in an inverted manner, and was so discovered inside-out'.[24] A number of sleeves have survived from children's costumes, and were apparently separately attached as required to tunics and dresses.

The tomb of Tutankhamun contained a large number of children's clothes and accessories, probably those the boy-king wore in his youth. There are

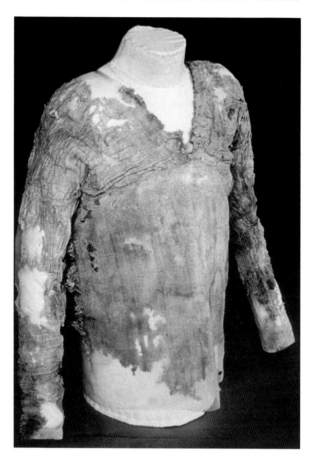

4 Child's fine linen tunic from Tarkhen, Egypt. *Courtesy of the Petrie Museum*

underclothes, caps, scarves, gloves, belts and a beautiful robe which was marked with the year it was made, the seventh of the reign of Tutankhamun's father Akhenaten, about 1343 BC. Made of exquisitely fine linen, it takes the form of a simple folded rectangle, seamed at the sides with open slits for the armholes and a roll-hemmed neck opening just large enough for a baby's head. The piece measures 1.64m by 1m, enough fabric to clothe an adult, and may have been a sort of 'christening robe'. Howard Carter described in some detail the process of excavation of a cache of clothing discovered in a painted casket from the antechamber of the tomb. Beneath some sandals, a gilt head-rest, and a beaded robe:

> there was a mass of decayed cloth, much of it of the consistency of soot, thickly spangled throughout with rosettes and sequins of gold and silver.…There were at least seven distinct garments. One was an imitation leopard-skin cloak in cloth, with gilt head, and spots and claws of silver; while two of the others were head-dresses, made in the semblance of hawks with outstretched wings. Bundled in with the actual garments there were a number of other objects – two faience collarettes of beads and pendants, two caps or bags of tiny bead-work

which had almost entirely fallen to pieces....Below the garments there was a layer of rolls and pads of cloth, some of which were loin-cloths and others mere bandages; and below these again, resting on the bottom of the box, there were two boards perforated at one end for hanging, whose purpose is still doubtful. With very few exceptions...the garments it contained were those of a child.[25]

Another symbol of childhood in ancient Egypt was the way in which the child's hair was arranged. Both boys and girls are depicted with a plaited sidelock of hair on the right side of the head, the rest of the scalp being cropped short, until the

5 An Egyptian family hunting among papyrus reeds. Note the differences in hairstyles and dress of the small girl standing in front of her father and her elder sister (kneeling). After a wall painting from the tomb of Nakht, at Thebes, Eighteenth Dynasty (1567-1320 BC)

age of about ten (5). The hieroglyphic symbol for child or youth was a schematic S-shaped sidelock of this type.

The mummy of a royal prince aged about five from Deir el-Medina, and another aged around 11 from the Valley of the Queens both wore sidelocks which have survived. Fashion and preference seem to have played a part, however, as depictions of other hairstyles include single or multiple pigtails, all-over crop cuts, wide plaits and full heads of hair. Hair slides and pendants were used to decorate and to control the hair. The removal of the sidelock, when worn, seems to have been part of the rite of passage from childhood to puberty. King Tutankhamun's sidelock was preserved in his tomb, labelled clearly as his boyhood hair. It may be that the ceremony of shaving off the sidelock was associated with the act of circumcision which may have been carried out between the ages of ten and 12 or so. Girls may have changed their hairstyles when they began to menstruate, or when they were deemed to have reached marriageable age.

The clothes of Greek and Roman children represented in paintings and sculpture seem to have been simpler versions of their parents' garments, usually tunics, long for girls and short for boys. One of the most important days in an upper-class Roman boy's life was the one on which his father took him to exchange his toga praetexta, or boyhood clothing, for his toga virilis, or first toga of adult manhood, usually around the age of 15 or 16.

Similarly, a rite of passage for boys in later periods would be the day when they were 'breeched', the moment when their childish petticoats were put aside in favour of male costume, or even more recently, when they progressed from short trousers to long ones. For girls, maturity was recognised by the wearing of supporting undergarments, full-length skirts, and by the putting up of the hair during the eighteenth and nineteenth centuries.

The stages at which these changes occurred in the presentation of children varied from period to period and society to society but, in general, differentiation seems to have been made in most societies between children still being nursed and children who have been weaned, and then sometimes at an intermediate stage (often around five to seven years old) when they were regarded as more independent, able to contribute to the family's labour or able to benefit from more formal education. Virtually all societies seem to have some sort of customs to mark the onset of puberty, or the emergence of the young adult from the adolescent stage. Most of the information on this subject is however historical and documentary, rather than archaeological.

TOYS AND GAMES

Modern children are presented with a vast range of toys, games and pastimes for their entertainment and education, but even without formal toys, children tend to create playthings for themselves, often versions of adult tools and equipment.

Play is generally agreed to be the child's way of 'trying out' activities and ideas observed around them in a way that makes sense to him or her. The concepts and ideas behind adult activities may not be understood at all by the child, or only dimly grasped, but the behaviours can be learned and copied. Typically, these efforts to imitate adults are met with great excitement and approbation by the parents ('What a clever girl, to hang out her dolly's clothes to dry!', or 'My Johnny tries to mend his toy car just like his Daddy!'). The child's mimicking of adult behaviour is thus reinforced by approval, and he or she learns the behaviours that equate to social norms and community membership.

Children are notoriously imaginative in their choice and interpretation of objects for play – the cardboard box is often a much more exciting toy than the expensive article it contained! Children's interpretation of the use and possibilities of everyday objects is unconstrained by what adults consider suitable or appropriate. This suggests that finding playthings in archaeological contexts is unlikely to be a simple matter. The famous 'Millie's Camp' experiment carried out in Canada studied a recently abandoned Indian camp site. The aim was to record and interpret the site as if it was a prehistoric investigation, and then to check the results by interviews with people who had lived there. Among the conclusions drawn was that a small wooden and wire bow was a tool used for snaring animals to supplement the group's diet, but was actually identified by Millie herself as a child's toy used as a hobby-horse; dynamite wire has similarly been gathered by young boys for a variety of games and 'symbolic' carvings on a telegraph pole were the artistic doodlings of Millie's teenage daughter.[26]

Another problem in identifying toys from the past is that just because an item is small, it does not mean it was made for a child. Miniature votive objects are found in many cultures, and take the form of pots, models, statues (easily confused with dolls) and tools and weapons. On the other hand, not all miniature objects are ritual in nature, and there is plenty of evidence to show that even in the earliest societies, children made toys or had toys made for them. As today, many ancient children's toys are tiny versions of adult possessions and the games played with them are imitations and explorations of the adult world. Many, too, are simply playthings – balls, hoops, kites, tops, yo-yos, skittles and the like. But remembering that '…children redesign toys through the ways that they are used, ignore toys that do not suit them, and create toys from non-toy objects',[27] how are we to tell toys from the other major group of miniature objects and figures – the objects used in ritual and religious contexts? The tiny figure of a saint, or a crucifix, are clearly not toys in our society – we know their significance and would not confuse the two. We do not know what objects may have held significance in prehistoric societies, and so we are always in danger of misinterpreting the things we find. Additionally, a child may turn a figure of a saint or a crucifix into a toy, being unaware of their religious meaning. There are also ambivalent objects, even today, whose religiosity may not be immediately obvious. Some years ago I saw displayed for sale in Ste-Anne-d'Auray in Brittany a small figure of the saint. On closer inspection, this turned out to be a pencil sharpener: the pencil was to be inserted beneath the saint's skirts!

At Ovcarovo in the Czech Republic, a remarkable find consisting of a collection of tiny items was made. There are two small clay figures of stylized people, decorated with incised lines suggesting skirts or short trousers and jackets, a tiny table, what may be highly decorated beds, some pots and some rotary querns, or grinding stones, just 2cm across (6). These were not found in association with any ritual activity, and although originally recorded as part of a 'cultic scene' are more likely to represent the contents of a dolls' house. What is remarkable about these objects is that they date from the Neolithic period, the time of the first farmers, before Europeans started to use metals. Other objects interpreted as toys from the Czech Republic include a carved animal, perhaps a bear or a pig, from Prague Vinor dated to the Early Bronze Age, a Late Bronze Age clay rattle in the form of a bird found at Prague-Stresovice (7), and tiny pots from Jenstejn.[28]

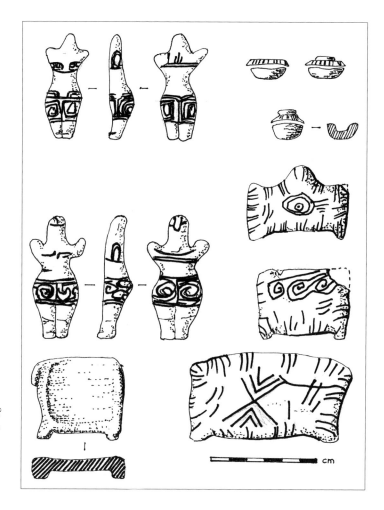

6 'Cultic scene' or Neolithic dolls' house? Miniature figures, pots and furniture from Ovcarovo, Czech Republic. After Turek, accessed 2003

7 Pottery rattle in the shape of a bird, approx. 8cm high. Prague-Stesovice. After Turek, accessed 2003

It may be possible to understand more about prehistoric play by comparing these forms of evidence with ethnographic material from modern or recent simple societies. A number of investigations into ethnographic and archaeological evidence for play in Inuit societies have identified both toys and the sorts of games which would not leave archaeological evidence. Records from the nineteenth century of Inuit children's play list activities such as ball games, hide-and-seek, races and a game of tag called variously 'Wolf and Raven' or 'Caribou and Wolves' (it is perhaps interesting that wolves feature greatly in children's games and stories over much of the world; in modern England, most children know the story of Little Red Riding Hood, and 'What's the time, Mr. Wolf?' is played in many a school playground). Songs and stories featured in Inuit play too, and they also played that game much beloved of all parents; seeing who could stay silent the longest! Toys included noise makers such as 'bullroarers', drums and whistles; some archaeological examples of possible 'bullroarers' have been identified. Spinning tops and balls made of wood or stitched skins are known.

As elsewhere, many Inuit playthings reflected adult activities; these have been divided into three categories – playing house, playing with dolls and playing at hunting.[29] Both sexes played at building snow houses in winter; in summer, children used pebbles to lay out the plans of snow houses and finds of these pebble plans have been reported from archaeological contexts. Miniature lamps, pots and other containers, beds and knives represent the play of girls, often in the corners of the real houses. Wooden dolls dressed in caribou skin clothing are recorded; a girl might have several such dolls and it seems that this activity was encouraged by mothers as a way of teaching the skills of skin cutting and sewing that would be essential later in life. Miniature spears, harpoons, bows and arrows are evidence of hunting play; some ethnographers have suggested that both boys and girls might accompany their fathers on hunting expeditions, or engage in mock hunting play. Another form of toy that was probably popular was the transport toy – kayak or *umiak*, or sled.

There are, nevertheless, problems in identifying miniature objects as toys in archaeological evidence for early Inuit societies, particularly as miniature items were known to be used in two other contexts: as grave goods, and as the equipment of shamans. Several writers have recorded the practice of placing miniature models of artefacts in graves. 'A dead man's property usually descends to his relatives, if it is worth anything. Instead of his own possessions, they put into the grave small copies of the things they have inherited, these miniatures being carved in wood'.[30] This very thrifty practice should mean that only objects found in graves need be viewed in this light, but there is also the possibility that a child's toys might be placed in his or her grave, and in such a case the division between toy and ritual object becomes less clear. Shamans acquired miniature objects as symbols of power and connection with the givers, members of their community who, by offering such a gift, ensured their share in the shaman's power and influence. In such cases, it would be expected that the objects would be found either in the shaman's grave, or in connection with other ritual or magical objects in the shaman's house. The Thule culture emigrated from Alaska into Arctic Canada and Greenland around AD 1000, bringing with it new artefacts such as dog sleds and skin boats for open-water hunting. In the winter months, the people built semi-subterranean structures, which, when abandoned, collapsed, burying objects in permafrost and preserving them very well. Many miniature objects have been excavated from these house remains, and their contexts suggest strongly that these were toys rather than ritual objects. Among objects found in excavations at some 31 Thule sites are 99 dolls, 23 tiny lamps, 13 miniature cooking pots, 17 small sleds, 12 little kayaks, 29 children's bows, 16 harpoon heads and numerous other objects.[31] Beyond demonstrating the presence of children at these sites, the assemblage offers confirmation of some of their activities, and their learning, through play, of vital adult skills.

Ancient Egyptian toys include rattles, peashooters, dolls of all types and miniature animals, as well as dolls' house equipment. Many of the dolls and animal figures have moveable limbs, opening mouths and wagging tails, such as a model of a crocodile with snapping jaws dating from the second millennium BC and the wooden cat with crystal eyes and moving jaw with bronze teeth found at Thebes. Models of craftspeople at their work have been found. There is even a tiny mummy in a miniature sarcophagus. Many models were made quite simply from mud and include human and animal figures, balls, tops, hoops and boats; a fine collection of these may be seen at the Petrie Museum in London (8). It is probable that these mud toys were either made by the children themselves, or by their parents.

Dolls have been found, sometimes painted, and some had wigs made of flax or mud beads; some had moving arms. The Petrie Museum has such a doll recovered from the tomb at Hawara of a young girl called Sitrennut. By the Roman period in Egypt, cloth dolls were made, and three or four have survived. Egyptian children also indulged in sporting play. Athletic games are represented in paintings; at Mereroka, a sixth-Dynasty *mastaba* tomb has scenes of balancing games, a tug-of-war, a race, fighting games, a girls' ring game and dance, and rattles. Ball games are also shown on tomb walls and a number of actual balls survive. These were made of stitched leather, cloth, wood or papyrus and were stuffed with yarn, hair or straw. Some of the balls were gaily painted, like examples in the British Museum. A child's grave at Naqada produced a complete set of stone skittles and balls, with a marble 'gate'. Juggling is shown in a tomb painting from Beni Hasan. Egyptian children are also depicted with their pets – kittens, birds and even gazelles.

8 Mud toy in the shape of a crocodile. *Courtesy of the Petrie Museum*

Hunting and fishing were apparently favourite occupations for boys, and several murals depict girls with mirrors, perhaps playing with their hair and make-up. Board games were also played; one famous example is the Serpent Game, which consists of a spiral arrangement of squares and seems to have involved a crouching lion figure and six round 'men', one for each player. Sadly, despite finding the pieces and having depictions of the game being played, we do not know the rules![32] Tutankhamun's tomb contained a chest full of toys and pastimes from his boyhood. The chest had been disturbed and its contents scattered, perhaps by ancient tomb-robbers, but among the items recovered were pocket ivory gaming boards, slings, archer's wrist guards, some mechanical toys and a painting set. Elsewhere in the tomb were hunting weapons and more gaming boards and playing pieces.

9 Knucklebones game. Ceramic, late sixth century BC. Height 8.5cm, length 11.1cm. From Baeotia (original in the Louvre Museum, Paris)

Greek and Roman pastimes included such evergreen favourites as knucklebones depicted, for example, in a ceramic model of the late sixth century BC now in the Louvre Museum, on a fine red-figured crater dated 420-410 BC in the British Museum and in the same collection, Southern Italian ceramic figures of knucklebone players of about 340-330 BC (9), and yo-yos, shown on vase paintings like the example dated to 440 BC now in the Staatliche Museen Preussischer Kulturbesitz, Berlin (10). The Museum of Archaeology in Dijon has a Roman period wooden yo-yo, 6cm in diameter, in its collection (11). Various rattles and noise-making toys for babies have been found. Ball games and juggling were equally popular among Greek and Roman children, sometimes using walnuts which were also copied in clay, perhaps as symbols of youthful joy in adult rites. Similar clay bags of knucklebones are known. Tops and hoops are shown on vases, and wooden tops have been excavated (12); these were operated with small

10 Youth playing with a yo-yo. From a Greek red-figure cup, c.440 BC

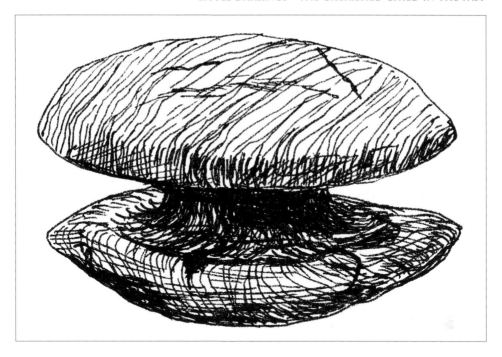

11 Wooden yo-yo found at Sources de la Seine Roman period. Approx.6cm diameter. *Musée Archéologique de Dijon*

12 Wooden spinning top, 4.8cm diameter, from the Gallo-Roman period. *Musée Archéologique de Saintes*

13 Child driving a toy chariot drawn by pigeons. A second child passes the driver a palm of victory. After a mosaic from Piazza Armerina, Sicily, fourth century AD

two-tailed whips. A really lucky child might have a miniature racing chariot, pulled either by an animal or by other children, and for Dionysic festivals, there were, it seems, junior racing circuits in Rome. It seems that these races were undertaken with all the seriousness and danger of the adult versions. A funerary inscription records 'It is I, Florus, who rests here; small child driver of a double yoke, quickly, while I ran the course, yes quickly, I fell and descended into the shades'.[33]

Dolls' house toys were made, a particularly fine set of amphorae, goblets and ladles in silver being displayed in Berlin, but other sets made of bronze, copper and ivory, as well as ceramic, have been found. Furniture is represented by items such as an ivory doll's bed reported by Pausanius. Whole rooms of furniture were made, and dolls also came with sets of equipment that would not compare badly with Barbie's ensembles. A young girl called Crepereia Tryphaena living in Rome around 150 BC had a 30cm tall articulated ivory doll, which had moving joints at the shoulders, elbows, hips and knees, and a full trousseau including little gold rings, mirrors, beads, combs and bone and ivory jewellery boxes. This girl died aged around 14, and her toys were placed in her tomb. Articulated dolls are found in Greece from the fifth century BC, made in moulded ceramic, at first with just the legs movable from the hips, but later with moving knees too. Over time, these became larger, from just 10cm tall to 25cm (*14*). Unlike ritual statues

14 Two bone dolls from Asia Minor, late first/early second century AD. The arms are articulated, and there are traces of painted detail

and cult figurines, these dolls are naked, ready to be dressed. In the Eastern Mediterranean and Asia Minor, a range of dolls, dated from between the fourth century BC to the third century AD, carry objects indicating particular attributes and identities, or in poses that suggest their occupations – there are dancers (male and female), musicians, soldiers and female gladiators or Amazons with spears and shields. Perhaps the dreams of little girls extended beyond the household roles their society usually planned for them, and were explored with these exciting figures.

Roman dolls were generally naked, with rudimentary modelling suggesting the shape of the chest, the navel and the genitals. Sometimes shoes are modelled on the feet. Some of these are identifiable to a period by reference to the hairstyle depicted. Dolls that have survived were generally made of bone, ivory or ebony (*15*); very few dolls are known from other parts of the Roman empire, such as Gaul, Britain, North Africa or Germany, where they may have been made from more perishable materials such as cloth or wood.

Some 253 Graeco-Roman contexts have produced evidence of dolls, and none of these have religious associations. About 203 contexts are generally

15 Two bone dolls, Italian, fourth century AD

domestic (houses, streets and storerooms), and 35 are tombs whose occupants are now unknown. Fifteen more are tombs containing the bodies of children, seven in the Western Empire and eight in the Eastern. Apart from Crepereia Tryphaena, we know the names of Hermofilis, who died in Rome aged just three months and fourteen days, and Claudia Victoria, who died in Lyon aged ten years, one month, and eleven days. An unnamed girl aged five or six was buried with her doll in Tarragona, and the mummified body of a seven- or eight-year-old girl was buried with her doll at Grottarossa (Tomb of Nerone), Rome.[34]

Animal toys were very popular too. Many children had pets including goats, dogs, birds and even hedgehogs; pottery and wooden models of animals include lions, horses (sometimes with riders and wheels), rams and more hedgehogs. Educational toys were also made, such as letters of the alphabet made of ivory or as little cakes.

Many toys represent ways for children to copy and explore the adult world through play, and as such are part of their general socialisation and community

16 Marble altar from Ostia, Italy, dedicated to the memory of A. Egrilius A.f Pal. Magnus, who died aged five years nine months, in the mid-first century AD. His pet goat is shown by his side

education. 'Toys and children-specific artefacts (such as toys, clothing, mugs, medicines, school paraphernalia, etc), when purchased or made for children, represent attempts, made by adults, to suggest and enforce certain norms of behaviour for children based upon their gender, age, socio-economic class and even socio-cultural ideals of beauty'.[35] This statement may well be true, but it is surely also the case that in buying toys, educational or not, parents were also expressing affection for their children, a desire to please and amuse them, that we can empathise with very easily. The fact that a market for toys existed, and that professional toymakers made a respectable living even in the ancient world, demonstrates the love of children by their parents in these societies.

Physical education was regarded as important, particularly by ancient Greek society, and among other sports represented in Greek art are hockey (on an Attic bas-relief dated 500-510 BC now in the National Museum of Athens) and various ball sports. A tombstone in York depicts the family of a Roman soldier; his son and daughter both died before reaching the age of two, and they are shown holding balls on the stone. Encouragement of sporting games is related in the classical world to the development of a healthy body as a prerequisite for the development of a healthy intellect, an attitude that persisted in British public schools well into the last century. Of course, parents might also encourage sporting activities as a way of letting children run off excess energy and thus be quieter and more tractable in the home!

It is to be supposed that children may have played board games that were also enjoyed by adults, such as the various early forms of backgammon or chess that are known from very early times in many societies. Egyptian paintings show a form of backgammon called *senet*; a model ship in the Ashmolean Museum has two figures playing the game among its details, and an ivory board with drawer for the pieces is in the British Museum. Various other Egyptian board games have been found: the '20-box game', and the '58-hole game' (played on a little carved table, with animal-head markers looking something similar to a cribbage board or, in at least one case, a blue hippopotamus); very similar examples come from the Graeco-Roman world. A number of board games are mentioned in Greek and Roman literature; the '*polis*' game seems to have been a tactical game, but we know little of the '*diagrammismos*' game mentioned by Pollux. '*Pente grammai*' seems to have been another tactical or battle game. The Romans also played '*latroncules*' which had two colours of pieces, black and white, and involved blocking and capturing pieces. The game of '*duodecim scripta*' was played on a board that is very similar to a backgammon board. Traces of board games also come from medieval contexts – the Lewis chess pieces are famous, and the game is found illustrated in the margins of manuscripts, such as the Flemish example from the workshop of Jean de Grise between 1338 and 1344.[36] Chess or draught boards were scratched into the cloister benches at Salisbury, Romsey and Saint-Hilaire (Aude). It is not impossible that the game was played by the bored and perhaps rather naughty school boys or choristers at these religious establishments, which also offered schooling. Dice are fairly common finds in many medieval contexts, and the homemade crudity of some suggests that they may have been made and used by young people.

Anglo-Saxon children could play rather noisily; there are a couple of records of 'noisy throngs' of children in the streets or by the sea, but we have very little evidence of toys from the period. In the graves of some children, there are miniature weapons like spears and axes. These may have been symbolic items, relating to the identification of the child's gender, future role as a warrior, or status of his parents, but equally, they may have been toys, played with as today's children play with toy guns. Girls' graves often have chatelaines or spinning and weaving tools, which may also have served to indicate gender and adult roles. It is possible that there were other items in these graves (toys such as dolls, stuffed animals, wooden tops) which simply have not survived because they were made of organic materials. We cannot therefore say very much about the play of these children archaeologically, although at Jarlshof on Shetland, in the same period, a miniature bowl and quern, carved from the local stone, have been found at a Viking farmstead.

Many medieval toys and games are known, and a great number are recorded for us in Breughel's painting 'Children's Games'; a close inspection of this painting demonstrates that much entertainment can be had without elaborate or specially made toys, as well as providing an illustration of many common playthings. There are dolls and windmills, tops, stilts, a hobbyhorse, knucklebones, hoops, bladders and mud pies. There is also a pretend wedding, a christening, a pretend shop, fights, round games, blind man's buff and much more; a personal favourite is the little girl in the foreground poking at an animal dropping with a stick!

In London, excavations and metal detecting on the Thames foreshore over the last 20 years or so have unearthed hundreds of toys including numerous figures. There is a fine hollow-cast mounted knight, dated to around AD 1300, with his helmet, armour and sword; from the late Tudor period there are several hollow pewter figures, some worked by strings like puppets, and some cheaper flat-cast versions found more often in rural situations. Mechanical toys are represented by, for example, a bird figure on a rod and bar, which, when rocked, sticks its tongue in and out – it comes from the fourteenth century. Dolls' house equipment such as miniature plates and jugs, griddles with fish on, and cauldrons are well represented. Working miniature guns and cannon must have been popular with boys, although the fact that they used real gunpowder and tiny cannonballs must have given their parents a few nasty scares – some have split barrels, showing that they had blown up in use! Model boats have always been favourites. From Viking and Norman levels in Dublin come wooden toy boats; later pewter models show Elizabethan warships, and finds of miniature anchors in the Thames suggest that many more boats were 'lost at sea'. By the seventeenth century, working toy watches are known, and we know of a Mr Hux and a Mr Beasly who specialised in the production of such items in the early eighteenth century.[37]

Professional toymakers are recorded as early as the fifteenth century; the first professional dollmaker is recorded as Nuremburg in 1413, and a woodcut of 1491 depicts a German toymaker. Fairings are mentioned in a variety of sources; these were offered as prizes for games, or could be bought as souvenirs and included wooden toys such as dolls, rattles and drums, and edible treats such as gingerbread men.

In the upper echelons of early modern society, the toys a child, particularly a boy, played with were related to their age as well as status. A clear demonstration of this can be found in the record of the toys and pastimes of Louis XIII during his childhood. As a baby, the list of playthings given to the young prince included active articles such as balls, tops, a hobbyhorse, a windmill, a tennis racquet, as well as creative toys such as a tambourine, and scissors and paper. There were also soldiers and a cannon, and male dolls; perhaps the baby was particularly fond of his clockwork pigeon! By the age of four, his social and military education began; approved activities included archery and balls games, parlour games and card playing. At six he was learning to play chess and charades, and by the age of seven he was expected to become a young gentleman, his dolls and soldiers were taken away, and instead he spent his days riding, hunting, fencing, shooting and learning to gamble. A structured progression was created for the child from babyhood towards the skills and accomplishments expected of a noble gentleman of the time – a progression that in our age we might regard as rather accelerated.

Disapproval of play was a feature of some of the stricter Puritan and other Protestant sects of the later medieval and early modern eras. The Puritan government during the Civil War passed laws against ball games, maypole dancing, public masques and street entertainments; surviving documentary material suggests that children were expected to give up play at an early age, turning their attention instead to the study of religion and useful work. In the nineteenth century, a popular event for apprentice boys, the Shrove Tuesday football match, was the subject of much disapproval by town dignitaries, and was eventually banned. The towns of Kingston and Dorking in Surrey both have records of drunkenness, fighting and civil nuisance associated with the event. Nevertheless, at Dorking (where the ball was ritually covered with blood at a local slaughterhouse at the start of the day-long game, to make it more slippery) it was some 20 years before the various injunctions against the game finally had their effect. Many people supported the games, regarding them as a legitimate and traditional 'perk' for young working boys.

Victorian attitudes to toys ranged from the approval of only the strictly educational (map jigsaws, Noah's Arks, and toys intended to teach children useful household and work skills) to elaborate and fanciful amusements with little obvious learning potential. Since that time, the toy industry has grown to one of the world's largest, assisted by the development of the ubiquitous plastic that replaces the organic materials of more ancient playthings. Despite the popularity of such modern items as mutant ninja turtles and Game Boys, however, traditional toys survive. Dolls and dolls' houses, miniature weapons (no longer fully functional, happily), model animals, balls, yo-yos and toy soldiers are still part of the child's armoury in the effort to make sense of the world in which they find themselves, and in many ways are very similar to those toys enjoyed in other societies hundreds and even thousands of years ago.

CHILDREN AND DOMESTIC SPACE

The space provided for children in the home is a reflection of social attitudes in a community. In upper-class European and American houses of the eighteenth, nineteenth and early twentieth centuries, separate suites of rooms were provided for children and the staff employed to care for them. There might be day and night nurseries, schoolrooms and quarters for nurses, nannies and governesses or tutors. Children led a separate life from that of their parents and were generally invisible to adult society. They might be produced, carefully cleaned and pressed, for inspection once a day, for a brief interview with their parents, and on Sundays would be brought by their nurse to church. Even once they had progressed beyond the stage of nursery and schoolroom, their interaction with their parents could be minimal. Boys would be sent to boarding schools or cadet schools; girls would remain confined to the schoolroom or tutored in household skills by servants or, later in the period, be sent to finishing schools abroad.

For the poor in the same period, a completely opposite situation was normal. Families often worked, ate and slept in the same room, sometimes the same bed. Children were an intimate part of adult life, always underfoot until they were old enough to be employed in the fields and factories, where they worked alongside adults.

It is this latter type of household that we tend to assume would have been normal in prehistory in many cultures, and indeed the thin scatter of child-related artefacts found on settlement sites seems to confirm this. Some study has been made of the spatial arrangements of prehistoric housing. It has been suggested that within roundhouses, the typical form of house in the British Bronze and Iron Ages, with their central hearths, space was organised around the axis between hearth and doorway. Many, if not most, of these houses appear to have had their doors facing between east and south, away from the prevailing westerly winds and allowing the maximum light into the building.

Some studies have suggested that the north and east sides of the interior, particularly the central part of the house, were 'male preserves' with the best light and warmth, where visitors were welcomed and social contacts were maintained. The darker west and south sides of the house, therefore, were the 'female' areas, where food preparation, cooking and other domestic activities were carried on, and, presumably, children were cared for.

Another possibility relates to the fact that many of the small farmsteads that typify settlement in British prehistory in many areas have a number of structures within their compound boundaries. Often there is one house larger than the others, with a porch, assumed to be the main dwelling house, and the smaller buildings grouped around it are variously described as animal sheds, storage huts and craft working sheds. Some of these smaller buildings have produced domestic artefacts. One suggestion for a smaller hut with domestic material is that it might have been a 'granny flat' for older members of the group. It is equally possible that such a structure might have served as a nursery, representing a form of division between the life of adults and that of children.

Romano-British villas, which succeeded some of the roundhouse settlements, display a change in spatial organisation. The design of villa houses seems to represent, over time, an increasing separation of domestic life from public life. This may have been a result of an increase in uncertainty, a formalisation of external relationships and the introduction of a much wider range of possible contacts. The owner of the villa, in contrast to the elder of a roundhouse settlement, had to deal with officials, civilian and military, local and foreign, as well as traders who might have come from all over the Roman Empire, and representatives of a much larger group of tribes and communities involved in local politics and administration. It must have been hard to know who was trustworthy, and what dangers might arrive at the door.

There was also, possibly, a much clearer distinction between people of wealth and status and their workers and slaves. It is suggested that towards the end of the period of Roman occupation, something like a feudal system was beginning to emerge in Britain. The houses reflect these changes by providing formal spaces for external relations such as imposing entrances, corridors, highly decorated reception and dining rooms. Domestic accommodation moved 'deeper' into the building, away from the public areas, both for reasons of safety and with regard to the impression given to visitors of gravitas and status. We assume that children would often be restricted from entry into the formal rooms and contact with visitors on most occasions, and that their world would therefore become less visible in adult social and business affairs, in a manner not dissimilar to the nineteenth-century upper-class world.

Upper-class medieval parents might also have provided separate spaces for children and their nurses. There are few records of how domestic interiors were arranged in castles and manors, but those that have survived suggest that, where accommodation was available, girls and their maids were housed separately from boys and their menservants. In some houses at least, attic rooms were designated as accommodation for children. From the later medieval period onwards, royal children were sometimes provided with whole separate suites of accommodation, and some rarely saw their parents. They had their own, often large, staffs of servants, and their care was the responsibility of designated guardians, as was the case for the young Elizabeth I.

Very little evidence of furniture specially designed for children has survived. A particular exception is the wooden cradle at Herculaneum that still contained the remains of a baby who had died during the eruption of Mount Vesuvius in AD 79. Here, the volcanic dust and mud had clearly preserved the form of the wood, a very rare occurrence. A few Greek depictions of furniture can be found painted on pottery, one of which seems to show a specially designed 'high chair' (*17*). Medieval illustrations also sometimes include depictions of baby walkers and high chairs, and there are a very few survivals of these and similar items from the Tudor period and later. Once again, we have to accept that if there were small items of furniture and equipment made particularly for children, they would have been of organic materials, thus rarely surviving. In the world of children, the old archaeological adage 'absence of evidence is not evidence of absence' is frequently to be invoked.

17 Depiction on a Greek plate of a mother with a small child sitting in an early form of 'high chair'

2

EDUCATION AND WORK

What is it all Mankind aim at in the Education of their Children? Certainly to give them such a Degree of Knowledge as will qualify them to fill some certain Post, some certain Station in Life: in short, to fit them for an Employment suited to their Condition, such as will make them happy in themselves, and useful to Society.

James Nelson, 'An Essay on the Government of Children' 1768

LEARNING

The education of children in ancient societies was, in most cases, almost certainly informal and related directly to the work roles they would assume as adults. Children learned by observation of adult behaviours and by practising basic skills during play or as part of chores. In some societies, a more formal system of learning and training existed, usually for the children of particular strata or classes. The motives for educating the young were sometimes academic, sometimes practical, and often related to instructing the young in the cultural and religious norms of their parents rather than specific vocational activities.

The evidence for education is usually restricted to written accounts, but, although rarely, can also be found in pictorial representations or graffiti. In literate societies, reading and writing were obvious subjects for the curriculum. Basic numeracy, too, was commonly taught, as were elements of the history and culture of the society, and its religious beliefs. Sometimes we have more detailed information about the subjects young people studied; Cato, for example, tutored his son, Marcus in the physical activities of wrestling, swimming and boxing as well as reading, writing, law and history. Much of the information we have relates to the education of children of the upper classes of their societies, children who were being trained not just for work, but for future roles in government, administration, the military and the priesthood.

From Egypt come 'Books of Instruction', texts containing rules of morality, justice, obedience and the like, often in the form of verses from a father to his son. The student would have learned these and, perhaps, practised writing by copying them. The Instruction of Ptahhotep includes advice such as 'Do not boast of your knowledge, but seek the advice of the untutored as much as the well-educated' and 'Be prudent whenever you open your mouth. Your every utterance should be outstanding so that the mighty men who listen to you will say:"How beautiful are the words that fly from his lips"'. There are clear parallels here with the kind of moral texts popular in Victorian school primers in England and the United States.

Literacy was important in Egypt as it was the key to a range of careers in civil, religious and military administrations. In early centuries, boys were probably educated at home by their fathers or respected elders. By the time of the Middle Kingdom, schools are mentioned, with one of the most important being at el-Lisht, near the residence of the pharaoh, to which the sons of high-ranking courtiers were sent. There were also schools which catered for children of less exalted parents, designed to provide candidates for future employment among the rank and file of the civil service. Biographies of officials recorded on statues and in tombs suggest that schooling began around the age of five or six and would consist of four or more years of primary education, followed by up to ten years of apprenticeship. Less robust children were perhaps considered particularly suitable for a life as a scribe, while their huskier brothers might be encouraged to join the military. Primary education included numeracy as well as literacy, and corporal punishment was used to stimulate learning. An ancient Egyptian quip runs: 'A boy's ear is upon his back; he hears when he is beaten'.[1]

Excavations at the village of workmen at the necropolis of Deir el-Medina show that some of the artisans were literate, and it is probable that there was a school for their children nearby. Much of the learning would have been done as it is today in Islamic schools, with chanted readings and recitations, and copying exercises were set which had the dual role of encouraging the practice of clear handwriting, and the inculcation of moral sentiments. A number of these exercises were worked on *ostraca* (*18*), fragments of stone or pottery, which were cheaper by far than papyrus, and as a result some have survived and have been recovered in archaeological contexts.

It is unclear whether girls were literate, but again at Deir el-Medina there are indications that some, at least, could read and write. The ostraca from the site included letters sent by or to women about everyday topics such as ordering underwear, which appear to have been written by the women themselves. Certainly some women learned decorative arts such as painting, and depictions of princesses sometimes show them with painting palettes. Painting skills were also practised by boys apprenticed to tomb decorators, sculptors and other craftsmen. A few pictorial copying exercises survive, with the master's original on one side and the inexpert or incorrect learner's copy worked on the reverse; practice drawings of hieroglyphic signs and human and other figures have been found.

18 Front (top) and
reverse (below)
of a limestone
ostracon from Deir
el-Medina. The
front shows the
master's example,
the reverse the
pupil's copy;
note the reversal
of symbols in
the right-hand
cartouche

The ancient Greeks began educating their children around the age of six or seven; before this age, children's time was devoted to play, and there are many depictions of games and toys on painted vases. The Athenians were obliged by law to educate their children, even the very poor, and teaching was provided freely. Literacy was a prerequisite for participation in Athenian political life; each citizen needed to be able to read and write in order to cast their votes in elections. Writing was practised using wooden tablets or sometimes even broken sherds of pottery. A fourth-century BC piece of a storage jar upon which a dictation exercise was written can be seen in the British Museum. Education was provided by private tutors, with schools set up in their own houses. Jar paintings and figurines show pupils with their paidagogoi or teacher, such as the example dated between 375–50 BC in the Metropolitan Museum of Art in New York. In the fifth century BC, the curriculum consisted of basic reading, writing and calculation skills, followed by the reading and learning of poetry and sections of plays; music was important, with most children learning to play a lute or flute, or a cithar, and to sing. At the age of 14, boy children were expected to start regular gymnastic training, especially wrestling, running, jumping, and throwing sports with javelin and discus. Again, vase paintings offer many illustrations of these pursuits. For the Athenians, a healthy body was a prerequisite for a healthy mind. It is believed that girls were educated at home, and the skills of textile working and domestic management were deemed particularly important. There is, however, a depiction of two girls, apparently on their way to school, on a ceramic drinking cup in the Metropolitan Museum of Art's collection, although there is some dispute over whether this means girls really could be educated in schools, or whether the image was intended as a joke at an all-male drinking party.[2]

The upbringing system of the Spartans has become very well known, because of its apparent brutality. Weak or disabled children were disposed of at birth; at the age of seven, boys were taken from the family home to training schools where they learned to fight and excel at gymnastics. The boys were lightly clothed (from 12 years old they went barefoot and bare headed all year round), their hair was cut short, baths were only rarely allowed, and they slept on simple straw palliasses without covers. They were poorly fed, and were encouraged to steal; part of their training was seen to be the successful learning of skills of evasion and guile practised on food raids. Beatings and whippings were given for failure and to toughen body and spirit – no expression or exclamation of pain or distress was allowed. No formal lessons in literacy were given, but music lessons encouraged patriotic songs and tunes. Younger boys were assigned older boys as mentors, who taught them both physical and social skills, and frequently inducted them into sexual activity.

Spartan girls also participated in gymnastics and learned singing and dancing. Like the boys, they participated in public sporting championships; for these sports they dressed in very brief sleeveless tunics, a costume the Athenians found shocking.[3]

Roman children were taught to read and write, and were introduced to basic numeracy and history, across all social classes; slave children and the children of the poor could all be given schooling. Graffiti demonstrates that literacy was general in Roman society; messages are scratched in wet clay by tilemakers, used on pottery to advertise the contents or the seller, daubed on walls to comment on the attributes of courtesans or gladiators. Richer children would have tutors at home, often well-educated slaves. Slaves were also educated to act as secretaries, accountants, annalists and civil servants. But there were also small schools available in both poor and wealthy neighbourhoods. Horace mentions a teacher called Flavius who ran a school in his home town of Venusia; this school catered for 'boys of pretensions, sons of prominent centurions, [who] went there with their school bags and writing tablets slung over their left arms'.[4] These boys, Horace tells us, paid their school fees on the Ides of each of the eight months of the school year. Schoolmasters kept discipline by means of the cane, it seems. Martial writes a plea to one of them:

> Sir Schoolmaster, show pity upon your simple scholars, at least if you wish to have many a long-haired boy attendant upon your lectures, and the class seated around your critical table love you. Then would no teacher of arithmetic or swift writing have a greater ring of pupils around him. Hot and bright are the days now under the flaming constellation of the lion; and fervid July is ripening the bursting harvest. So let your Scythian scourge with its dreadful thongs, such as flogged Marsyas of Celaenae, and your formidable cane – the schoolmaster's sceptre – be laid aside, and sleep until the Ides of October. Surely in summer time, if the boys keep their health, it is enough.[5]

In the post-Roman period in Northern Europe, formal education appears to have been abandoned, except for those young people dedicated to a religious life in nunneries and monasteries, particularly those of the Celtic Church. The Irish communities, in particular, were renowned for their scholarship, and from these, ultimately, derive the few surviving manuscripts of the period, such as the Book of Kells and the Lindisfarne Gospels. Most people, however, were illiterate, and the ancient skills of storytelling and learning by memorising the spoken or sung word enjoyed a revival.

King Alfred of Wessex is said to have arranged for the education of children as early as the ninth century, and by the late Saxon period it is clear that literacy was once again highly valued, with great reliance and importance being vested in written charters, agreements and wills. In the medieval period in England, written sources tell us that the sons of noblemen were educated at home by tutors, while grammar schools existed from the late eleventh century for boys of slightly lesser status. Winchester College was founded in 1382 as such a school. Basic education began to become available to the lower classes, particularly the offspring of urban artisans and householders. In many towns and villages, the local priest supplemented his income by giving elementary lessons to poorer children, both male and female, for a minimum rate; these classes were often held in the church bell tower room or in a room above the church porch. Monasteries and nunneries often had boarding pupils, and we know of a few female schoolmistresses such as the Londoner who paid tax in 1441 called Elizabeth Scolemaystres.[6] By the High Medieval period, monastic and cathedral schools were not restricted to children who were intended to enter the Church, although a religious path was the best way for a likely pupil to advance in his career. Children were first introduced to the arts of reading and writing, and then to the *Trivium* – grammar, logic and rhetoric, the first three of the 'Seven Liberal Arts'; more advanced education consisted of the other four arts, the *Quadrivium* – arithmetic, geometry, music and astronomy. Attention was ensured by the use of corporal punishment. For the most part, it was the skills of embroidery, weaving and home management that were taught to girls, but at least a small number did benefit from a good education. There is some evidence to suggest that from the thirteenth century onwards, mothers had a role in instructing their children in literacy, and therefore in godliness, and this impression 'would appear to derive powerful support from the growing number of depictions of the Virgin being taught by her mother, Saint Anne'.[7] The role of mothers in the teaching of reading is discussed by Orme, who notes the rise in popularity of St Anne.[8] Some existing manuscript illustrations show the saint reading to her daughter (*19*), and a medieval window at Standford-on-Avon, Northants., also shows the scene. A wall painting from Bradford-on-Avon has a similar picture.

Queen Margaret of Scotland, a descendant of King Alfred, was recorded in the eleventh century as teaching her children Christian precepts, presumably from manuscript texts. Nunneries, generally far less favoured than monasteries in terms of economic gifts, utilised a number of strategies to increase their income, including providing nursing care, accommodation for women and children, and schooling. The nunnery at St. Mary's, Winchester, at the time of the Dissolution in 1536, had in its charge some 26 girls, many daughters of knights, who were receiving an education there.

Older boys who had sufficient wealth or patronage could then go on to university. University education began in the twelfth century at cathedral schools; there were no formal entry qualifications, either of ability or age, so many students were quite young and not necessarily of a very studious bent. They studied such subjects as theology, medicine and law in colleges and lived in hostels under the care of senior students and their tutors. The behaviour of students was notoriously bad – drunkenness, fighting between the students of rival colleges, and crime were often rife in university towns, leading to poor relations between the citizens and the college authorities, a divide between 'town and gown' that has persisted into the modern era in some places.

Some early fifteenth-century school notebooks survive, introduced to replace wax tablets when paper eventually became cheaper and more plentiful. They reveal that pupils spent their time copying Latin texts, and working on

19 Saint Anne teaching her daughter the Virgin Mary to read. From the Dunce Book of Hours

exercises. Some contain rhymes or songs in English.[9] There are translations, rules of grammar and fragments of notes and descriptions, generally reflecting a high standard of scholarship. Children of high class might also be taught Greek, French, Italian, Spanish or another language, religious philosophy, music, dancing and practical arts such as fencing, archery and swordsmanship. Some girls also received the benefit of a good education; a most notable example of female scholarship was Elizabeth I.

Professional tutors were employed, many, though by no means all, being clergy. Parents also took an interest in educating their children, and some wrote books for them to read, such as *The Book of the Knight of the Tower* written around 1371 by Geoffrey de la Tour Landry for his daughters. The education of wealthy children began early, perhaps as young as four or five. Primers were published, containing alphabets, word lists and prayers. Some horn books, a sheet of paper or parchment containing reading material protected by a thin sheet of horn and mounted in a wooden frame with a handle, survive from the fifteenth century, and there are manuscript illustrations of 'alphabet boards' of a similar type from earlier periods. For the very rich, extraordinary teaching aids could be produced, such as the alphabet made of letters of gold belonging to the five-year-old Jeanne, daughter of the duke of Orleans, in 1415.[10] An excavation at Saint-Denis, near Paris, has uncovered an alphabet disk used in a local school, and an inventory for the castle of Angers includes, in the room set aside for the education of the children living there, 'a great board on which there are alphabets' in 1471.[11] By the sixteenth and seventeenth centuries, the production of bright and interesting teaching aids was being promoted, such as playing cards with letters drawn upon them, and mechanical wheels which revealed letters as they were turned.

Much basic education took place in the houses of the teachers. In medieval France, teachers hung signs outside their doors to advertise their classes, and a few survive. Some of these signs offer speedy education and a gentle approach, and there seems to have been some competition, even the offer of free education to the poor. The accommodation appears to have been rather basic in many cases, often unheated and dark. Little furniture was provided; records suggest the children sat on the floor, partially protected from the chill by strewn straw. A record from Lyon dating from 1545-46 notes the decision to install a proper floor in the college, as the rooms were 'paved with stone and make the little children very cold'.[12]

Education for children was, of course, offered in many societies beyond Europe, the Chinese system in particular being developed very early. In ancient Mexico, all children attended school for some time in their teenage years. Every town or district had a school for ordinary children, called a telpochcalli, where boys, at least, boarded. It is not known whether girls boarded too, or attended as day pupils. The genders were separated for lessons, which included music, singing and dancing; boys undertook community work projects such as building and repairing roads, temples and bridges, and were trained in the military arts.

They then undertook practical training, at first as orderlies for soldiers, and later as fighters.

Children of the upper classes, or specially favoured commoners, attended a different sort of school, the calmecac. These were associated with major temples and stressed military and religious skills. The pupils learned a range of subjects, including astrology, astronomy, music and military arts, equipping them for adult lives as priests, government officials and army leaders. A Spanish friar recorded that large beautifully painted books were provided from which the children were taught their lessons.

Aztec discipline was quite harsh; idleness was greatly disapproved of and other shortcomings for which punishments were given included telling lies, being rebellious or failing to correct bad behaviour. The punishments handed out could be severe – beatings, canings, being pierced in the body with spikes of the maguey cactus, and forcing children (as young as 11) to inhale chilli smoke, which the Codex Mendoza recorded as being a 'serious and even cruel torment'.

It is perhaps interesting to note that many societies have accepted the need to educate children from a young age, while at the same time recognising that children themselves are likely to resist the process!

WORKING

Archaeology provides, on the whole, very little direct evidence of the education of children, but of course indirect evidence is obtainable from general evidence of levels of literacy and numeracy in adult society, on the premiss that most people would have learned their skills as youngsters.

It can also be difficult to discern evidence of the labour of children from archaeological sources, but it is clear that in most societies at most times, children were actively engaged in subsistence and economic work as a matter of necessity.

In modern western society, there is a general feeling of disapproval about the employment of children in all but a few limited spheres. Since the mid-nineteenth century, there has been a great deal of emphasis on the creation of laws to protect children from exploitation, to ensure their safety and to encourage their education. There are strict rules about how much paid work children are allowed to do, the form and type of work considered suitable, and the supervision and duration of it. The result of this well-meaning series of concerns has been to remove children from participation in adult work situations; they make no economic contribution to the family or society. We have created a concept of childhood nurture that has sanctified the notions of education and play, ascribing notions of innocence, purity and happiness to this period of life that in some ways has the effect of demonising adulthood and adult responsibility. This has, it may be argued, effectively marginalised the existence of children within their own communities. They have become a separate, non-producing but highly consuming group outside of mainstream life. Children rarely have the opportunity to participate in and learn about the world of work, and adults who are not parents can spend their working lives with no or very little experience of the needs or potentials of children.

In global terms, this is rather odd. Outside the developed world, children are intimately concerned with the subsistence and employment activities of adults from an early age, and take an important place in many economies, both urban and rural. Before the modern era, this was also true of children almost everywhere.

It has become a widely-held assumption that the employment of children is somehow wrong, immoral and dangerous for a society; our history books stress the evils of satanic mill owners in grim industrial towns of the Victorian era, or the fate of matchgirls and chimney sweeps. Novels such as Charles Kingsley's *The Water Babies* or Charles Dickens' *Oliver Twist* have created an impression so strong in our minds that the very notion of a wage-earning child has become synonymous with cruelty and suffering. It is of course sadly true that many children are dreadfully used, to the extent of kidnap, physical abuse and actual slavery in a number of industries such as carpet weaving and garment making, and in areas such as domestic service and prostitution. Stories about the fate of such children create international outcry, rightly, and serve to underline the view that child labour is necessarily unacceptable.

That this is an unbalanced view must be obvious. Children at work in many societies are valued, cared for and regarded as a positive force. Their role in the support of their families is central, not as an asset to be exploited, but as an opportunity for their own socialisation and entry into adult life. Their work is a way of learning and creating their own opportunities for later success and acceptance.

It is, indeed, possible that in divorcing children from the world of work and adults we are doing both them and society in general a disservice. Western children display higher levels of delinquency and antisocial behaviour than those of more traditional societies. They also suffer more frequently from a fear of joining the adult world that manifests itself in symptoms such as anorexia and self-harming. Constantly bombarded by advertising, they lack the ability to earn the money needed to satisfy their desires and so are more easily led into petty crime or, if met with disappointment, alternative behaviours ranging from angst and depression to drug abuse. They often find it difficult to adjust, once they leave school, to the need to earn a living and are often seen as a liability by employers. They are untrained and unprepared for the adult world, and yet we are surprised by their acts of rebellion and their refusal to conform. Physically mature, they are relegated to a second childhood as junior employees.

This does not happen in traditional societies to anything like the same extent. It has been noted, nonetheless, that there may be considerable variation in the way children are engaged in work in simple societies. Studies of the children of the Hadza people of southern Tanzania, a community which maintains a lifestyle based on hunting and foraging, show that they are engaged early in the struggle for subsistence:

> Hadza children appear to be given many errands and to perform useful tasks, bidden and unbidden....Children of either sex may be asked to hold a protesting toddler when the mother leaves camp to forage....Children commonly are sent to fetch water and sometimes firewood....Even toddlers are sent to carry things from one house to another or one adult to another....Hadza parents use physical punishment, and we see and hear them shout prohibitions and commands at children.[13]

In contrast, the children of the !Kung people, with a similar economy, 'seldom allocate work to children, seldom utter commands, and seldom ask children to run errands'.[14] The life of !Kung children consists of play in and around the camp – they are not even asked to mind younger siblings. The economies of these two societies are generally comparable to each other, and the choice to employ or not employ children within the labour of the community therefore seems to stem from social attitudes rather than necessity. How and why these attitudes have developed are questions that remain unanswered, but which are surely deserving of more research.

We have very little evidence for the work of children in the prehistoric past, but we can suppose that they would have been involved in a number of the activities noted among the Hadza in many cases such as helping to forage, hunting small animals, caring for younger children, running errands, fetching and carrying. A common activity for boys in pastoral communities is minding stock. Small children might be given responsibility for poultry in the barnyard, while older boys look after sheep and cattle, an activity recorded in societies as diverse as fourteenth-century France and the twentieth-century Masai. Jean de Brie for example, at the age of seven, was responsible for the care of the geese and goslings, at eight minding pigs, at nine helping a cowherd and by eleven in charge of eighty lambs in a medieval French farmstead.[15] Girls in many parts of the world learn from household chores the skills of caring for the family, or the arts of dairying, weaving and pottery making. The life of Saint Alpaix records that in her twelfth-century childhood, as the eldest child of a peasant, she was expected to help with the ox plough team, and carry baskets of manure to the garden and fields while her younger brothers watched the cows and sheep.[16] This type of activity tends to increase in complexity and responsibility as children mature and is a form of apprenticeship for their world and preparation for adult life. It can help to free parents too, to accept external cash employment outside the home and village to boost the family income.

There are forms of employment that are open to children simply because they are more suitable in size than adults, or because of their dexterity; chimney sweeps' boys have been mentioned above, as have modern carpet weavers. Modern figures for child employment in Kenya show that rural girls aged between nine and sixteen work on average 41 hours a week, and boys work 35 hours, and in countries including India, the Philippines and Senegal, seven-hour days are worked by children as young as five in occupations that vary from industrial and craft work to street vending and shoe-shining.[17]

The evidence for the work activities of children is likely to be very ephemeral in most situations; we can only use analogy with more recent societies to guess at the levels of assistance they gave their parents in daily or economic tasks. Thus we can imagine that Palaeolithic children accompanied their mothers on foraging expeditions, like the Hadza children, learning what places and seasons offered food and materials for tools, how to find plants and roots, how to trap and hunt small animals and birds, where to find safety and how to avoid hazards, and when old enough, accompanied hunting parties after larger game.

An ethnoarchaeological study of the Meriam Islanders suggests that the foraging activities of children may, in fact, be different enough from those of adults to be archaeologically visible. The researchers observed that the way in which the children gathered shellfish was different from the strategies of the adults, and they thought this was partly because of the constraints of the children's physical size and ability, and partly because their goals were actually rather different from those of their parents. Children are not so easily able to gather the larger species of shellfish because these tend to live out of their reach, on offshore rocks or in deeper water; they choose, therefore, to gather more of the smaller species, and gather a wider range of species than adults. Nor can they process the shells they gather as easily, so they tend to take them home and sit near the house to winkle the meat out of the shells, thus leaving more rubbish on the midden pile than their parents. This means that if we find a prehistoric shell midden with many small shells and a wide variety of species, especially where we might expect people to be able to find larger and more attractive species, we may be looking at the remains of children's food gathering activities rather than adult subsistence strategies. The researchers also noted that the children tend to go foraging on their own, in 'play groups' rather than with the adults, and that 'when it comes to subsistence, children learn mostly from other children, not adults'.[18]

If this holds true for other foraging societies, we might therefore expect children's activities to be responsible for a range of food remains at camp sites; bones of small mammals and birds, nut shells and fish bones and scales representing exploited species that adults might not necessarily consider worth collecting because of the effort needed both to gather and prepare them for eating. In the eyes of children, however, these might be species that are easily found and whose gathering and processing are worthwhile in the context of a game or because of the time they have available to undertake the work.

Remarkably, there may be some evidence of the learning and practising of essential skills in the manufacture of prehistoric flint tools. At Solvieux, in the Dordogne in France, analysis of the debitage or waste material produced by making flint tools, has suggested that at three separate locations an experienced flint knapper sat with a novice, who perhaps first watched a demonstration of the method of turning a flint core into usable flakes for knives. The novice then worked on two cores, creating his or her own debitage, before abandoning the rather mangled results of the attempts to copy the master's work. Also in France, at Pincevent in the Paris Basin, pieces of debitage have been refitted to study the process and skill of the flint knapper. The work of learners was made evident through collections of particularly thick flakes, with nasty hinge fractures instead of clean breaks, wandering angles of work and unsystematic approaches to working around the core. Some examples of debitage spreads were completely refitted, showing that despite all the work, there had been a failure to produce a usable tool that could be taken away. Sometimes the cores were abandoned before all the good flint had been removed; perhaps a young person's patience had been exhausted by their lack of success. It seems that their teachers were economical with materials – 'apprentice knappers appear to have had limited access to good quality raw material; they either worked inferior material or reworked material that had been abandoned for one reason or another by more accomplished knappers'.[19] A study at another site has suggested that there were several ranks of proficiency in flint toolmaking; nearest to the hearth in the centre of the working area, debitage was sparse and fine, suggesting the products of experienced and skillful workers – perhaps the older members of the group, who through their age and ability, claimed the right to work nearest the fire. Beyond this group were scatters of waste flakes that demonstrated a perfectly adequate but less fine technique, carried out by adults who were producing workaday tools. Further out still, the waste material was rough, with broken and incomplete material, and it has been suggested that the young people who were learning the skill sat furthest from the fire, practising alongside their elders. Ethnographic studies have occasionally noted the learning of these types of skills – in Tierra del Fuego children began learning to make slate and quartz arrowheads from three years old, according to one study.[20]

The identification of children's work in flint is beset by many problems. There is always an assumption that poorly made tools represent young, inexperienced workers, despite the obvious possibility that adults can be clumsy and inept too. Sometimes it is thought that small tools must necessarily be made by and for small hands. Again, this must be challenged. Children often lack the control necessary to manipulate very small items, whatever the dimensions of their hands. It is also true that making small fine tools requires a particular appreciation of the effects of strength, something that is generally learned over an extended period of time. Observations of adults and children working with clay have demonstrated to the author that it is adults who will choose to make the finer, more fiddly pieces, while children will often be happier manipulating larger lumps of the material (often with rather more force than is strictly necessary). Experiments are ongoing at the Lejre Experimental Centre in Denmark into the flint working of children and the relationships between the material produced by inexperienced knappers with archaeological evidence.

By the Neolithic period and the start of farming, children must have helped with the chores around a more permanent home, herding, helping to plant, harvest and process crops, and possibly helping to supplement the diet by foraging and gathering around the farmstead, as country children still do when they go mushroom gathering or blackberry picking.

Another innovation of the Neolithic period, some 5,500 years ago, was the introduction of pottery. Pottery offers us another potential source of evidence for the involvement of children in craft activities, through their fingerprints. Experimental work, combined with studies of pottery from actual archaeological sites, has demonstrated that there is a correlation between age and size of the ridge breadths in fingerprint patterns. Fingerprints are formed by the seventh month in the womb; from that time on, the only changes are in size of the ridges and furrows. Measurement of the gaps between the ridges is affected by numerous factors – the ethnic background of the subject, their gender, physical body and hand sizes can complicate the picture, as can the tendency of clay to shrink as it dries. It is still possible to differentiate age ranges within a population by measuring the prints, as was demonstrated in a study of ceramic figurines and pots from the Sinagua people of northern Arizona, a farming society that predates the modern Navajo and other peoples of the region. At the pueblos or villages of this society, a number of small clay figurines representing animals are found. Many of these are crudely made, lumpy pieces, in contrast with the fine cooking and storage pots also excavated. Analysis of fingerprints suggests that the average age of figurine makers was between 11 and 13. Some of the pieces were made by adults, perhaps parents or friends of the child, whilst others were made by children younger than eight-and-a-half. The pottery was mainly formed by adults, although some was made by people who could have been as young as ten. 'The corrugated vessels … appear to be made primarily by adults, although the range of producers included some children. Several rather sloppily-made vessels had smaller ridge breadth values and may represent children who are still in the learning stages'.[21] This fascinating technique of analysis has yet to be carried out on a large scale on European prehistoric ceramics, but it is possible that we could learn much about the involvement of children in production of ceramics for both domestic and trading use from such a study.

A further example of fingerprint evidence comes from an excavation carried out in August 2003 at Moston Hall, near Manchester; a brick dated to perhaps as early as AD 1590 was found to hold an impression of the fingerprint of a child aged about ten, suggesting the employment of children in this industry.

Indirect evidence for the labour of children in much more difficult conditions comes from an important Bronze Age site in Britain. Near Llandudno are the Great Orme Mines. During the eighteenth and nineteenth centuries, the copper ore here was worked on an industrial scale, but the miners were several times surprised to find themselves breaking into much older shafts and caverns, in which they found prehistoric tools. Since the closure of the mines and the cessation of commercial production, a great deal of research has been carried out both inside the workings and outside, under the waste rock left scattered over the area by the mining operations. So far, over 4 miles (6km) of tunnels have been explored, and over 3,000 stone hammers and 30,000 bone picks and shovels have been found. Carbon dating shows that the mine was being worked 3,500 years ago, with deep vertical shafts and adits hundreds of metres long cut into the hillside. Many of the tunnels are extremely small, too small to have been cut and worked by an adult. The conclusion must be made, therefore, that it was children who climbed and crawled down in the darkness, perhaps lit by torches or simple lamps of animal fat, to labour at breaking away the ore from the limestone rock and drag it to the surface. The dangers of this work cannot be underestimated: rockfalls, bad air, no safety equipment, rope or wooden ladders, darkness, water and the toxicity of the copper itself must have offered constant hazards.

Were the adults who sent the children down the mine callous or cruel? Probably not. It is doubtful that they would themselves have been wholly aware of all the dangers, and they willingly faced them themselves. In the Bronze Age, two materials were vital – the copper ore and the tin with which it was alloyed to make the metal bronze, a metal that was highly valued both for making tools and weapons that were felt to be far superior to stone, and for the wealth and status that ownership of bronze goods implied in contemporary society. The families who controlled and mined the copper ore must have had great advantages; the work was probably seen as a co-operative effort for the good of everyone involved, and while the children faced great danger and hard work, they also had the security of an occupation that could provide steady wealth and freedom from hunger and want. It would be dangerous to try to apply modern values to such prehistoric events, and it would be almost certainly unfair to these Bronze Age families.

Aristotle records that children carried out a variety of tasks in classical Greece. Gender separation in Greek society was very marked, so the work done by boys and that carried out by girls was different; both sexes, however, carried out jobs normally done by slaves, as 'some menial duties are honourable for free men if performed when they are still young'.[22]

The Codex Mendoza is a painted pictorial manuscript commissioned in the 1540s by the Spanish Viceroy to the Indies as a means of showing the king of Spain something of the life and culture of his new Aztec subjects. It contains a number of scenes which depict the working education of the children and describes the stages through which they passed. By the age of five, girls began

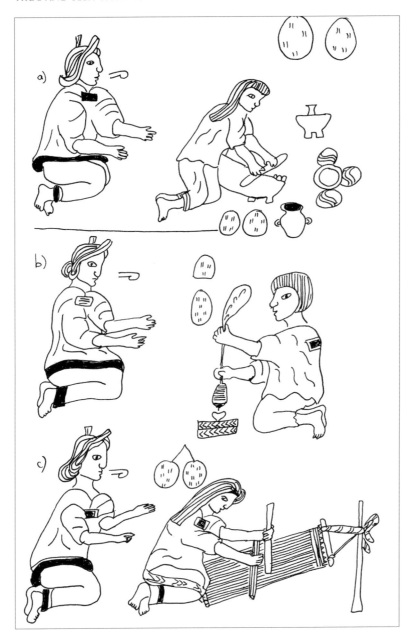

20 Aztec girls learning crafts from their mothers: a) making tortillas – the lobed object on the right is a griddle, and the girl is said to be 13 years old; b) spinning; c) weaving. After illustrations in the Codex Mendoza

their training in the preparation of cloth. All Aztec women, of all ranks of life, made textiles and at birth a girl baby would be presented with a distaff and spindle and basket, as well as a broom; her umbilical cord would be buried under a maize grinding stone or metate. The first stage of training would simply be how to hold the tools. The little girl would be spinning cotton by the time she was seven. Other pictures show girls grinding corn and making tortillas, and weaving on a backstrap loom (20).

21 Aztec boys learning crafts from their fathers: a) carpentry; b) lapidary; c) metal-working;
d) painting; e) feather-working. After illustrations in the Codex Mendoza

Five-year-old boys were expected to carry firewood and goods to the market,
and by the age of seven to use nets for fishing. They were expected to be warriors
but also to be farmers or to carry on a craft, usually that of their fathers. The
Codex Mendoza shows boys sitting in front of their fathers watching and learning
the skills of woodworking, cutting and mounting semi-precious stones, using
a bowl furnace for metalworking, writing or painting on a tablet and working
with feathers. (21) The making of feather mosaics for fans, clothing and cloaks,

headdresses and shields was a highly prized art form; featherworkers lived in neighbourhoods called calpolli in the major cities, and the whole family had roles in the production of the artefacts. Children made the glue, women sorted and dyed the feathers, and men prepared designs and made up the finished articles. The communities had their own temples and schools, and people not part of an established featherworking family were excluded from joining the profession, much like the system of medieval guilds.

Other crafts that Aztec children would have learned include reed sandal making, pottery making, stone carving, and the production of obsidian tools.

Egyptian tomb paintings and reliefs show children at work at a number of useful activities, including domestic chores, minding siblings, gleaning in fields, scaring birds away from crops, ploughing and sowing seed, and herding cattle, and as mentioned earlier, some ancient Egyptian children served apprenticeships. One picture from a Middle Kingdom tomb depicts a boy working with two men in a kitchen. This 'cartoon' is accompanied by text which tells us that the boy is being sent to tell others food is ready, and that he is agreeing to the order. Children also had more formal employment as workers in vineyards and as domestic servants. Others worked as dancers and entertainers. Some of these servants were slaves, in some cases Nubians, depicted with different hairstyles to those of their Egyptian contemporaries.

Medieval European children who did not stay at home to work in the household or on the land often entered into service at about ten years of age. Many worked in the households of richer families. Boys would be employed in the stables, as pages and valets, in kitchens or as porters, while girls worked in sculleries, dairies, as childnurses or maids. Others worked in trades such as weaving, silkmaking, metalworking, brewing, baking, blacksmithing and milling. Some of the labour these children undertook was very heavy. In the fourteenth century, children worked in the mines of the Montagne Noir in France, leaving their small footprints in the clay in the Caleil cave. Children whose parents could afford to buy them apprenticeships could expect, at the end of their servitude, to enter into a profession as a registered journeyman; poorer children might learn a trade as well, but their future would be as members of the unregistered workforce, or as servants to guild members. Like apprentices, these children would often have been bonded by their parents to remain with their master for a set period of time, and would live in the houses and workshops of their employers.

The larger households would often employ several members of the same family from the locality, or indeed, members of poorer branches of their own family as domestic servants. This was seen as a generous way to support unluckier relatives.

Apprenticeships generally lasted between seven and ten years, and children generally embarked upon them in their early teens. Young people often had little choice in the profession they were to learn; much would depend on their family's connections and degree of influence. The system was very formal, with contracts and bonds of surety, and parents would pay a fee to the master for the child's acceptance and support during the period of training. Apprenticeships were registered with the appropriate guilds, and a young person would need to have a sponsor, who would be willing to pay a fee if they failed to learn or work properly, stole from their master or ran away. Both boys and girls entered into apprenticeships; many more professions were open to girls and women in the medieval world than is sometimes recognised. Girls might, in particular, become trained in various cloth industries, apothecary practices and, above all, brewing, a particularly female profession, under the tutelage of an 'alewife'. A number of documents survive from the period 1380 to 1480 relating to apprenticeships in the region of Orleans in France, and these show most boys began their servitude between the ages of seven and twenty, most in their mid-teens, while girls were apprenticed generally before the age of 12. Surviving accounts suggest that in most cases, care was taken to provide a reasonable standard of living for these young people, and to ensure that they learned their trades at a reasonable pace according to their abilities. In 1255 apprentice potters were sent to gather light sticks for firewood at Brill; blacksmiths' apprentices worked the bellows and apothecaries' assistants ground the herbs and held the bowls while their master bled the patient. Much of the training consisted of fetching, carrying and above all, watching. Eventually, the apprentice would be allowed to work on simple pieces under supervision. A particular trade, that of the illuminator, has left us with a variety of surviving trial pieces, some very crudely made and others, clearly made by more practised (or talented) youngsters. Some pieces are actually signed with the child's name and age, and examples of work by children as young as 11 survive. Others found the work boring, and have doodled in the margins, or written complaints and jokes on waste scraps of paper or parchment.

Industrial employment of children in the West has left a wealth of historical material and depictions, and also some occasional archaeological evidence in the form of buildings designed to house child workers, such as those preserved at Quarry Bank Mill, Styal, the premises of the philanthropic employer Samuel Grey (22). The census information on child employment from 1851 however demonstrates that most children in Britain were working in more informal settings. The statistics show that 28.4 per cent (120,000) of boys and 7.2 per cent (12,000) of girls under the age of 15 were employed in agriculture, probably close to home. The textile industries were the largest employers of the girls – 41.3 per cent (98,000), followed by domestic work: 30 per cent (71,000). Other sources of work for girls included the fashion trade, metalworking, dockwork, the pottery industry and shop and tavern work. For boys, after agriculture the textile mills were the largest employers – 19.4 per cent (82,000) and dockwork: 10.9 per cent (46,000), with mines, metalworking and manufacturing, fashion, shop and tavern work, the building trade, the pottery industry and domestic work all offering other jobs. In

22 Child 'harriers' working in a mine. After an illustration in a nineteenth-century parliamentary commission report

all, 423,000 boys and 237,000 girls were earning a living in 1851 in the United Kingdom.[23] Figures for France between 1839 and 1843 show that 143,665 workers were under the age of 16 and represented 12.1 per cent of the total workforce.

American slave-owners are said to have regarded slave children aged below ten as a liability, and they were not normally made to labour until the age of 12, because the field work typical of the slave plantations required both size and stamina. However, poor immigrant children of even younger ages were set to work in sweat shops and manufactories in such centres as New York and Boston, sometimes in appalling conditions, a practice which continued until late into the nineteenth century legally, and illegally to the present day, according to some reports.

The visibility of children in the workforce is not high in archaeological terms, but it can sometimes be discerned or inferred. The importance of children's contribution to labour, however, should not be underestimated; it may often have been a crucial element in family or community survival, as it often is today in the Third World. And it is likely to have been ubiquitous; every form of work would probably have had a job for children to do, a small part but an essential one of the whole. The work of children may fall into the category of unrecognised labour that used to also comprise the work of large numbers of women; it is often largely carried out within the domestic sphere or close to home, it is informally organised and does not carry the same recognition or benefits as adult employment. Children are not members of unions, guilds or pressure groups. Having accepted the importance of female labour and tasks, it surely must be time to recognise the same for those of children, whether that labour is self-supporting, part of the communal family effort or in the commercial and industrial spheres.

23 Children working at cotton spinning machines, Macon, Georgia, USA. From an early twentieth-century photograph

TRAINING FOR LEADERSHIP

In many societies, children of higher classes undergo a different form of training or apprenticeship from the offspring of workers. They need to learn the process of command and the skills of man management, and their education in these respects often begins very early. We have noted something of the special provision for such children already – their toys, their tutors and the like, but other forms of preparation for such life roles can be briefly mentioned. Warrior training has often been deemed particularly important for a boy whose birth predestines him for leadership. From Tutankhamun to Louis XIII of France, martial toys and activities have figured strongly in the artefacts and records associated with their boyhoods. A notable system for the education of young leaders existed within the Royal Navy during the eighteenth and earlier nineteenth centuries, both for officer ranks and for non-commissioned ranks. A promising lad might start as an officer's servant or cabin boy at the age of ten or so, rising in time to become a master's mate and from there to master, purser or gunner, important ranks on a fighting ship; occasionally, such boys could be entered as midshipmen and rise to the officer class. Boys from more privileged backgrounds would start as midshipmen, sometimes only nominally (being 'on the book' of a particular ship, perhaps commanded by a family friend or acquaintance, without actually going to sea until a few years later) but often in actuality. The captain, among his other duties, was duty-bound to arrange for the education of these 'young gentlemen', subjects including Latin and Greek, history, mathematics, religion and geography, as well as the more vocational mapping, navigation and sailing lessons. Nevertheless, these children were expected to take their place as leaders during fighting actions, to direct cannon fire or small boat operations, to care for and be responsible for the men under their command, and to maintain their authority and superiority over sailors old enough to be their fathers and grandfathers. Rather surprisingly, perhaps, the system worked, in many cases very well, producing some of the best naval officers in history.

For the child 'born to the purple', no amount of preparation can sometimes serve to secure their futures. The unhappy examples of Nero and his ilk are well known; and to the Romans we can add Dom Pedro II of Brazil and Pu Yi Xuantong, last emperor of China.

Dom Pedro II – in full 'Dom Pedro de Alcantara João Carlos Leopoldo Salvador Bibiano Franciso Xavier de Paula Leocadio Miguel Gabriel Rafael Gonzaga de Bragança e Borbón' was born in Rio de Janeiro on 2 December 1825 and was the second and final emperor of Brazil. His father, Pedro I, abdicated in 1831 when Pedro II was only five years old and abandoned the country for Portugal, leaving his infant son and Brazil to be ruled by a series of regents until Pedro II reached his majority. As Pedro I had been a known womaniser and philanderer, the regents decided that Pedro II would follow a different course and employed tutors specifically to raise his consciousness and morality. As a result, the young Pedro became an accomplished linguist with an abiding interest in comparative religions.

While Pedro II was growing up, Brazilian politicians engaged in various power struggles which were beginning to affect the state of the nation. Because of this it was decided that Pedro's majority would be declared early in order that he could ascend the throne and bring stability. And so in 1840, the 15-year-old Pedro, now a tall, blue-eyed and fair-haired youth, was declared emperor and took control. Pedro II will be most remembered for starting in train motions that eventually led to his daughter, Princess Imperial Isabella, abolishing slavery. This, however, caused the downfall of the Brazilian royal family; the powerful landowners rebelled and caused a revolution, leading to the establishment of a republic. Pedro and his family were exiled to Europe.

Pu Yi was Manchu (originally a nomadic people from Manchuria) and a member of the Qing Dynasty which had ruled China since 1644. The Manchus considered themselves superior to the indigenous Chinese and retained their

24 Dom Pedro II (centre) and other juvenile heads of state, caricatured in a nineteenth-century print

own separate language, clothing and settlements and refused to allow Chinese settlers in the Manchu homeland. The Qing Dynasty was in trouble by the time Pu Yi was born on 7 February 1906, as China had become dominated by westerners. Dowager Empress Tzu Hsi ruled the country after imprisoning the titular emperor for conspiring against her. It is said she had him poisoned in prison. As she was on her deathbed, she named Pu Yi, nephew of the murdered emperor, as her heir. He was only three years old when she died. His father, Prince Ch'un, acted as regent but was disliked as he had no interest in politics and dissenters considered him spineless. In 1911, revolution swept through China against the foreigners and the hated Manchu government, forcing Prince Ch'un to abdicate in favour of General Yuan Shih-k'ai who suggested it was a good idea that Pu Yi also renounce the throne. So on 12 February 1912, the six-year-old emperor abdicated. He was, however, afforded great respect and allowed to remain within the walls of the Forbidden City where he grew up.

Eunuchs ran the Forbidden City and it was two years before Pu Yi even saw another child. Although no longer the emperor, Pu Yi was still treated as though he ruled and afforded great formality. Wherever he went he was accompanied by an enormous entourage ready to perform his slightest bidding. Although surrounded by a vast number of people, he hardly ever saw his parents; indeed he did not see his mother at all from age three to age ten, and his father only visited every couple of months, staying only for a few minutes each time.

The Second World War saw the beginning of the end of the Chinese Imperial Family with Pu Yi first of all coming under the control of the Japanese and then the Russians, before ending his days working in the gardens of the Academy of Sciences' Institute of Botany in Beijing. Artefacts and clothing of the last emperor are still displayed in Beijing today, although the message they carry is reinterpreted by the current regime to expose the decadence of the imperial system rather than to illustrate the strange life of a small boy emperor.

Modern ethnographic evidence clearly demonstrates that children all over the world are regularly employed in a vast array of paid or contributory labour, and indeed there are some jobs which are almost exclusively reserved for children because of their particular attributes, such as small size. It is a mistake to assume, from our modern western standpoint, that the capabilities of children at work are limited by ignorance, inexpertise or frailty. Given the opportunity, children can happily carry out complex and energetic tasks that most adults would be pushed to achieve; I recall particularly an extremely wet and unpleasant couple of days' excavation some years ago when the Surrey Young Archaeologists, aged between 8 and 12 years old, looked at the struggles of the adult volunteers to complete a very large trench, and rejected out of hand the offer that they could stay in the tent and do art work. Instead, they organised themselves into 'The Bucketeers' and worked the whole period taking full buckets from the diggers to the wheelbarrows, emptying them, and pushing the barrows to the spoilheaps. They refused to stop until the adults did, and the only adult help they accepted was assistance to upend the barrows to empty out the spoil. They ended up tired, aching, extremely dirty, and very proud that they had made a real contribution to the archaeology. You can imagine how proud we were of them! The identification of the need, the organisation of the workforce, and the decisions about how to carry out the tasks were all made by the children themselves. We should never underestimate the capabilities and determination of children, nor the contributions they can make.

3

PARENTS, CHILDREN AND DEATH

Perfect little body, without fault or stain on thee,
With promise of strength and manhood full and fair!
Though cold and stark and bare,
The bloom and charm of life doth a while remain on thee.

Thy mother's treasure wert thou; – alas! No longer
To visit her heart with wondrous joy; to be
Thy father's pride; – ah, he
Must gather his faith together, and his strength make stronger.
(From 'On a Dead Child' by Robert Bridges)

The provision of nurture, education and playthings by parents for children demonstrates their care for, and interest in, their development. Actual physical evidence for demonstrations of affection and love are, naturally, more rare, and often only become visible archaeologically in the treatment offered to the body of a loved child who has died. These moving testimonials are among the most emotive discoveries made by archaeology. Who can doubt the grief of those who laid to rest the body of a young woman and child of the Ertebølle culture at Vedbaek, north of Copenhagen, around 5000 BC? The woman's head lay on a cushion ornamented with snail shells and deer's teeth and beside her lay a new-born infant, resting on the wing of a swan. A tiny flint blade by the baby's side suggests that it might have been a boy.[1]

A study of the way in which children have been laid to rest in a society offers much information about the organisation of its social relations and its beliefs. For the archaeologist, the burial practices adopted for children often represent the only visible evidence available for the presence of children in a society at all, and so have been studied with rather more regularity and depth than other aspects of the life of ancient children.

Recently the intact skeleton of a four-year-old child has been discovered in the Lapedo Valley, 136km north of Lisbon. In the earth floor of a rock shelter, the bones were discovered sealed below a layer 21,000 years old. It has been speculated that the child died 26,000 years ago, during the early Gravettian period of the Palaeolithic. This find is important because it represents the earliest anatomically modern human people in southern Iberia, moving into an area previously inhabited by Neanderthals, and because of the treatment of the body, demonstrating that beliefs and rituals were part of the lives of these first modern human societies. The child's body was accompanied by a marine shell pendant around its neck, some animal bones, and a thick coating of red ochre, possibly originally coating an animal skin blanket laid over the corpse, a treatment not before found in western Europe. A well-known anthropologist, Erik Trinkhaus, has hailed this discovery: 'Even though these are the remains of just one small child, we'll now be able to make reasonable predictions about the biology of the people who lived in Iberia not long after the Neanderthals'.[2]

Further early evidence for burial practices relating to children comes from the Grotte des Enfants, at Grimaldi in Italy. Remains were first found here in 1874 and 1875; the bones of two small children were recovered. Dating studies suggest they were laid to rest over 12,000 years ago. Several techniques were employed to establish the age and state of development of these children, including the amount of calcification in the bones and teeth. Children's bones are soft, and as they grow they harden and become stronger but more brittle. Estimates of the degree of hardness can offer an educated guess about age. The results achieved for the two children from the cave (GE1 and GE2) are shown below:

		GE1	GE2
Dental age		3 years +/- 12 months 4 years +/- 12 months	18 months +/- 6 months
Bone age	Skull	24-36 months	12-24 months
	Mandible	more than 12 months	more than 12 months
	Limbs	36-48 months	18-24 months
	Spine	around 36 months	12-26 months

25 Age estimates for the children found in the Grotte des Enfants, Grimaldi, Italy. After Gambier, D., 1995, p.813[3]

The discrepancies shown in the estimates in the table result firstly from individual variations in the way particular children's bones grow, and secondly from the sheer antiquity of the samples measured. Taking the evidence as a whole, it is possible to suggest that child GE1 was about three or three-and-a-half years old, while child GE2 was perhaps just under two. Attempts were also made to identify the gender of the children; this is very difficult to do with such small children, and the researchers were also not sure whether factors that apply to modern humans would have applied to Palaeolithic children. In the end, they felt it likely that both children were of the same sex, and one analyst believes that this was female. The younger child, GE2, had particularly robust bones, raising questions about its parentage and relationship to GE1. Shockingly, the way this strong young child died was evident; lodged in one of its vertebrae was the point of a stone arrowhead. No evidence was recovered about how the other child died, although it is worth remembering that many wounds can cause death without leaving a mark on bones. Both children had been carefully laid side-by-side deep in the cave; there are some traces of colour which may suggest that they were annointed with ochre, a natural earth pigment often found in ancient burials.

Across and around the bodies were more than 1,700 pierced shells, which had been strung in longitudinal groups to form something that may have been like a grass skirt in shape. Bones of a young deer may represent an offering.

Perhaps we can interpret this site as the record of an ancient tragedy – a small family of roving hunter-gatherers are attacked by a rival clan. The adults escape but two children are caught and killed. Recovering their bodies, their parents laid them to rest in the deep security of the cave, wearing their best shell jewellery and with a fawn as an offering to the spirits of the afterlife.

An analysis of burials of the Natufian people (10500–8500 BC), one of the earliest farming cultures in the Levant, suggests that there was little formal organisation in the disposal of the dead. Nevertheless, there are a few incidences of both children and adults being buried with grave goods and some elaboration of ritual. Whilst adults may earn status during their lives, it is hard to see how children could have had the opportunity to do so, and therefore it may be possible to assume that these elaborate children's graves represent evidence of a society in which inherited wealth and status have already become important.[4] The same analysis goes on to chart the increase in the frequency of children's graves as farming became more important across the region; there are clues to social organisation to be discerned in the different ways in which the bodies of adults and children were treated. The Early (Pre-Pottery) Neolithic period (8100–5600 BC) saw a difference in burial practice, as adult bodies were often decapitated and their remains were interred in particular locations, whilst children's bodies retained their skulls but were sometimes simply dumped. In the following centuries it became the custom in some areas to collect adult skulls after death and to plaster the bones into the semblance of the living face, perhaps indicating an ancestor cult. This was never done with children's skulls.

The next period saw the invention and use of pottery (5600–4000 BC), and in the Northern Levant and Mesopotamia, elaborate and rich burials of children are recorded; at the Nahal Qanah Cave, the grave of a young child included over 1kg of gold decoration and artefacts. Across the Levant, jars began to be used as containers for the bodies of infants and foetuses. There is some thought process at work here about preserving the remains in a discrete form, keeping the whole body together in one place. Contained burials of adults do not appear until the following Chalcolithic (or Copper) Age, when the bones of adults were collected for secondary burial in pottery containers placed in cemeteries near the settlements. Children are seldom found in these cemeteries, but their bodies are sometimes found within the villages.

Children do appear in European Neolithic cemeteries, such as those of the Linearbandkeramik cultures. Study of these burial communities gives us some opportunities to address issues of child mortality and survival rates. (26) gives some data on a number of cemeteries of this period and the relative numbers of child and adult graves identified. Several of these cemeteries had incidences of both inhumation and cremation rites, and many of the population in some of them have either not been studied, or were not sufficiently well preserved for identification to age or gender.

Site	children ages 0–14	infants 0–1 also included in first column	juveniles 15–20	adults 20+	male: female
Kleinhadersdorf	1			11	7:3
Rutzing/Haid	6		2	9	8:2
Nitra	22	(5)	8	43	27:23
Bruchstedt	20	(0)	7	34	17:23
Sonderhausen	12	(0)	3	32	17:18
Wanderleben	72	(10)	26	118	65:80
Wittmar	3		2	11	3:7
Niedermerz	1	(0)	11	17	
Rixheim	6	(2)	3	14/5	7/8:11

26 Demographic composition of selected LBK cemeteries[5]

These figures show that about half the deceased in these burial grounds were children or juveniles, and in several cases the proportions of children under 14 years old represent about one third of the total. These levels of mortality are not uncommon in preindustrial societies.

The point at which a child becomes recognised a full member of society is reflected in the manner chosen for the disposal of the remains of children who have died. In many societies, children under a certain age are excluded from adult burial places. There are a number of possible reasons for this. In communities where infant mortality is high, the cost of providing a funeral for a small child may be too much to bear, particularly if such costs have to be met year after year. In other societies, small children may be regarded as not yet fully human, and therefore not eligible for burial rites. A particular group of special children's cemeteries are found in the west of Ireland. Under earlier Roman Catholic law, children who die before they can be baptised could not be buried in hallowed ground. Their parents did not want, however, to dispose of them without some care, and so small isolated plots of ground came to be utilised from the medieval period as *ceallunaigh* or killeens (children's cemeteries), some of which have been the subject of research, especially in Co. Galway and Co. Kerry. The name derives from the Latin *cella*, a word used to describe a sanctum or small chapel. These sites were sometimes shared with other deceased people for whom normal burial was thought inappropriate, including stillborn babies, suicides, shipwrecked sailors whose religion was unknown, strangers, murderers and victims of murder whose spirits might be unquiet. In the medieval period, there was much debate about whether the souls of unbaptised infants went straight to hell or to a particular kind of infant's limbo.

Killeens were sometimes sited at abandoned churches, holy wells, wayside shrines and crosses; others were placed close to sites with much more ancient associations – menhirs, ringforts and 'burnt mounds', areas of fire-cracked stones possibly representing ancient feasting sites. Examples include the killeen on Illaunloughan, where the burial site developed next to an ancient oratory, and Caherlehillan, at an early medieval ecclesiastical enclosure, and beside an ogham stone at Kildreenagh. In the middle nineteenth century, each parish might have several of these burial grounds, and the graves were often provided with rough stone markers. In recent times, it is recorded that the burials usually took place after dark, and that often they would be carried out by the father of the child. Despite the secretive and unceremonial nature of the interment, some have been found to consist of stone-lined cists. Coffins of pine were also found.

There is some evidence from the Neolithic and Bronze Ages for special children's cemeteries in Britain; a small burial ground was discovered at Eastry, Kent, dating from this period. There were three adult burials, all from the last period of the site's use; before that, six children aged between six and 12 had been buried there, and there were also two cremations of new-born babies.[6] There are also some isolated graves – at Durrington in Wiltshire, grave G7 was the unusually deep burial of a young child. The grave also contained a deposit of cremated bones, plus a length of antler interpreted as a favourite toy, perhaps a teething tool, or a comforter, which had areas rubbed quite smooth.[7]

Special areas also seem to have been reserved for children within communal burial places in the Neolithic period. West Kennet long barrow in Wiltshire (27) dates from approximately 3600 BC and contains five chambers. Fully excavated in the 1950s, the remains of approximately 45 individuals varying in age from babies to the elderly were located within these chambers and 'it is noticeable that all of the chambers contained children (ranging from infants up to juveniles) but the SE chamber stands out for the ten juveniles contained in it'.[8] This chamber must therefore have been a special area for certain members of the community, those who would never reach adulthood.

At the passage tombs of Fourknocks, in Co. Meath, there is evidence to suggest that after the main use for adult burials, the sites were employed for the burials of children. It would appear that a series of cists were inserted into the passage of the small Fourknocks I mound after it had been infilled. The remains of 21 children were found, three cremated. Seven of the children were newborn, six were under 12 months old, three under 24 months, and one child was about five years old. The seventh body was too damaged for a determination to be made. During the Bronze Age, further soil layers allowed the insertion of four secondary cists; Cist I contained the crouched burial of an eight-year-old child with a Food Vessel pot. In Cist II a series of burials had been made, each disturbing those that had gone before. The remains of a five year old, a two year old and a seven year old were identified. A two-year-old child had been buried in Cist III. Fragments of other bones were found in and around the mound.

27 West Kennet long barrow. *Photo courtesy of S.P. Dyer*

In the Fourknocks II mound, adult graves were found in a rock cut trench; children's remains were only found in the passage. All eight were aged under five, most being neonates. In a number of cases, it is clear that the original burial monument was disused or even falling into disrepair when the children were buried.

A similar pattern of the reuse of chambered tombs for the burial of neonates is recorded from the Point of Cott chambered tomb on Westray in the Orkney Islands, and also at Isbister and at Quanterness. It is possible that the killeens are a similar response to these Neolithic and Bronze Age examples. People who had lost a child wanted to bury their remains within some form of sanctified ground; denied access to the normal or adult burial places, they chose a place of ancient meaning and holiness. In this way, they honoured and cared for their children at the last, despite their exclusion by other parts of the community.

The provision of ornate monuments for children's graves is a generally rare phenomenon; they do occur, however, in several societies and periods, notably in Rome and its provinces where ornate sarcophagi and stone grave markers are fairly well represented, and in eighteenth- and nineteenth-century Europe and America. There are some examples in Britain today; teddy-bear shaped stones, for example, although these are often frowned upon by the church authorities.

Clearly we would not think that a teddy-bear shaped memorial stone would be a suitable monument for an adult, or even a teenager. Perceptions of attitudes to children at various ages and stages of life are evident in burial practices. Babies' bodies are often treated differently from those of older children, and children's graves are sometimes substantially different from those of young adults or older people. The stages of difference vary between cultures and periods, but they must reflect cultural and social divisions and perceptions within societies based on age and growth of children.

It is not at all uncommon to find that the graves of babies or unweaned children are placed in very different situations from the rest of the community. The Dyaks of New Guinea place the bodies of young infants who have died in the branches of a tree. They believe that humans spring from trees, and that such babies have left their trees too soon and must go back to them. Their souls were not yet ready to take on human form, but if the soul resides in the tree a while longer, it will be more prepared to enter the mother's body later and result in a healthy child.

In the Roman world, newborn infants were often buried beneath the overhanging eaves of houses, and indeed these were the only burials officially permitted within the confines of Roman towns. This reflects the Roman view that children in the first month or two of life were not yet really human beings. The Etruscan civilisation seems to have buried babies in separate cemeteries, using places like abandoned farmhouses to do so. Once again, children are not always included in the cemeteries of the 'normal' population.

The evidence for prehistoric customs of this type is sometimes to be found in the absence of infant burials in other collections of graves. It is hardly surprising that we should find very few interments from the Palaeolithic period; after such a vast period of time, very few bodies survive, let alone those of children, although amazingly there are a couple of Neanderthal examples. In a Syrian cave, the body of a two-year-old Neanderthal child has been found, accompanied by a piece of worked flint; a deliberate burial of a Neanderthal baby has been found at the Amud cave in Israel, where the evidence seems to suggest that 50,000 years ago, the body of a baby less than a year old was carefully placed in a niche in the cave wall, with the jaw bone of a red deer, and the niche was then walled up. Various other deliberate Neanderthal burials of children have been claimed, although there is much discussion over whether these truly represent a funerary ritual, or were much more casual depositions.

It has been calculated that in preindustrial societies, a normal rate of infant mortality should be about 15–30 per cent of the total deaths, but in fact in most Neolithic grave groups, there are very few infant remains to be found. Chalcolithic and Early Bronze Age cemeteries in Europe display a similar lack of infant burials, and it is therefore possible that there was a substantially different burial rite for young children at the time.

This is not always the case; the Ertebølle culture of southern Scandinavia around 5000 BC buried infants and young children in communal cemeteries, often with grave goods, sometimes with adults, and sometimes alone. Infants and young children account for some 10 per cent of the cemetery populations in this culture, a figure which seems a little low. This may suggest that the bodies of some young children, at least, were treated differently. The Vedbaek cemetery included a group of pits within a circle of stones which was kept open throughout the settlement's use-life, and contained a group of mixed ages:

> At the bottom of one was a newborn on a tray with lumps of ochre under the head, and another three contained ochre-covered children with flint axes and blade knives, one also possessing two sets of red deer teeth, and in a fifth was a child accompanied by a jaw and other red deer bones and ochre. Of the same date are two cremation graves: one was in a pit, with the collected and cleaned bones of an adult placed on a wooden tray with an unburnt blade knife on top, the bones being only a small part of the original number, although all elements of the skeleton were present; the other contained the bones of two young adults, perhaps of opposite sex, a youth, a 5-year-old and a newborn, with some indications of dismemberment and defleshing having taken place before the cremation, along with the burnt remnants of three duck-feet, a wing from a bird of jackdaw size, a small piece of amber, red deer and fox tooth pendants.[9]

The funerary rituals carried out here were obviously complex; the evidence can be variously interpreted as including rites to destroy the body (perhaps to free the soul) before cremation, or to pacify the spirits of those violently injured and killed, using amuletic artefacts that may have been meant to allow a damaged body to reach the afterlife, or to prevent haunting by angry ghosts.

Cave sites seem to have been chosen as suitable burial places for children in a number of societies after the Palaeolithic, such as the Mesolithic group who used the Franchthi Cave, in Greece, and the Neolithic people near Abruzzo in Italy who placed several children's bodies in a ceremonial pattern in the Grotta dei Picconi. In the Levant around 7000 BC, infants were buried alongside others of their community at the Shukbah cave in Judea, which held the remains of young children from the Natufian culture, the period of the very beginnings of settled villages and agriculture in the region. Other Natufian communities, however, buried infants (and other children and adults) within the floors of their houses. This was also the case at the European late Starcevo/early Vinca culture (*c.*4500 BC) site of Obre I (Bosnia) where burials within the settlement are all of children. At the Linearbandkeramik site of Vedrovice in Moravia, five burials of young children were found beside the western walls of houses. At Ezero in Bulgaria, a settlement tell of the period 3500-2200 BC had 16 burials associated with it, ten of which were newborn babies which had been placed under the floors of houses or at the edge of the settlement, in stone-lined pits or ceramic urns. Urn burials of babies were found also at similar sites at Yunatsite and Gulubovo. However, infant burials were not found in the normal cemeteries of this culture.

The choice of the domestic setting for baby burials has been variously interpreted as relating to control of the environment: 'The young were buried in the settlements and under houses not because they were insignificant, but because they had a special kind of significance which expressed itself through the dialectic involving the domestication of death and the domestication of the processes of the living environment'[10] or relating more to the emotional comfort represented, as suggested by Ian Hodder: 'I expect that the house was always a safe haven, providing warmth and security, the focus of a child's early life, and the centre of domestic production'.[11] Another view suggests that burial of the very young in or near houses was conceptually linked to the continuity of the settlement, retaining the life force within the community.[12] An element of this notion seems to have been retained in the ancient Greek world where babies were also buried under house floors 'where their souls could be reborn into the women of the same family'.[13]

In the ancient Egyptian pyramid builders' town of Faiyum, excavated in the late nineteenth century by Sir W.M. Flinders Petrie, many baby burials were found under the floors of the houses. They had been placed in boxes or chests previously used for other purposes such as keeping clothes, and some chests contained two or three bodies. On the other hand, a cemetery close to Deir el-Medina contained the bodies of over 100 children, some interred in coffins, others placed in baskets, chests or amphorae. Many were accompanied by amulets, jewellery, and jars of food. In addition, there were burials of still-born babies, placentas and foetuses. Slightly higher up the hill were graves of older children and adolescents, and higher still were adult graves. Among the burials of small children and infants, some of the burial containers included the names of the families to which the children had belonged, and various grave goods such as a razor or a sandal. One child, buried in a box, was named Ariki. He was severely deformed, but his parents had nevertheless gone to some lengths to provide him with a proper funeral. The box was painted yellow with black borders, and carried written inscriptions on its side.[14] The evidence from Deir el-Medina seems, overall, to point to a concern that the souls of children be accorded the same care as those of adults, and although the funerary rituals were generally less complex and expensive for children, they were presumably as well prepared as the families could afford. There is no sense in which the evidence suggests that children were not accepted as fully human and spiritual beings.

The evidence for later periods in Europe tends to show young children appearing more regularly in general cemeteries and burial places; a distinct change has been observed between the practices carried out in the Middle Bronze Age and those of the Late Bronze Age in Central Europe. In the latter period there is a considerable increase in the percentage of children being included in general cemeteries, and having their own graves rather than being inserted into the grave of an adult. It seems that at this time, children's burials were being accompanied with the same types of rituals accorded to their elders. 'The … increase of interhuman contacts during the Bronze Age may have been followed by an easier acceptance of membership of a given social group…. The relaxation of conditions of initiation led to small children being treated as group members with full rights'.[15] A similar pattern is observed at Owslebury in Hampshire in the later Iron Age and Romano-British periods. Burials of very young children at this site accounted for 35 per cent of the total.[16] However, variations in the pattern occur. Nearby, there are different distributions to be found at two sites in or close to Winchester. In the Victoria Road cemetery in the city, which was a fairly typical Romano-British burial ground, there were very few burials for very young children in what may have been a Christian site. However, the site at Oram's Arbour near Winchester is a prehistoric enclosure which was abandoned late in the Iron Age. It began to be reused from the second century AD, when burials were introduced in the centre and ditches of the site. Fifty-two of the burials, all in the ditches, were of newly born babies, forming 77 per cent of the total. There was also a burial of a woman who had died in childbirth, two double baby burials, and one of a man with a baby at his feet. Unlike the adult graves, the baby graves were shallow and less carefully dug.

Another site with baby burials in a ditch is Kingdown Camp, Somerset, also late Iron Age/Romano-British, where ten small children were interred. Several other similar sites have been reported, encouraging speculation that there was a particular meaning in the placement of babies who died in the first weeks or months of life at the edge of settlement areas, perhaps because their spirits represent a danger to the living. The differences in placement of babies' graves may also be a reflection of the different population of the various settlements, with older British customs and ideas occurring in the more rural sites, and new Romanised practices being more common in the towns which might have had more mixed cultures and rituals.

Other Roman period sites in England have a much more normal distribution of adults and children, or even rather high numbers of children in comparison to adults in the same burial ground:

Site	No. adults	No. juveniles/ older children	No. infants/ young children
Winterton, Hants.	6		26
Rudston, Lincs.	6	I	16
Old Winteringham, Hants.	4		22
Baldock, Herts.	17		43
Catsgore, Som.	3	3	+20
Bradley Hill, Som.	20	I	34

28 Populations of some Roman period cemeteries in England. After Scott, 1999:116[17]

The statistics shown in (*28*) suggest that 67 per cent of the population died before reaching four years of age and 25 per cent died at or near birth, statistics comparable with the developing world and early modern Europe where the relevant mortality rates are in the region of 250 in 1,000.

In central Italy a number of infant cemeteries found from the late Roman period and one in particular attest to superstitions concerned with the loss of small children. At a long-abandoned villa in Teverina, the tiny victims of a malaria epidemic were buried around AD 450. Most of the 47 children were either premature or newborn, but six were aged up to five to six months and one was a toddler. Analysis of their bones suggested that this was a community under stress, either caused by poor diet, or perhaps by an inherited condition, either thalassemia or sickle-cell anaemia. The use of the old villa recalls the Etruscan custom mentioned earlier of utilising abandoned farmhouses for child burials.

The honeysuckle flowers placed in the graves demonstrated that the children had died in summer, when malaria epidemics endemic to the region usually reach their peak. The spirits of such young children were regarded with fear by the Romans – they were possibly polluting and malevolent. It is clear from the evidence at the site that several different rituals were undertaken to pacify

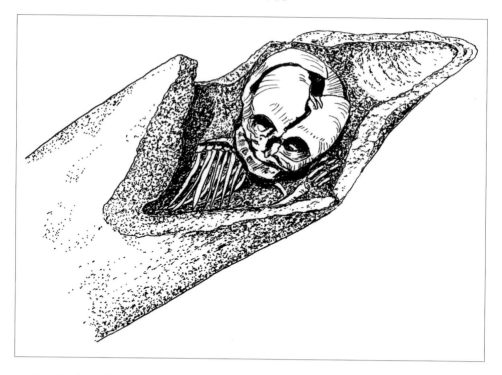

29 An infant buried in a broken amphora at the Lugnano villa ruins near Teverino, Italy

these spirits and those of the dangerous deities of the underworld. At various places between the graves were found talismans against evil: the talon of a raven, a toad, an inverted pot, a limbless doll figure, and in particular, the bones of 14 young puppies, many of which had been decapitated. These puppies, each 5-6 months old, seem to have been killed and buried near the children as sacrifices to the underworld. The association with dogs and the realm of death is a fairly common one, from the Roman Cerebus guarding the gates of the Underworld to the Hounds of Hell of later medieval tradition. The tradition of dog sacrifice is mentioned by Pliny, and dog and puppy skeletons have been found in 'ritual' shafts in many places, including Staines and Southwark, in the Roman period. It is believed possible that the offerings were made to the goddess of the darkness, Hakte, so that her canine consorts would lead the souls of the children away from the world. This was important, because according to Tertullian,[18] if the souls did not move on, they could be used for evil purposes by black magicians.[19]

Small children are also rare in the cemeteries of Anglo-Saxon England, both Pagan and Christian, but some *are* found, and this begs the question of why this should be the case. Studies in Kentish cemeteries have found very different population ratios – just one child under five at the Dover Buckland cemetery,[20] and two aged between two and six at Lyminge, out of a total of 44 burials. At Polhill, with a population of 125 burials, just 16 were of small children, and none were babies. Other studies show a similar disparity.[21] Clearly, these figures are unlikely to represent all the deaths in these age groups, so some other form of burial rite may have been practised for most children, or else the bones of children simply do not survive. There may be a number of reasons why the skeletal remains of children disappear more quickly than those of adults; burial may be in shallower graves, or it may be that the composition of small children's bones is more prone to rapid decay.

Bones are made up of minerals and protein; over time, a person's bones become harder and more mineralised, until old age is reached, when excess mineralisation leads to brittleness. Babies' bones are soft, to allow for growth. They are also more porous than adult bones, so acid ground water could, in theory, penetrate more easily and help to destroy the bones more quickly. It certainly seems to be the case that in acid soils, bones of children are less likely to survive. This means that in areas of sandy or gravel soils, preservation is not likely to be good and children are likely to be under-represented in surviving cemetery samples, while in areas of chalky or clay soils, preservation is likely to be much better. There are exceptions to this rule, such as Great Chesterford in Essex. Here, the Anglo-Saxon cemetery contained a large number (40.1 per cent) of graves of children under five years old which had survived in a sand and gravel soil. It is also the case that small bones are more likely to be lost or unrecorded, and whilst this is unlikely with modern standards of excavation, it may well have been the case in earlier investigations. A recent paper has noted the increase in the recovery of children's bodies from Anglo-Saxon cemeteries in recent decades with the adoption of better techniques, and perhaps more awareness of the value of looking for the remains of children. The same paper also suggests that the apparent increase in the number of children represented in cemeteries of the later Saxon period is more a reflection of change in settlement location than in burial ritual for children.[22] Many early Saxon settlements are on light soils in southern and eastern England with sandy areas; it is possible that later settlements have a greater tendency to be located on slightly heavier, less acidic soils which create better conditions for bone survival.

However, evidence from Merovingian France also shows a lack of small children in cemeteries – for example, four sixth-century graveyards in Lower Normandy produced no graves of any children under the age of four. Not until the Carolingian period, in the eighth century, do children begin to be represented in numbers that make demographic sense in French cemeteries. Where children's burials are found, they tend to be concentrated in specific areas, for example along the boundary wall at St Martin de Trainecourt (Calvados), near the southern extension of the building at St-Lucien church, La Courneuve, and the church of St Barthelemy at Saint-Denis, and under the southern rain gutters of the church at Saint-Etienne, Rouen. One reason for burials under the gutters here (and at other sites, such as Dassargues near Montpelier) may be the notion that the rainwater pouring onto these graves was purifying.

It may have been the case that where loss of children was a frequent occurrence, the sheer cost of providing a proper funeral was simply too great. To provide grave offerings, burial clothes, food and drink, fuel for the pyre, and perhaps social rituals for one child might have been prohibitive; if families could normally expect to lose up to five children in a generation, it would have been beyond their capabilities if they were not to compromise their surviving children's chances.

It follows, therefore, that those children who did receive funeral rites must have been special in some way. As they were too young to have achieved status on their own, their specialness must relate to the status of their families; it has been suggested that identifying family grave groups that do include the graves of very small children may be a good way of finding out how much status a community might have within it, perhaps more reliable than looking for high-status or expensive objects like brooches or swords.

The goods placed within a grave to accompany the body of a child can also have a great deal of significance not only for assessing the wealth of the family, but for identifying the child's gender and the role or roles ascribed to it by adults in its society.

These areas of research have been particularly addressed in relation to pre-Christian Anglo-Saxon children's graves. It has been noted that the older the person in a grave, the more often grave goods accompanied the body. In a sample of graves of this period, 36.8 per cent of those of children under five years old had received grave goods, and 48.9 per cent of children between the ages of six and ten did so. The figure for the 11–14 age group was 57.9 per cent, while for the 15-29-year-olds it was 74.7 per cent.[23] It was also noted that the older the deceased person, the larger the number of items were deposited in the grave. Relatively few children under 10 had items of value in the graves, usually beads of amethyst or amber, or old Roman coins pierced to be suspended as jewellery or amulets. Nevertheless, a variety of objects do appear with the bodies of children, including knives.

It is rare that items appear in these British graves that are apparently specifically intended for children, but at a cemetery in Sewerby, Yorkshire, two infants' graves held tiny iron brooches not represented elsewhere. At Abingdon in Oxfordshire, the grave of a child aged around 12 (possibly a girl) had a small iron spearhead that seemed to have been ground down from a larger normal one. In Europe, however, there are examples of a number of playthings, including dolls made of ivory, balls, spinning tops and pottery figures of animals and birds.

Many children were buried without any grave goods at all, which makes the few richly furnished examples particularly interesting. Of the 19 children's graves found at Finglesham in Kent, 12 had no grave goods, others had one or two items, and three contained expensive necklaces. Grave 7, of a probable female child aged between two and five years old, contained a pottery bottle with a piece of glass inside which may have been a rattle, a Roman flagon, a knife, a chatelaine, a pouch, and an elaborate necklace which included a gold solidus coin.

The inclusion of a chatelaine with such a young child is highly unusual; however, older girls (aged upwards of 10 or so) more often have this artefact in their graves. These may have a single key attached to them. Other items in the graves include spindlewhorls, and weaving swords or battens. Adult women are often buried with this equipment, but tend to have more keys and other items attached to the chatelaines. 'Adult women, if the number of keys in the burial ritual is anything to go by, accumulated wealth and boxes to put it in. The single keys buried with the youngest girls may represent their first box in which to put their treasures – broken brooches, pretty pebbles and single beads, partly in play, and partly to begin to learn the importance of ownership and the skills of personal responsibility'.[24] They were also learning the textile making techniques that would be essential in adult life to clothe their husbands and children.

Boys' graves sometimes included weapons, although the definition of 'weapon' is open to challenge. Knives, for example, were essential personal tools for everyone in the Anglo-Saxon period, and they are found in the graves of babies, children and women as well as men. Other, more certain, weapons are not found in the graves of boys under the age of seven, at which age spears begin to appear. Spears and shields are more common in the graves of the 12-20 age group, while swords rarely appear in any but adult graves. It has been argued that weapons in children's graves are symbolic items, related to status and the future roles of children as adults, but this ignores the fact that boys from much younger ages serve as soldiers in a number of modern armies, and up until the end of the nineteenth century, young boys fought alongside adults in the British Army and the Royal Navy on a regular basis. Some of the cabin boys, midshipmen and powder monkeys on the ships that fought at such battles as Trafalgar were as young as eight years old.

Another aspect claimed for Anglo-Saxon graves was the provision of 'amuletic' items for children in their graves. At Marina Drive in Dunstable, Bedfordshire, the list of these items includes beaver teeth, cowrie shells, a faceted crystal, an ox rib and a piece of quartz. Elsewhere, polished pebbles, baby teeth and other items have been found. There is no real need to see these objects as in any way magical, however, as they may simply represent the kind of unusual and fascinating small treasures that a child might have been attached to in life. In early medieval Friesland, where cremation was the usual funerary rite, it has been noticed that among the remains placed in the burial urn are a number of examples of astagali (or knucklebones) of sheep. Some of these had been decorated with circle-and-dot patterns. At least some of these knucklebones come from the graves of children, and it seems likely that they were used in games of a type still popular in the Netherlands, although they may also have been used for fortune-telling.[25]

A further concern of the Anglo-Saxon period was, however, the prevention of hauntings. This was a superstitious age, and even into the Christian period, some graves demonstrate that extraordinary measures were deemed appropriate to protect the living from the unwelcome attentions of the dead. A common practice was to place large stones on the body and this has been observed in the graves of four out of the nine children at Winnall II, Hampshire and in several children's graves at Lechlade, for example. Prone burial, too, may have been a measure against phantom activity; at Lechlade again, this was carried out with the remains of a 10-year-old and a 15-year-old. Similar actions were taken with some adult graves, but the incidence of such practices in children's graves is relatively high, suggesting that the early deaths of children might have been regarded as particularly threatening and likely to result in supernatural activity. The ancient Greeks shared this fear of the newborn, especially if the child had shown any evidence of disability. Children at birth are new and strange, not yet quite human, and still attached to the world of the gods or spirits. They have not yet become people, they cannot walk or speak, and sometimes they have an almost uncanny appearance of listening to or looking at things that we cannot hear or see. It is perhaps hardly surprising that in a number of cultures it is believed that infants have a foot still in the supernatural world, where human rules do not apply. And the spirits are capricious and dangerous, and perhaps could easily act through the baby to harm people in the everyday world. Babies are liminal, existing in both the normal and supernatural realms but belonging to neither.

Why were some children so much better provided for at death? It is unlikely that very small children had achieved particular status and recognition in their society through any act of their own. It seems, therefore, that these rich items in graves show us that the communities from which they came included people of more wealth and importance than others in the same group, and that this wealth and importance was inheritable. It has been argued that the shift from individual adult burials to family burials containing children and infants in Europe in the fifth and sixth centuries AD is evidence of the emergence of a new aristocracy for whom the production of heirs was becoming a mark of status.[26]

French children's graves demonstrate this trend towards special treatment of some individuals, such as the fourth-century burials of a six-month-old and a three-year-old child in expensive lead caskets at Lisieux. A child's grave of the sixth century found beneath the later cathedral at Cologne contained a small chair, and other German graves have produced a further seat and small dishes containing food, particularly hazelnuts.

Children were differentially treated according to the standing of their parents, and that difference accrued to them even in death. We might expect such evidence of inheritance among the families of the aristocracy, perhaps, but it may be surprising to find it among communities that otherwise seem to be more uniform. Either the aristocracy were happy to bury their children in the common cemetery among peasants and farmers, or those peasants and farmers had a clear hierarchy amongst themselves.

Even after the adoption of the Christian burial rite, children's graves were more likely to contain artefacts or be treated in a more traditional manner. A site in medieval Italy demonstrates the desire to place the graves of children in places which had been of previous ritual importance. At Monte Gelato in South Etruria the population was buried in cemeteries accompanying and postdating the late-Roman and early-Medieval church. In the earlier medieval phase (around the tenth and eleventh centuries) infants were almost entirely absent in and around the church. Infant graves begin to appear after the building was demolished, and were placed predominantly in the baptistry. Eventually, some 20 children under 10 years old were buried in this area.

The later medieval period saw an increasing trend towards the recognition of the importance of lineage and descendants. This is demonstrated in grave memorials of the period, where depictions of children begin to appear on memorials to their parents. 'In the early stages, ties of affinity could give rise to confusion: the tomb image of Henry III, Count of Sayn (d.1247), with his miniature daughter, now in Nuremburg, appears to have prompted the tradition that the count, a kindly giant, had inadvertently killed a child by patting it on the head'.[27] In an age when many children failed to survive infancy, heirs became more and more important, and children 'became as manifest a sign of achievement as the bearing of arms and a loyal marriage'.[28] Children are depicted raised on pedestals, as in the example of the memorial brass at Stoke Fleming in Devon of John Copt (who died in 1361) and his granddaughter Eleanor, who followed him to the grave thirty years later. The importance of heirs to carry on the family name and control of estates and influence was particularly important for royalty and the great houses, and as we know, became all-consuming in the case of Henry VIII.

The death of a child is also particularly tragic because of the lost potential life represented, the may-have-been person who will now never grow up, and because of the innocence of the child. It is natural to ask why death should come to one who has done nothing wrong, who has never sinned or taken risks. It was this vision of stainless purity that particularly touched the hearts of those parents who erected sentimental and elaborate monuments to their lost children in churches and graveyards in later centuries. The memorial to Anne Burton, who died at Oakham in 1642 at the age of 15, provides one example of such sentiments:

> Reader, stand back; dull not this Marble Shrine,
> With irreligious Breath : the Stone's divine,
> And does enclose a Wonder Beauty, Wit,
> Devotion, and Virginity with it.
> Which like a Lilly fainting in its Prime,

30 The tomb of Penelope Boothby, who died in 1791 aged nine, at Ashbourne, Derbyshire

Wither'd and left the World ; deceitful Time
Crop it too soon : And Earth, the self-same Womb
From whence it sprung, is now become the Tomb,
Whose sweeter Soul, a Flower of matchless Price,
Transplanted is from hence to Paradise.

There are less fulsome and more achingly poignant monuments, too. The memorial by the sculptor Thomas Banks dedicated to Penelope Boothby, aged nine, at Ashbourne, Derbyshire, depicts a little girl sleeping gently on a cushioned bed. The inscription reads:

She was in form and intellect
Most exquisite

The unfortunate parents ventured
Their all on this frail bark
And the wreck was total.

INFANTICIDE

Why do people deliberately kill children (outside of religious sacrifice)? Infanticide can be as simple as murder, by parent, family member or stranger. Children die at the hands of others in many ways, some of which have at least partially understandable causes, such as postnatal depression, stress, doubts about paternity, or jealousy. But in some times and places, the killing of young children has seemed to have been more institutionalised and common. In modern China, reports suggest that because of laws restricting families to just one child, many babies have been abandoned or killed. This may be because the baby showed some kind of deformity, and the parents would rather it died so they had a chance to try again for a healthy child, or because the baby was the wrong gender. In Chinese society, particularly in rural districts, girls are regarded as of very little value, so a girl baby may be disposed of in the hope that the next child will be a son. It is apparently not uncommon for tiny bodies to appear on the streets of some Chinese cities early each morning, and Western observers have noted with shock that the Chinese crowds on their way to work seem not even to see them. Cultural attitudes vary greatly across different societies and places, and this is a fact that the archaeological interpreter cannot afford to forget.

Archaeological evidence for infanticide presents many difficulties of interpretation, not least because of the poor survival of many infant bones, and the ease with which a child can die in ways that leave little forensic trace on the skeleton. The most common ways in which babies are killed include being overlain, being smothered accidentally or deliberately with a pillow or similar object, or simple neglect, either as a result of being abandoned in an exposed place, or left unfed and without warmth at home. It is frighteningly easy to strangle a baby, or to shake it sufficiently to cause brain damage leading to death, as a couple of recent highly publicised cases have demonstrated. Babies also commonly die in the bath or the garden pond; they can drown in an inch or two of water, and once again, the death may be accidental or criminal.

The first few days and weeks of life are fraught with danger; as we have seen, in some cultures babies are not even named until this dangerous period has been survived. So what can we use to identify those children who have been deliberately killed as part of a social practice?

There are surviving documents to provide evidence for institutionalised killing in some societies. An ancient Roman medical treatise by Soranus offers advice on how to recognise whether or not a baby is worth rearing, advocating the disposal of any child born weak or with a deformity. That this was regarded as perfectly normal Roman practice is perhaps confirmed by the way in which Tacitus notes that among the Germans 'to restrict the number of children, or to kill any of those born after the heir, is considered wicked', obviously contrary to what he thought normal.

Babies of the wrong gender were also liable to be killed; in the *Metamorphoses* of Ovid, we hear of Telethusa who hid the sex of her baby girl from her husband, raising the child as a boy rather than killing it as he had instructed her to do. Her husband's decision was related to his poverty as girls were much more expensive to raise and provide with dowries. In ancient Athens, it was only males who could inherit property or live a social life; girls and women lived in virtual seclusion, and it seems that some girl babies were killed or exposed rather than their families having to bear the cost of their support. In Sparta, children and slaves were regarded as state property, not that of the family. The state could decide which infants to rear and which to kill.

It was the right of the Roman father to decide whether the newborn should be raised or not. A papyrus letter, sent from Oxyrhynchus in Egypt by Hilarion to his wife Alis, dated 1 BC, says:

> I send you my warmest greetings. I want you to know that we are still in Alexandria....I beg you and entreat you to take care of the child and, if I receive my pay soon, I will send it to you. If you have the baby before I return, if it is a boy, let it live; if it is a girl, expose it....[29]

In Viking Scandinavia a similar practice appears to have occurred. An instruction from a husband in the Gunnlaugs Saga tells the wife: 'It appears...that you are with child. If the baby is a girl, it is to be exposed, but reared if it is a boy.'[30] At several Viking sites, the bones of babies have been found in rubbish heaps or among the outer stones of cairns, and this has been cited as possible evidence of infanticide, although, as we have seen, differential burial rites for small children may explain these finds without such an interpretation.

Another possible way to identify infanticide as a practice is when the majority of infants found in a particular burial place are predominantly of one gender. It would not be normal for natural perinatal death to be confined to just girls or boys, so another cause may be sought.

A study of data from the Mokrin Early Bronze Age cemetery north of Belgrade, Yugoslavia suggested a realistic population in terms of sex and age of death with two significant exceptions. There were no newborn babies, and there were more female children than male. Does this mean there was preferential male infanticide? If females were regarded as having more value, there might have been more females living (and so more dying).[31]

In the Roman period, a large number of infant bodies ended up in a sewer in the Israeli city of Ashkelon.[32] There were about 100 newborn babies in the sewer, which served a bathhouse. Techniques using DNA have been able to ascribe gender to 19 of these children; 14 were male and five were female. The suggestion has been made that the bathhouse was in fact a cover for a brothel, and that these children were the unwanted results of the prostitutes' trade. More girls might have survived because they could be raised and employed in the brothel in their turn. Such conclusions are extremely speculative; it is unclear whether or not the bathhouse was definitely a brothel, or that the deposition of the babies occurred when the bathhouse was in use, and the very small proportion of babies in whom gender could be identified casts doubts on the possibility of there having been a gender preference.

A number of Romano-British cemeteries seem to have a disproportionate number of adult males, such as the Trentholme Drive site in York where the male to female ratio was 4:1; at Cirencester it is recorded as 5:2. Was this the result of preferential female infanticide? Or does it suggest better treatment of male infants? Similar results have been recorded for Natufian adults, people who lived in the Near East at the very beginning of agriculture up to 5000 BC, where two thirds of the bodies found were male; in early Europe several other sites have provided similar ratios, such as Branc where the ratio is in favour of adult males, and Tiszapolgar–Basatanya in Hungary where an absence of females and children has been noted, the ratio in Period I being two males for every female. Can such figures make a possible case for widespread infanticide in prehistory? Of course, there is simply insufficient evidence at the moment to be able to decide one way or the other, but it is not beyond the imagination that infanticide was practised at some periods.

Several studies have been made of the phenomenon noted at various British sites of the Roman period of large numbers of baby burials. At the Hambleden Villa, in Buckinghamshire, a corridor house within a courtyard, the excavator noted that:

> A remarkable feature of this excavation was that the ground, roughly speaking throughout the northern half, was littered with babies. They number 97 and most of them are newly born, but an occasional one is rather older. A few of them were laid at length, but the majority were evidently carried and buried wrapped in a cloth or garment, huddled in a little bundle, so that the head was almost central, and the knees above it; usually, therefore, the whole of the scanty remains came away in one spit. As nothing marked the position of these tiny graves, a second little corpse was sometimes deposited on one already in occupation of a spot, apparently showing that these interments took place secretly, after dark.[33]

At Barton Court Farm, in Oxfordshire, 47 infant burials were unearthed, all but six in an agricultural processing area in the outer yard. The burial of babies were also found in association with foundations of new additions to villas such as Sparsholt and Brixworth in the fourth century AD, and at Winterton and Catsgore associated with so-called 'corn-driers' or malting floors in the same century, where they might have served as so-called 'foundation sacrifices'.[34]

One explanation could be that the babies were those of slaves, not allowed to keep their children by their owners, but this would not necessarily explain the apparent secrecy of some of the burials. The evidence from Barton Court and elsewhere points towards an adopting of ritual behaviours different from previous times, alongside other social changes such as an increasing trend towards enclosure and protection of villa sites. At Barton Court Farm three burials of newborn babies were accompanied by the skulls of two dogs and a sheep, and another pit contained the jaw bones of a dog, cattle and sheep laid in the bottom. At Star in Somerset, shallow pits in corners of rooms contained apparently ritual deposits of sheep and pig bones, or a mixture of fragments of human and sheep skull bones; one contained remains of an infant's skeleton mixed with sheep bones. It would appear that the bodies of babies were playing increasingly significant roles in ritual and votive activities.[35]

This has been interpreted by some as evidence of a change in the ritual behaviour of women in fourth-century Roman Britain, women whose sphere of action had become increasingly circumscribed in a world of growing uncertainty:

> Increasingly enclosed by architecture, walls and enclosures, did women in villa settlements revive memories of rituals in order to renegotiate their place in the changing world? Were they making linkages between the new dead, fertility, agricultural production, processing space and domestic commerce – an ideological link between themselves and the outside world, as the physical barriers rose around them?[36]

It is possible that these rites were carried out by women as a means of trying to gain some sort of control over their lives in a period of increasing stress and uneasiness. By carrying out rituals associating farming activities with human fertility in the form of babies, women were trying to make connections that would establish a form of power over their worlds, a way of exerting influence over agricultural production that gave them importance in a male-dominated world. Similar suggestions have been made for infant burials in the Iron Age in western Spain.[37]

Also in the fourth century AD, very young children begin to appear in normal cemeteries, probably as a result of the adoption of Christianity if the statistics are significant, though not everyone believes that the small numbers recorded actually mean a great deal, and that they are really a reflection or survival of evidence rather than change of practice.[38] The Christianity of the fourth century was a religion which disapproved of abortion, contraception and infanticide, and in AD 370 Valentinian I made infanticide illegal in the Western Empire. The rights of the unborn child were first clearly set down in the sixth-century AD *Digest of Justinian* which stated 'The foetus in the womb is deemed to be fully a human being, whenever the question concerns advantages accruing to him when born, even though before his birth his existence is never assumed in favour of anyone else.'

In the succeeding Anglo-Saxon period it is clear that even those children born with deformities were given every chance to survive; there are a number of examples of children who survived at least for a while (even to adolescence) despite major birth defects, and artefacts such as the pot apparently designed for the feeding of a baby with a cleft palate mentioned earlier have been found.[39] There was even the provision of weregeld for the life of an unborn child – a judicial payment imposed on anyone causing the death of the child:

> It is undeniable that perceptions of the past are encultured. Likewise, cultural perceptions of infanticide are determined by socially embedded and constructed roles of parents and children. These attitudes influence our recognition of infanticide as 'good' or 'bad'. As a result it is very difficult to see beyond our socially conditioned, emotional response to infanticide, yet this is necessary in order to understand its role and social efficacy.[40]

The decision to commit infanticide can never have been entirely easy. Choices may often have been pragmatic – does the baby have a chance to grow up or not? If not, then is it not kinder to end its life before it begins to know suffering? Infanticide as a result of social preference may also have a pragmatic cause, as in modern China, struggling with its demographic explosion. The cost of raising, endowing and protecting a child of one gender may endanger the chances of survival of its siblings, and there may well be social penalties that would result if one tried to do so. The demands life made on people in the past from time to time offered them some very hard choices.

4

THE DIVINE CHILD

Babes at birth
Wear as raiment round them cast,
Keep as witness toward their past,
Tokens left of heaven; and each,
Ere its lips learn mortal speech,
Ere sweet heaven past on pass reach,
Bears in undiverted eyes
Proof of unforgotten skies
Here on earth.
(From 'Olive' (addressed to Olive Miranda Watts, aged nine years)
by A.C. Swinburne 1837-1909)

In many societies, children have become important in ritual behaviours. The reasons for this are concerned with various attitudes about the nature of childhood and the relationship between birth and the supernatural. Childhood is often regarded as liminal, neither death nor true life, which is only reached at adulthood or when the child reaches an age or size that indicates it is likely to survive into adulthood. Refusal to recognise the child as a full human being may be related to high levels of infant mortality; it can be a strategy that protects the parents from the emotional distress associated with the death of many young children in communities that lack advanced medical facilities or which regularly face nutritional stress or disease. Children, too, may not be economically useful and can be regarded as easily replaced.

There are also attitudes which see the child as being closely related to the supernatural dimension, having only recently left it and being unsullied by the physical and adult worlds. Children are perceived as having a closeness to deities and spirits that is lost later in life; they may retain something of the nature of those deities. They are innocent, pure expressions of humanity until they reach certain stages of development, such as being weaned, or puberty and sexual readiness.

Thirdly, children are regarded in most societies as valuable. They are the future of the society, and they are dear to their parents beyond all other forms of affection. Thus, they can acquire particular forms of reverence and power in ritual behaviours.

Each of these sets of attitudes can be seen in different cultures and in the ways in which those cultures have approached the supernatural. The liminality of children makes them suitable for use as conduits to the gods; it can also make them appear expendable and appropriate for utilisation in this way. Their closeness to the 'otherworld' and their perceived purity is considered to make them particularly pleasing to the gods. Their value makes them the ultimate form of offering to appease or propitiate deities.

This is evident in many religions, not least Christianity. Christians have likened Jesus to a shepherd, and children are the lambs in his flock; Jesus himself is the Lamb of God. This metaphor obviously contains many elements of youthfulness, innocence and purity. Among the angels, intercessors between God and mankind, the cherubim are in the first circle of heaven, alongside the seraphim. There are numerous hagiographies of child saints and martyrs, but the most powerful image is, of course, that of the Christ child and the Nativity, represented in thousands of carvings, paintings, illustrations and other forms across the world. Here all the elements of ritual belief associated with children are combined; there are lambs for purity and innocence, there is worldly and spiritual wealth (gold, frankincense and myrrh), there are supernatural powers in the form of angels and stars, there is the association with sacrifice and blood, the mystical nature of conception and birth, and the means of intercession with God being given to ordinary people.

We can trace many of these elements in the beliefs of other cultures, but it is perhaps worth remembering right at the start that we may struggle to understand all of the meanings of the clues we find through archaeology for the practice of ancient rituals. One has only to consider the iconography of Christmas to realise just how complex and interrelated religious and cult symbols may become. If we found evidence of our Christmas celebrations in a few thousand years' time, and if we had no surviving written record to explain what was going on, what would we make of the juxtaposition of images of a woman and baby with robins, trees with candles on them, Middle Eastern villages and Victorian stage coaches in the snow, along with turkeys, puddings and mistletoe? We could easily end up with a very strange idea of belief and worship in the twenty-first century! We would probably decide that there was no direct connection between many of the elements; we might even decide that tree worship was prevalent!

So in interpreting clues to past beliefs and rituals, it is best to try to understand them as broadly as we can, and to recognise that much of what actually happened, was felt or thought, we will never know.

SACRIFICE AND MAGIC

To most modern people the idea of killing a child for religious or magic reasons is appalling and unimaginable. In the summer of 2001, however, the discovery of the torso of a young boy in the Thames led police to suspect that this killing was part of a ceremony performed by members of an African 'muti' cult for whom magical rites intended to bring either sexual power or longer life, or such benefits as a kind of divine motor insurance for vehicles, involve similar murders. The body and blood of a small child are thought to bring extreme potency to the incantations of the shaman, placating and propitiating the spirits who control the desired gifts.[1]

Recent reports[2] have noted an apparent rise in the use of children in tantric magical rites around Gwalior in India. Tantric mystics have been accused of encouraging believers to murder children in rituals designed to enable childless couples to conceive or to lift curses from people. Some two dozen child sacrifices have been recorded over a six-month period in the region, despite police efforts to end the practices. A similar spate of deaths occurred in West Bengal in the 1980s, as a result of the activities of another sect, the Anandmarg cult, who were sacrificing children to appease the goddess Kali.

There is nothing new in such beliefs. Child sacrifice has occurred in many different cultures at different times. The idea of sacrifice is a complex one. The motivations behind a sacrifice may include and combine acts of gratitude for favours granted, propitiation for favours desired, acknowledgement of power, fear of future and possible dangers, and marking of important events by a sacred rite. The choice of what to sacrifice is based on the degree of importance of the ceremony, request, thankfulness or fear, and the system of values a society maintains. At one extreme are the sacrifices of human beings or costly animals or goods; at the other, the notion of sacrifice has been abstracted so that tokens of little real but great conceptual value are acceptable, namely replicas, miniatures, or acts of contrition.

A widespread context for the sacrifice of infants is in so-called foundation sacrifices – the placing of the body of an animal or baby under the foundations or threshold of a new building. A number of instances of apparent foundation sacrifices of infants have been recorded from Iron Age and Roman Britain. In the Early Iron Age, the body of a boy aged about 12 years old was cut into quarters and the quarters were placed in pits, along with the butchered remains of two calves and two sheep, under a house that was being built at Hornish Point, South Uist.[3] Excavations at Wandlebury hillfort in Cambridgeshire discovered human bones in disused storage pits including the dismembered torso of a six-year-old boy whose legs had been hacked off.[4] At the great hillfort of Maiden Castle near Dorchester, Dorest, the body of a young child was found buried in a pit just outside the entrance to a circular building that may have had religious significance[5] and other baby skeletons have been retrieved from beneath the ramparts of other hillforts.[6] The bodies of an adult and a child were found beneath a circular structure in a Late Iron Age cemetery at Harlyn Bay, Cornwall.[7]

Other examples of possible child sacrifice in prehistoric Britain are even earlier. The body of a four-year-old child was discovered in 2003 near Kettlewell in Upper Wharfedale. Provisional dating suggests a Bronze Age date for the remains, which had been placed in a stone-lined cist within a ring cairn. Pebbles had been deliberately placed by the child's head and feet, and a hair pin had been placed in the grave. The excavator considers it possible that child sacrifice may be a possibility in this instance. The skeleton of a child was found buried in a pit at the centre of the enigmatic monument known as Woodhenge, near Amesbury in Wiltshire; the likelihood of a foundation sacrifice here seems quite strong.

At the Roman legionary fortress of Reculver in Kent, the bodies of infants were placed in the foundations of barrack buildings, and the body of a child had been buried in two parts under the floor of an extension to the large public baths in Wroxeter. During the second century AD the head of a teenaged boy was defleshed with knives before being placed in a pit outside a temple in Verulamium (Roman St Albans, Hertfordshire)[8] and in the same town, one infant burial had been enclosed in a cist made of roofing tiles and placed in the corner of a building. Mortimer

31 The Neolithic site of Woodhenge, Wiltshire, which has a child burial at its centre.
Photo courtesy of S.P. Dyer

Wheeler believed that this was a foundation burial marking rebuilding in the third century. At Springhead in Kent in another religious enclosure also dating to the second century AD, the bodies of babies, cattle and horse skulls had been placed in pits dug to hold timber posts which were apparently set in a free-standing line.[9] Beneath shrine IV in the complex, in a room approximately 3m by 4.5m, with the base of a cult statue in its centre, four more children had been buried, one in each corner of the room. Two of these burials had occurred at an early stage, those in the northwest and southwest corners. One of these two children (in the southwest corner) had been decapitated; they were about six months old, and were buried lying on their sides. Some ten years later, in a new building phase, two more children were placed, one in the northeast and the other in the southeast corner of the room; again, one child, that in the northeast, also being decapitated.[10] At Witham in Essex another temple had an infant burial placed in its surrounding ditch and another associated with the building lay with a deposit of eggshells, possibly associated with some sort of fertility rite. These are both thought to date from the mid-fourth century.[11]

There seems to be a particular correlation between infant burials and later 'aisled' farmhouses in the Romano-British countryside. Aisled houses of later Roman Britain consist of a floor plan divided by rows of posts into a 'nave' with two flanking 'aisles'. This design is thought by some to have Germanic origins; it is a departure from the winged corridor designs or courtyard villas that developed from more standard Roman provincial forms, and they appear from the third century AD onwards. In the fourth century AD, infant burials become much more common at these sites, along with other burials of animals (such as the decapitated sheep, probable pair of chickens and a goose placed under a tegula roof tile beside a wall at Cocks Farm villa in Surrey) and of objects such as hobnail shoes. It is possible that:

> these rituals are signposts for fertility. The proliferation of infant burials associated with malting floors, hearths and the walls of agricultural buildings in late Roman Britain may be understood in this light. In a number of traditional societies the 'spirits' of babies who die peri-natally or neo-natally are deemed to live on, awaiting rebirth....There can, in effect, be a perceived connection between infant death and fertility.[12]

A problem that must be faced is that in many societies, is that as we have seen in chapter 3, burial of infants within houses was a normal custom; infants are often rarely found in general cemeteries. It may not necessarily be easy to distinguish an ordinary burial of this sort from foundation sacrifices. Another difficulty is that we do not know in most instances whether the child buried in a ritual deposit died of natural causes, or was deliberately killed for the rite. In the brief span of time these children lived, chronic diseases will not have had time to make their marks on the bones; neither would it be possible to ascertain whether a baby had been deliberately smothered or starved to death.

The phenomenon of foundation sacrifice is not confined to European contexts. The Americas also provide a number of examples of dedicatory child sacrifice. At Aspero, on the Peruvian desert coast, a temple dated between 5000–3000 BC revealed the body of a small child, wearing an elaborate beaded cap, and wrapped and placed on a bundle of textiles under an inverted metate or grinding stone that had been covered with red colouring, in what seems to have been a ritual deposition. A contemporary site to the south called La Paloma had a number of elaborate child burials in special houses, notably different from other burials in the area.

In around 400 BC a child was buried under the corner of a stone structure at Ancón in Peru; its eyes had been replaced by sheets of shiny mica, its stomach by a gourd and its heart by a lump of clear rock crystal, a substance often associated with magical powers. Children's bodies were found associated with the splendid burials at Sipán. This adobe mound in northern Peru was built by the Moche people some 1500 years ago to house the tombs of the royal rulers. Tomb 1 contained the body of a 40-year-old man (the 'Lord of Sipán') in a wooden coffin containing hundreds of objects including a tunic covered in sheet gold plaques, silver and gold beads, gilded copper sheet metal figures, a gold headdress and much more. Around this burial were further burials of servants who accompanied their lord into death, two men (one with a dog) and three women, and a child's body near the head. A second tomb also contained a man in a wooden coffin; his ornaments included a necklace of ten gold beads, each with a web on which sat a golden spider with a human face on its back. Other men and women were buried around this coffin, and again, there was the body of a child. It seems unlikely that these small children were servants – it is more likely that they were offerings. [13]

Child foundation sacrifices may also have occurred at Huaca de la Luna, a massive sacrificial precinct on the north Peruvian coast, built by the Moche people. There are three ceremonial platforms connected by corridors, plazas and terraces, built of adobe; changes were made to the structure during Period IV of its life (around AD 540-655). An extension was built to the north of the main platform. When this had been completed and before the walls around it were raised, a ceremony took place which involved the burial of three children into the surface. The skeleton of the first child was complete, laid out on its back on a north–south axis; it was between two-and-a-half and three-and-a-half years old. No signs of trauma were visible but there were possible indications of periostitis. A second child had been laid out on an east–west axis, with a large seashell lying by its side. This child had been decapitated, and had been about a year old. Paleopathological analysis showed that the child had been suffering from severe periostitis or osteomyelitis, from which it could have died. A third child was also laid out on a north–south axis, close to the north wall of the platform. Aged about three, this child had also been decapitated, and had been covered by textiles. It was holding a whistle in each hand. A little later, walls were built

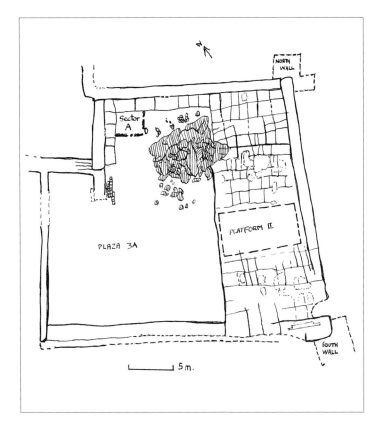

32 Sketch plan of Plaza 3A, Huaca de la Luna, Moche Valley, Peru. The sacrificial burials of children were discovered in the northwest sector, close to the natural rock outcrop in the centre, which may have been the sacred focus of this plaza. After S. Bourget

which enclosed the area in which the children lay. Some time later, a great many other people were sacrificed at the site – males aged between 15 and 35, probably prisoners of war.[14]

There are a number of Moche ceramics which depict adults, or sometimes skeletons, carrying children and blowing on whistles, or whistles themselves have depictions of children being carried. There are also pictures of bat-like creatures carrying children. Bat creatures have been linked to ritual bleeding and sacrifice by decapitation, and children shown being carried by bats often have closed eyes, perhaps indicating that they are already dead. It is thought possible that whistles are linked to women, and other evidence suggests that women were closely concerned with preparing victims of sacrifice for the ritual and carrying out funerary rites afterwards. It is probable that women would have carried these children to the sacrificial site.

It is interesting that two of the children at Huaca de la Luna display evidence of illness. We do not know whether they died or were killed for the ritual, although strong evidence for sacrifice by decapitation exists in many parts of ancient Central and South America. Were these children chosen because of their illness – because they were unlikely to survive anyway? One of the main concerns of the worshippers at this site was to ask the gods for help to control

33 Moche ceramics from Peru depicting (left) a skeleton figure carrying a child, and (right) an elderly woman(?) also carrying an infant whose eyes are closed, perhaps signifying death. The skeleton figure is actually a musical instrument, the sound coming from the eyes and mouth, which the female figure appears to be whistling. Whistles are often found buried with victims of sacrifice

the weather. The region suffers extreme droughts and torrential rainstorms, and periodically subsistence, largely based on fishing, is devastated by El Niño events. People lived in constant danger of natural disaster, and it must have seemed to them that no sacrifice could be too great to combat the awful powers of the elements that came to threaten their very existence; perhaps, though, they chose to offer to the gods only those children whose loss could more easily be borne because of their pre-existing weakness.

Sacrifice of children could occur as a result of legal penalties; an Assyrian contract recorded on a clay tablet in the seventh century BC includes a penalty clause for failure to meet the conditions laid down; the 'malefactor' would be obliged to burn his eldest son in the sacred precinct of Adad.[15] Inscriptions of the tenth century BC on a palace at Tell Hâlaf in Mesopotamia warn that anyone who defaces the names of the royal family would have seven of his sons burned. Other ancient writings attesting to child sacrifice include references in the Old Testament, examples of which are reference to the worship of Ba'al through the burning of children (*Jeremiah* 32:35), the sacrifice of a son as a burnt offering by the Moabite king when besieged by the Israelites (2 *Kings* 3:27), and of course the intention of Abraham to sacrifice his son before he received the Ten Commandments (*Genesis* 22:10-13). Further references which may have their origins in the eighth and seventh centuries BC suggest the existence of a cult based in Jerusalem which centred around the making of burnt offerings, mainly infants and children. These include the passage from *Exodus* (22.29) that records Yahweh demanding 'You shall not delay to offer from the fullness of your harvest and from the outflow of your presses. The first born of your sons you shall give to me' and again 'Consecrate to me all the firstborn; whatever is the first to open the womb among the people of Israel, both of man and of beast, is mine' (*Exodus* 13.2). Later Biblical passages suggest that a concerted effort was made by the authorities to stamp this practice out, and to ascribe these sacrifices to worshippers of Ba'al (for example in *Jeremiah* 19, 4-8), or Molech. This may be a corruption of the Phoenician word '*mlk*', meaning sacrifice. The Bible records that one of the places for child sacrifices was called Topheth – the word tophet came to be used generally for sacrificial cemeteries in the cities of the Phoenicians. The original 'tophet' cemetery was a fire sacrifice site in the valley of Ben Hinnon, outside Jerusalem. The numerous exhortations to the Israelites to refrain from sacrificing their children would tend to suggest that this was an enduring and widespread practice, at least until perhaps the eighth or seventh centuries BC.

The practice of child sacrifice also existed in early Rome. Dio Cassius records that Lucius Sergius Catalina, who led a rebellion in 63 BC, 'sacrificed a boy, and after administering the oath over his vitals, ate these in company with the others'.[16] The traditional laws supposed to have been made by Romulus (who, with his brother Remus, had been exposed to die as a baby) included injunctions that all male children and first born female children were to be brought up (unless a committee of five neighbours agreed that the child was too weak or deformed), and that no child under the age of three should be killed (although exposure was not forbidden). After the age of three, Roman law allowed fathers the right to kill their offspring at any age, until reforms changed this in the first century BC. The literature of the Greeks contains a number of tales of child sacrifice, particularly of maiden daughters, perhaps the best known being the refusal of Agesilus to sacrifice his daughter Iphigeneia at Aulis, thereby dooming his expedition against the Persians.

Perhaps the most well known incidence of child sacrifice is that associated with the ancient city of Carthage, on the North African coast, and with other locations in the Mediterranean, including Hadrumetum in Tunisia, Cirta in Algeria, Motya and Lillebeum in Sicily, Tharros in Sardinia, and elsewhere (see 35). The 'normal' method of burial for adults and children in these societies in the period from around 750 BC to around 150 BC, is thought to have been inhumation in general cemeteries. However, cemeteries of inurned cremations, often marked by stelae, consisting almost exclusively of the remains of children under about four years old, have been found in these places, and have been identified as 'tophets' similar to those recorded in ancient Israel. The 'tophet' in Carthage was about 54-64,000sq ft in size, and perhaps 100 burials took place there each year, with some 20,000 being identified for the period between about 420-200 BC. Earlier burials (before the fifth century BC) are dedicated to the god Ba'al Hammon; later dedications are to the goddess Tanit alone or to Tanit with Ba'al Hammon.[17] Many are marked with inscribed stones. Occasionally, the infant burial was replaced by a substitute, usually a lamb or a kid, and this was recorded on the stelae above the interment. The Carthaginian site, like that of Cirta, became crowded – the area of burial was extended, and at least twice the cemetery was wholly or partially levelled up with sand, earth and clay to allow more burials.

The historian Diodorus Siculus reports of the Carthaginians, when they were at war with Syracuse in 310 BC, that they had a bronze statue of their god Kronos with them. The god stood with arms outstretched, the palms of his hands open but tilted towards the earth, so that an infant placed in his hands would roll from them into a pit lined with fire.[18] Apparently, the god had become angry when children of low status had been sacrificed, and allowed the Syracusans to besiege Carthage. The Carthaginians therefore proceeded to sacrifice 200 children from their noblest families, and to pledge a further 300 to placate the deity. Earlier in the period, dedications on the stelae suggest that the deities being propitiated were Ba'al Hamon and Tanit, with Kronos-Saturn being of later importance. There are versions of the Carthaginian sacrificial rite which suggest that the children were stabbed to death before they entered the fire – Plutarch[19] tells us this was done at the foot of the altars, and musicians played loudly to drown out the cries of anguish of the parents. One stela shows a man wearing a ceremonial headdress holding an infant in the crook of his left arm, with his right arm raised. Mothers were supposed to be present but to make no sound or protest. Other versions suggest that it was the sound of the parents' anguish that was most pleasing to the god, as it proved the degree of sacrifice made. However, Plutarch also suggests that childless couples would buy children from the poor in order to make a sacrifice, and some double urn burials may be records of the dilemma of parents who, having promised a child to the god, found that their own offspring was stillborn or died of natural causes before the ceremony, so that they had to provide a baby bought for the purpose to supplement the burial of their own child.

The dedications on the stelae, the presence of children in normal cemeteries, and the fact that none of the children in the tophet cemetery were newborns, all help to confirm the interpretation of this as a site of sacrifice. The Romans, having conquered Carthage during the Punic Wars, destroyed the city and banned the rites, but according to Tertullan[20] they continued in secret for a long time afterwards, perhaps as late as the third century AD.

Why did the people of Carthage kill their own children? Some of the stelae make references to vows being fulfilled; people must have propitiated the god for something important, that would be paid for by this most extreme sacrifice. The story about the Syracusan siege also suggests that sacrifice in the name of the community good was obligatory, and the purchase of poor people's babies or the use of young animals as substitutes certainly suggests that not all parents were willing to make the offering wholeheartedly. It is possible that entry into certain groups or levels of society or cult status was dependent upon the sacrifice, and perhaps it could have been a necessary cost towards the achievement of local power and position. Child sacrifice by elite Carthaginian families may also have been a means of regulating family size and maintaining their socio-economic status, by reducing the breaking up of estates between many heirs; appeasement of the gods was a useful additional benefit.[21]

34 Stela from Carthage, thought to depict a priest carrying a baby for sacrifice

It has been pointed out that '… the Carthaginians used infanticide in a very open and determined way. It was not hidden; it was even commemorated on stelae. Sacrificing parents knew what they were doing and had time to think about it. The decision was made out of piety with culturally accepted religious motivation and may even have been admired'.[22] It was a practice that lasted for a very long period of time, and was certainly not casually undertaken. The archaeological material allows us to assess the evidence for this assertion:

> 'It required planning, as evidenced by the inscriptions stating that the child was offered because of a past vow and by the careful burials and the 'custom-made monuments.…The vessels and other paraphernalia depicted on sacrificial stelae indicate as well that there were rituals associated with killing and burying a child victim that required planning, preparation, and, presumably, professional assistance'.[23]

Nevertheless, the Romans utilised the practice in a way that has remained familiar to us throughout history. They drummed up support for the campaign against Carthage (in reality based on trade competition) by crying for the banning of the infant sacrifices as a barbaric horror. Of course, the hypocrisy of the Romans is clear; their own record for cruelty is well known, but the accusation of barbarity towards children has been a rallying cry in many conflicts, from the suppression of the Templars who were said to eat babies to Germans in the First World War allegedly spitting babies on their bayonets, to similar apocryphal stories from Bosnia, Rwanda and other more recent wars. One of the earliest records of this type of myth appears in a second-century AD work of Pausanius[24] which tells the story of the Gauls under their leaders, Orestorius and Comboutis, accusing them of killing and eating the babies of their Greek enemies. The Romans' accusations were designed to shock and disgust, but like many other examples of propaganda, they cannily divorced the effect of the sacrifices from an intention which may seem alien to us but was nevertheless both acceptable and pious to the people of Carthage.

Other Mediterranean regions have produced an interesting parallel to the Carthaginian rite. In Cyprus, and also parts of Phoenicia, Greece and Etruria, the offering of votive statues in the form of children occurred between the fifth to fourth up to the second centuries BC. There are variations in the nature and design between regions and periods that may represent different beliefs and rites. Some 200 'temple-boy' statuettes are known from Cyprus. Most of them depict a young boy sitting on the ground, with one knee raised, and about half are wearing a tunic drawn up to expose the genitals. They are also shown wearing a necklace or chain with heavy pendants in many cases, while some without a necklace have traces of paint where such an ornament might have been represented. Only two so far have been found to carry specific dedicatory inscriptions, both to Apollo, but the figurines have also been found at temples or sanctuaries of cults of Haracles-Melqart and Aphrodite/Astarte. These statuettes

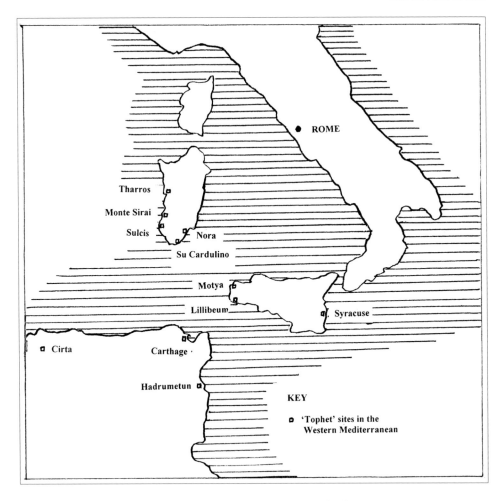

Tharros

Monte Sirai

Sulcis

Nora

Su Cardulino

ROME

Motya

Lillibeum

Syracuse

Cirta

Carthage ·

Hadrumetun

KEY

◻ 'Tophet' sites in the
Western Mediterranean

35 Some excavated 'tophet' sites in North Africa and the Italian islands

appear to represent children aged from about one year to perhaps eight or nine. One explanation is that they were offered as part of a rite of passage, perhaps to mark a ceremony of circumcision.

Similar figures have been found more rarely in Greece, but they are much more varied – standing and sitting poses occur and both boys and girls are depicted. The boys are usually unclothed, while the girls usually have on a chiton (a finely woven tunic dress). The find spots of these pieces are equally various, but at least some of them come from sanctuaries associated with healing, and so may have been offerings asking for help for a child in times of illness.

Etruscan figures come in two main forms – very young children wrapped in swaddling clothes, or a child sitting on the ground. As is the case with some of the Greek examples, some children are depicted holding a little bird, while others have balls or pomegranates. Some of the statuettes may display signs of

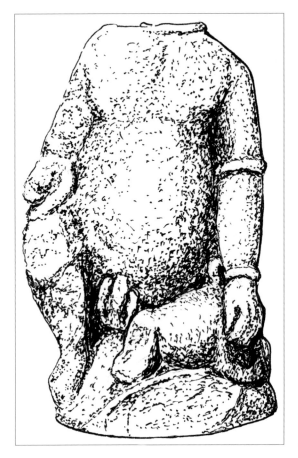

26 'Temple-boy' figurine in the Cyprus Museum. Limestone, height 21cm

congenital illness, and again, the purpose of these offerings may have to do with prayers for the health or future success of children.

In recent years, a series of child sacrifices have come to light in the Andes of Bolivia, Chile and Peru. Early Spanish records suggest this practice was still going on in the seventeenth century AD; there is an account of an Incan girl who voluntarily agreed to be entombed alive as a gift to the god of the sun. Young children in the Inca world were regarded as being close to the gods, still partly attached to them rather than the normal world of humans. Thus their sacrifice was thought to be particularly pleasing to the spirits, returning the child to the gods rather then keeping it. 'The capacocha children were accompanied in death by miniature animals moulded in precious metals, a ritual celebration and adoration of the smallness of youth and the learning play associated with it'.[25]

The ancient peoples of the Andes were very much at the mercy of natural forces, and thus, in their perception, of supernatural beings. Very little of the land produces crops, water supplies are at a premium, the altitude is extreme, the region is subject to earthquakes, tidal waves and even occasional volcanic eruptions. As noted earlier, there are also severe El Niño events leading to devastating floods. The mountains were regarded as either gods or the homes of gods, and the thunder and earthquakes were their voices. Precious water came from the mountains and mountain lakes were viewed as ancestral homes. Sacrifice was a part of a reciprocal arrangement between people and the spirits – as the gods supplied people with food and water, so people gave back flesh and blood to feed the gods. Capac hucha or capacocha ('solemn sacrifice') of children occurred through the Inca-controlled areas of the Andean chain. The remains of these children have been found high up on the mountains or in the mountains lakes such as Lake Titicaca. As well as the precious metal animals mentioned above, the children may also be accompanied by miniature figures, dressed in tiny clothing, which occasionally seem to have been substituted for an actual child, but an increasing number of child mummies attest to the prevalence of the rite. Mummification was in fact an accidental process; the children's bodies were placed in caves or rock shelters at very high altitudes, and were in effect 'freeze-dried', leading in some cases to astonishing levels of preservation of skin and facial features, and beautifully woven and embroidered textiles.

Some bodies, like two on the Nevada Ampato volcano in Peru, had been destroyed by lightning strikes, and the forces of lightning seem to have been regarded as of powerful importance, both as destroyer and bringer of rain. A third body found on Mount Ampato was that of a twelve- or fourteen-year-old girl, nicknamed 'Juanita'. A young boy who was frozen to death high on Cerro El Plomo, in Chile, had red ochre and jagged yellow lines painted on to his face, possibly to represent lightning, and the zigzag motif is also found on some of the textiles clothing the figurines found with the sacrifices. This boy had been placed in a stone-lined crypt; he was wearing a llama wool tunic, and with him were a silver clothed human figure with a headdress and a small gold llama. One remarkable fact about this boy was that it was discovered that he had a viral infection that would have resulted in warts; this was the first time a virus had been identified in pre-Columbian America.

Recent finds of two girls and a boy high on Mount Llullaillaco in Argentina are thought to be 500 years old and were accompanied by some 36 statuettes of gold, silver or Spondylus shell, about 50 per cent clothed, as well as bundles of gorgeous textiles, embroidered moccasins and pottery vessels still containing food offerings. The bodies of the children were astonishingly well preserved, allowing the possibility of DNA, paleopathological and dietary studies, to establish their family relationships, state of health and lifestyle. They were aged between eight and 14 when they died. The textiles that were found may be particularly useful in identifying where the children came from, by comparisons with a range of local styles and design elements. One girl was wearing a white feathered headdress and a yellow textile cloak with a geometric motif over her outer tunic. Some researchers have speculated that the children involved in capacocha sacrifices were offered drugs (possibly coca) or alcohol to render them insensible before they died. Some children seem to have been strangled, while

37 Mummy of an Inca girl found in 1999 on Mount Llullaillaco

others show evidence of blows to the head; some mummies seem to demonstrate that the individuals simply froze to death.

The rituals associated with these and other forms of child sacrifice in the ancient Inca empire demonstrate their importance for society. There would have been processions and ceremonies, and the sacrificial victim would have been feted and treated like royalty. Their parents became highly honoured members of society, and the children themselves were regarded, after their death, as godlike themselves. Their sacrifice was recorded in local memory as a great and memorable act.

Records of other Inca child sacrifices seem to lack the apparent degree of consent and celebration of these mountain rituals, although that is probably a rather subjective view. The Spanish chronicler Juan de Betanzos wrote in 1557 that when the Temple of the Sun in Cuzco was dedicated, the local aristocrats were ordered to produce llamas, maize, fine vestments and boys and girls for sacrifice. A huge fire was built to burn the clothes and corn, and the heads of the animals.

The children were dressed in fine garments and jewellery, and then buried alive in the temple. On the death of the Inca, 1,000 five- to six-year-old children were gathered from all over the empire, finely dressed and, if possible, coming from high status families. They were to be carried in litters in great processions of chiefs, priests and warriors, to meet the Inca and to present offerings. The Inca would reciprocate with gifts and then the children were returned to their home towns where they were sacrificed, either by strangulation or having their throats cut. Other records suggest that a similar ceremony involving ten- to 12-year-old children took place every four years; parents were said to offer their children happily; they would become lords in their communities, the child would join the ancestors in a blessed afterlife, and would be venerated as a deity.

Sites in Central Italy, at Abruzzo, may suggest an even more macabre set of rituals involving children in the Neolithic period, although the evidence is capable of a range of interpretations. The normal burial rituals of the time and region seem to separate child and adult burials, with most child burials occurring within or near houses, and children not being generally represented in more formalised adult cemeteries near settlements. However, the human remains found in a series of caves seem to be evidence of a different set of activities. In several caves, unusually, bones of adults and children are found together. In one case, S. Angelo at Monti della Laga, a cave contained only the bones of children and juveniles. Partially burned bones were scattered across the early Neolithic surface level and in several pits which also included burned animal meat bones, pottery and bone and stone tools, and the carbonized pips of wild apples or pears. At this site, and at the Grotta Scaloria in Apulia which contained a pit full of split and burned human bones, the practice of cannibalism has been suggested as an interpretation of the deposits. Cremation does not seem to have been practised except at cave sites and for the bodies of children.

At the Grotta dei Piccioni, children's remains are associated with apparently carefully arranged assemblages of rocks and objects. The cave had been used for a series of depositions over a long period, the earliest being the placing of a child on the floor in the Early Neolithic, during the late sixth millennium BC. About a thousand years later, in the late Neolithic layers, excavators found a large flat rock slab near the back of the cave, upon which had been set out 11 rough circles of stone on a shallow layer of soil. The earth around the circles was darkened by charcoal and ashes. Inside the southernmost circle was the skeleton of an infant; at the other end were the skulls of two more children and a few head and body bones of a third. The bones had not been covered. In and around the circles were animal bones, pieces of pottery, stone and bone tools and shells; these objects were grouped with a concentration at either end of the line and another in the centre. It seems clear that the bones of the children had a special significance that was respected by the placement of the other material. Among the items deposited was a red painted triton shell which may have come from the shores of Liguria, 500km away, which had been pierced for suspension and modified to form a trumpet. Other examples of these shells, similarly treated, have been associated with other cave burials. 'The numerous animal bones, represented especially by meat parts, strongly suggest that feasting took place in the cave, an interpretation which is perhaps supported by the predominance of bowls in the ceramic assemblage and the evidence of burning from around the circles'.[26] Caves, it is suggested, were special places; they were close to the 'otherworld', liminal and therefore appropriate settings for particular rituals. In addition, the caves of the central Italian region are themselves sited on the edges of the utilised territories of the Neolithic communities, on the edge of or just beyond normal daily activities and life.

This liminality, this sense of being just on the edge of something beyond normal human experience, may help to explain what was going on in these caves. It is suggested that the caves were the places in which initiation rites were held, ceremonies marking the change from childhood to maturity, or other changes or acts of reinforcement of status and power relationships within the community. In the secrecy and dark of the caves, perhaps lit by flickering fires that revealed the carefully placed sacred bones and objects, young people may have been led to face rites that changed them into adults, sharing in the knowledge and mystic experiences of their parents and grandparents for the first time.

BOG BODIES

The bodies of some young people have been found among the preserved remains found in peat bogs in northern Europe, particularly Ireland, Britain, the Netherlands, Denmark and Sweden. The bog bodies include many adult, even elderly people and the interpretations of their depositions are numerous. In some cases, however, it appears that individuals who suffered from particular physical disabilities may have been specially selected for a ritual killing, perhaps a sacrificial offering to the gods of the underworld. Many legends have been told about bottomless pools and dangerous mires, eerily lit by 'corpse-candles' of marsh gas, and capable of swallowing up people and animals in minutes, drawing them down into the Underworld. It must have stood to reason that powerful spirits were at work in these places, and that they demanded great sacrifices from the people who lived by them or crossed over them. Perhaps the regular sacrifice of a chosen victim would serve to sate the hunger of the spirits and protect other travellers. Perhaps the spirits of the bogs had power over the sky that is often so strangely reflected from the surfaces of the marshes, and controlled the weather and the fertility of the crops.

The girl found in a marsh at Yde in the Netherlands had been about 16 years old; she had suffered from an extreme curvature of the spine. The right side of her head had been shaved. Her death was certainly not natural; a garrotte made of a woven fabric belt was found around her neck and there was a knife wound near her left collarbone. A boy aged between eight and 14 was discovered at Kayhausen, in Schleswig-Holstein. His feet had been bound up in a cloak, and his hands tied behind his back. A length of cloth had been passed between his legs and then wound tightly around his neck. He, too, had suffered deformity, and probably had been unable to walk properly in life. Other victims of bog burial, child or adult, do not exhibit deformities in the bones, although they may have been handicapped in some other way.

It is possible that impaired people were seen as having been 'touched' by the gods in some way, and therefore seen as appropriate choices for sacrifice. Alternatively, they may have been selected because they were seen as expendable, unlikely to be able to make a full contribution to their societies in any other manner. In some cases of adult bog burial, it may have been the case that the killing and placing of an individual in a marsh in a specific manner was a judicial punishment. This may explain the double burial made in the late Bronze Age or early Iron Age at Derrymaquirk, in Co. Roscommon in Ireland. A woman and an infant were buried together, with a large stone having been placed on the woman's pelvis; perhaps this was a punishment for adultery.[27]

Tacitus mentions that the shaving of the head was used as a punishment and mark of adultery among Germanic tribes. The case of the young girl found in a bog at Windeby, also in Schleswig-Holstein, offers several possible explanations. Pathological assessment of the body revealed that she had suffered several episodes of arrested growth, possibly rendering her handicapped in some way. Half of her head had been shaved a few weeks before she was killed, some time in the early centuries AD. Additionally, she had been blindfolded with a brightly-coloured fine woven belt, a practice sometimes associated with people thought to be seers. Her body had been weighted down into the bog with birch branches and a large stone. So was she killed because of her possible deformity, because she had committed the crime of adultery, or because she was a mystic or witch?[28]

These sacrifices and burials give us many problems. It is all but impossible for us today to comprehend, much less accept, the killing of children for religious reasons. What we cannot do, however, is have the arrogance to bring to bear our own notions of morality upon the acts of people in the past. Some forms of child sacrifice seem to have been acts of love, giving the child back to the gods and the spirits and thus sparing them the suffering of everyday existence. In other cases, these were acts of great piety, meant for the good of the whole community, sometimes even to ensure its very survival, and thus sparing others pain and distress. Some parents may have acted from a less admirable concern with their own status and importance, of course, and others have shown a callousness in the selection of a poor woman's child to replace their own for the ceremony. But none of these acts was careless. The people who sacrificed children all did so for a reason in which they believed wholeheartedly. They were not being deliberately cruel or murderous. By their own lights, most of them were consciously trying to do a good thing. We must remember that when we hold these acts up to judgement.

SAINTS AND MARTYRS

The Christian Church has a long tradition of holy children and stories associated with children. The birth of Jesus is itself associated with an incident which recalls the kinds of sacrifice recorded in the Old Testament – the Massacre of the Innocents. Upon hearing that a new king had been born to Israel, we are told the King Herod ordered the slaying of all male babies in Bethlehem. The reason for this, ostensibly, is to remove the threat to his own throne, but this is unlikely; Herod at that time, after all, owed his throne to the Roman occupiers of Judaea. The story may be a garbled record of a sacrificial event, perhaps even aimed at the eventual removal of the Romans in the same way that sacrifices were made by the Carthaginians. This is highly speculative, of course, but the long history of Jewish child sacrifice allows at least the possibility of alternative interpretations. Rather less likely is the interpretation of the unknown picture restorer who, given the task of repairing Breughel's 'Massacre of the Innocents', mistook the subject matter and replaced the children who are being put to death in the painting with young pigs. This version of the picture hangs in Hampton Court Palace.

Numerous relics exist that are supposed to be the remains of, or are associated with, child saints and martyrs. A recent report from St Louis in the United States, lists some of the relics held by the motherhouse of the Sisters of St Joseph of Carondelet. These include the bones of a number of saints including St Aurelia and St Discolius, said to be child martyrs whose bones originally rested in the Roman catacombs. St Discolius' remains are accompanied by a crude stone slab with his name inscribed in Latin. There are also remains said to be those of St Berisimus, who was believed to have been a child aged about eight who was martyred in the Colosseum during the reign of Antoninus Pius. These remains, and others in the collection, are displayed dressed in Roman-style tunics of rich brocades, with wreaths on their heads and waxwork faces.

Other extraordinary relics claimed in the past by different establishments include Jesus' nappies (in the Aachen Cathedral Treasury), and his swaddling clothes (at Reading Abbey, Berkshire recorded between 1120 and 1190). A 'Holy Hand' preserved at the Royal Chapel in Budapest is held to be that of St Stephen, who was King of Hungary and died in 1038; scientific investigation has suggested, however, that it is in fact the hand of a ten-year-old child, mummified in an Egyptian style.[29]

Frederick the Wise of Wittenberg collected some 5,005 relics by 1509, including 204 portions of the Holy Innocents massacred by Herod (and a crumb from the Last Supper). The Treasury of Cologne Cathedral held many marvellous relics, but perhaps the most amazing was the skull of St John the Baptist when he was 12 years of age!

It is said that in May 1802 excavators working in the catacombs in Rome found a shelf-tomb sealed with terracotta slabs. Three inscribed tiles held pictures of a lily, an anchor, a lance and arrows, and the legend 'LUMENA/PAXTE/CUMFI', which when rearranged was seen to read 'PAXTE/CUMFI/LUMENA' or 'Peace unto you, Philomena'. These symbols were taken to mean that the coffin held the remains of a virgin martyr. Upon investigation inside the tomb, the bones of a girl aged about 12 or 13 years were found, together with a small vial of dried blood. In 1805 the remains were transferred to the village church of Mugnano, near Naples, at the request of the local priest. Almost immediately, a series of favours and miracles became associated with the remains, and in 1837 this hitherto unknown girl was raised to sainthood by Pope Gregory XVI. She is said to be particularly efficacious on behalf of those involved in conversion of sinners, real estate, money problems, mental illness, food for the poor, expectant or destitute mothers, sterility, priests, and like St Jude, hopeless causes. This is a very unusual case; the Vatican normally spends a great deal of time and effort researching potential saints, but of St Philomena nothing is known apart from her name.

A better known child saint was St Simon of Trent. His cult was ratified in 1588 by Pope Sixtus V. Simon was born in Trentino in Northern Italy, and was said to have been murdered, aged about three, in 1475 by Jews 'out of hatred for Christ' although there was much dispute about this at the time. Child murder by unorthodox sects or rival religions is a fairly common phenomenon in history. Both the Albigensians and the Knights Templars were accused of performing unspeakable rites involving the murder of young children, and similar propaganda has been used time and again in warfare. In fact, there is little or no evidence that any of these claims has ever been true, and even the events surrounding the death of Simon of Trent were questioned by a number of church authorities at the time and shortly afterwards.

The cults associated with child martyrs and saints have nevertheless appealed to the popular imagination, and evidence in the form of statuary, shrines, reliquaries and pilgrim tokens attest to their veneration.

CHILDREN IN RELIGIOUS INSTITUTIONS

Rules about the acceptance of children into monastic houses, male and female, varied over time. A child of seven could wear the tonsure and serve as a clerk; up to the twelfth century it was customary for children aged five or six (sometimes even younger) to be entered into the convents. St Thomas Aquinas was sent to the monastery of Monte Cassino at the age of five in 1230. Until the eighth century, the age at which a child could make the decision to become a monk or nun was 14 for boys and 12 for girls. After this, the child's right of choice began to be lost; the parent's decision on behalf of the child was regarded as irreversible, effectively removing from the child any choice about the course of its life. Once dedicated to the church, even if this occurred before birth, the individual became the church's property. Doubts about this practice began to be raised, and in 1215 the Fourth Lateran Council made it possible for boys raised in the religious life to be able to leave without penalty when they were old enough. Before this the Cistercians had already raised the age for entry into the novitiate to 15 and then 18. Benedictine houses still accepted children; ostensibly this was for their education, but there was sometimes a very heavy moral pressure for the child to enter the religious life at the end of their schooling.

It was a fairly popular solution to the problem of the appearance of an illegitimate or a handicapped child to place it in a religious house during the medieval period. It was believed by some that in dedicating such a child to such a life, it would be cleansed of the flaws of its conception and birth. Children might also enter monasteries and convents accompanying widowed parents who had decided to retreat from the world, or as 'gifts to God' on behalf of their parents. It was not in the church's interest to take in all and sundry, however, and in most cases the child was only accepted if it was accompanied by a gift of money or land.

From the twelfth century onwards, many urban religious houses founded schools, not only for the children living within the precinct, but also, for a fee, for the children of burgesses of the town. In their early years, the houses of friars were opposed to accepting children into their orders, although by the mid-fourteenth century the Franciscans accepted 13-year-olds.

The age at which girls were placed in convents was not subject to so much legislation and change. Indeed, it was thought that the younger the girl, the more suitable she was for the life, as she would have been less tainted by the experiences of the outside world. Although in theory she could choose to leave at the age of twelve, in fact the girls rarely had anywhere else to go or any way of surviving outside the convent walls.

The life of the children inside religious houses was highly controlled, and in theory at least, very isolated from normal daily life. They were always to be under supervision, discipline was often harsh and physical, and few concessions were made to their youth. They were allowed some laxity in the observance of fasts and some periods of rest during observances. Nevertheless, they were fed, educated, given medical treatment, and provided with a generally safe environment. If their emotional needs were hardly met and their lives were constrained and hard, this was often also true of the lives of the adults around them.

It is perhaps not surprising that we do not hear much about sexual abuse in religious houses; nevertheless there can be no doubt that it took place. There are numerous accounts of monks being punished for 'unnamed vices' between themselves; the children must sometimes have been vulnerable to these. It must also be recognised, however, that there is likely to have been a measure of consensuality. Adults and children in such institutions would both have been in need of physical and emotional contact, and with no alternatives other than prayer and mortification of the flesh, it should not, perhaps, dismay us if such practices were adopted more or less willingly. Certainly, the various reminders to nuns that they should not allow certain shapes of implements and vegetables into their precincts suggest that forms of relief were utilised by religeuses too.

It does not, perhaps, immediately strike us, when we visit a monastic site that it was home to children as well as to monks or nuns. We know very little of what particular arrangements were made for their housing, feeding and education within the building plans. It is to be presumed that they did not normally share the dormitories of the dedicated members of the community and that therefore other sleeping arrangements must have existed. Did children eat in the frater (referectory) along with their elders? They certainly served them at meal times, and perhaps ate their meals a little earlier or later than the adults. Where were classes held? Were there areas where the children could run and play? Were children accommodated differently in infirmaries? There is much still to be understood about this topic.

DIVINITY MADE FLESH

In a number of societies, children have been regarded as living deities. Several Buddhist sects seek for the reincarnation of revered lamas among living children, including the successor to the Dalai Lama, on the death of the incumbent. The children, once identified, are removed from their families and brought up and educated in monasteries, until old enough to assume leadership of their spiritual communities. It is believed that the spirit of the dead lama enters into the body of a particular child, and thus is immortal and made continuing flesh.

Nepal also has a living goddess, the *kumari*, in Kathmandu. Equally revered by both Buddhists and Hindus, the *kumari* is chosen at the age of four or five by priests. She must be a member of the Sakya caste of gold and silversmiths, and display the requisite 32 characteristics, which include physical perfection, a calm disposition, and the ability to spend a night without showing fear in a room filled with severed buffalo and goat heads. Once chosen, the girl is taken from her parents to live in virtual seclusion for the next eight years or so, until she reaches puberty. She is regularly displayed, wrapped in costly garments and covered with jewellery, to worshippers, at a window in the palace courtyard. Once she reaches puberty, however, this rarefied existence comes to an abrupt end. She is returned to the parents she has not seen for many years without any great ceremony. Nani Sobha, kumari between 1961 and 1969, recalled that 'I didn't get to keep anything. The day that you stop being *kumari* they come and take away all the jewellery and give you pocket money and a few clothes'. The present *kumari*, Preeti Sakya, is reported to be on strike over a charge made by Kathmandu's Metropolitan Committee to foreign tourists for the opportunity to see her appearances; none of this fee has been handed over to Preeti's guardians and their own share of donations has fallen as a result, so they have not allowed the goddess to make her customary visits to the window as a protest.[30]

38 Preeti Sakya, aged six, the 'kumari' or living goddess of Kathmandu since 2001

In ancient Egypt, the pharaohs were considered to be god-kings, who ultimately became gods in their own right after death. Not only was the pharaoh the earthly representative of the sun god Ra, he was also the high priest of the cult of every other deity, and only the pharaoh is depicted making offerings to the gods in temple wall paintings.[31]

The best known ancient Egyptian pharaoh was, coincidentally, also a child – Tutankhamun. Ruling from approximately 1343 to 1333 BC, Tutankhamun, the younger son of the so-called 'heretic king' Akhenaten, ascended the throne at the age of nine or ten, following the death of his father and older brother. As was the tradition, he married his sister Ankhesepaaten (later known as Ankhesenamun), making her queen, but the effective rulers of the country, the powers behind the throne, were the generals (and subsequent pharaohs) Ay and Horemheb. Apart from the astonishing grave goods that were memorably found in Tutankhamun's tomb by Howard Carter in 1922, the young pharaoh is chiefly remembered for re-establishing worship of the pantheon of gods and goddesses that had been swept away by his father Akhenaten, who had tried to introduce a monotheistic cult dedicated to the Aten, or living sun.

Tutankhamun reigned for only nine years, and was probably still in his teens when he died. Damage has been found to his skull and circumstantial evidence seems to imply that he may have been murdered by a blow to his head; on the other hand, he may simply have suffered an accidental injury.

Very little is known of Tutankhamun's background. Records show that Akhenaten sired six princesses with his principal wife, Nefertiti, and it is thought that Tutankhamun was the child of one of his father's lesser wives. Up until Akhenaten's reign, it is rare to find depictions of royal children but, as well as attempting to change the religion of the state, Akhenaten also appears to have supported the introduction of a more realistic and informal artistic style, examples of which include representations of the royal couple playing with their children. The children are shown acting in normal ways for their ages, rather than as miniature adults; the parents look entirely comfortable and affectionate in their company. The message of the style may have been designed to reinforce the importance of the entire royal family and not just the pharaoh; the children and their mother are to be worshipped as much as the father.

The boy pharaoh's divine status is underlined by the careful curation and inclusion in the tomb of objects such as his childhood toys and clothing regarded as sacred objects in themselves, to be conserved and included in the paraphernalia of the afterlife. Two tiny mummies of stillborn babies, one possibly aborted at five months and the other about full-term, probably Tutankhamun's own children, were also preserved, wrapped in linen and enclosed in carved sarcophagi. One of these babies also had a gilt and gesso mask, a miniature version of the great gold mask of the pharaoh.

In ancient Rome, the tradition of deifying emperors began with the first, Augustus, in 31 BC, and continued until Rome accepted Christianity under the reign of Constantine I in AD 306. Of the more than 150 men who held the title of emperor, eight were less than 20 years old, and two were under ten when they came to the throne. Some of these young men are notable for their failure to reconcile their semi-divine status with the practical and sensible requirements demanded of the ruler of the known world. Perhaps the most notorious was

Nero (who ruled from AD 54 to 68). Nero was originally feted as a talented and charming boy, but by the end of his reign he was said to have become a megalomaniac, convinced of his artistic genius and guilty of the murder of members of his own family, including his mother and sister. Whilst probably innocent of starting the fire that destroyed much of Rome in AD 64, and indeed credited by some with heroic efforts to alleviate the suffering of the citizens as a result, general discontent with his reign eventually forced him to commit suicide.

Similar delusions of grandeur affected Commodus (emperor between AD 180 and 192) and Elagabalus (AD 218-222). Commodus, the son of the respected Marcus Aurelius, was 19 when he became emperor, and like Nero he began well, but later he started to identify himself with the god Hercules, wearing lion skins and carrying a club. He scandalised the Roman public by entering contests in the public amphitheatre with gladiators and ferocious animals, something that only slaves and condemned criminals were supposed to do. He was strangled in his bath at the age of 29. Elagabalus was not the real name of the 14-year-old grand nephew of the emperor Caracalla. Varius Avitus Bassanius was born in Syria, and upon ascending the throne adopted the name of a Syrian deity, who he tried to establish as the principal god of the Roman pantheon, supplanting Jove. He also had the habit of conferring upon himself honours without official sanction, and acquired a very bad reputation. Accusations made by a number of biographers including Herodian, Dio Cassius and Aelius Lampridus include effeminacy, bisexuality, transvestitism and being a male prostitute. Whatever the truth, he at least seems to have been guilty of being flamboyant, and was only 17 when the army decided they'd had enough and killed him.

Other boy emperors seem to have fared better, including Elagabalus' successor, the 14-year-old Alexander Severus (AD 222-234). Relying on the advice of his mother and grandmother, Severus seems to have stabilised the empire; his failure, and the cause of his early death, seems to have been due to his military inexperience and desire to avoid conflict in Germany by buying off the barbarians. Enraged by this policy, young Severus and his mother were killed by their own soldiers. Constans I (AD 337-350) was 17 when he became emperor, and showed great military ability; the first half of his reign was moderate and successful, but later corruption led to his murder.

The emperor Gratian was the son of Valentinian I. He was born in AD 359 and was only seven when he was awarded his first consulate. A year later, his father fell ill whilst on campaign against the fierce Alamanni tribe in Gaul and Germany, and young Flavius Gratianus was proclaimed co-regent, effectively becoming emperor at the age of eight. Apparently a scholarly lad, Gratian's disinterest in fighting made him less than popular with the army, particularly in view of the precarious state of the empire in the face of increasing barbarian incursions. On the death of his father in AD 375 Gratian became sole ruler of the Western Empire, with his capital at Trier. The army in Pannonia (modern Slovakia and Hungary) was facing barbarian onslaughts, and declined to recognise Gratian's sovereignty. The local generals then made a seemingly astonishing decision – they proclaimed Gratian's four-year-old half-brother Valentinian II as co-regent, claiming that he was closer to the trouble-spot of Brigetio (now Komarom-Szony, Hungary) than Gratian. In reality, this allowed the generals free rein to continue their battle plans without interference from above. Surprisingly, or perhaps not, given his peaceful nature, Gratian happily acquiesced to the army's demands.

Gratian now controlled the empire in the west (Gaul, Britain and Spain) while the little Valentinian II held the east (Illyricum, Africa and Italy). The empire, however, was not settled and the army was still discontented. In AD 383 the British troops declared their field general Magnus Maximus to be emperor and pursued Gratian in Gaul, Gratian was eventually killed by Maximus' men in Lyon on 25 August 383. In 384 Maximus named his infant son Victor as co-regent, and no longer recognised the 13-year-old Valentinian II. Valentinian nevertheless continued to rule and, with assistance, defeated and slew Maximus. He himself died in 392 at the age of 21, possibly by suicide as a result of the continual political wranglings of the imperial court.

Although it seems absurd to our eyes today that a child as young as four years old can become a 'ruling' emperor and be worshipped as a god by his subjects, it can be argued that such child emperors may have had their advantages. By being removed from the adult world of policies, decision-making, strategies and infighting, the child could become a symbol of unity for Roman citizens – a symbolic figurehead of 'incorruptible' purity and innocence. Sadly, for the children themselves, the hothouse environment of the imperial court rarely resulted in happy lives.

CHILD DEITIES

Child deities, although not common, appear in cultures throughout the world, often as youthful aspects of a deity more frequently revered in its adult form. Vishnu, a solar deity, is one of the major gods within the Hindu pantheon. It is said that he has reincarnated nine times so far, each divine incarnation known as an avatar. One of the most popular of Vishnu's avatars was his eighth, known as Krishna. Krishna himself incorporates a number of different characters and representations; as well as being mentioned in the Bhagavad Gita as a young charioteer encouraging the hero to succeed in battle, he was also the child-god of Braj, an area near Delhi, said to be his birthplace. Arguably the most popular Krishna manifestation is as the delightful but mischievous child-deity who exasperated his mother by stealing yoghurt and butter, and, in adolescence, seducing the Braj milkmaids away from their husbands.

It goes without saying that, for parents, a child often means the whole world to them, and this can be illustrated in a popular tale about one of Krishna's

39 Images of children from Roman coins: a) Ti. Claudius Britannicus, son of the Emperor Claudius, born AD 43, poisoned by Nero in AD 55; b) Nero, who became emperor aged 17 in AD 57; c) Galenius Antoninus, son of Antoninus Pius, who died very young in the mid-second century AD; d) Diadumenian, born in AD 208, declared Caesar with his father Macrinus in AD 217 and executed in AD 218; e) Valentinian II, born AD 371 becoming emperor in AD 375; f) Leo II, born around AD 467, who became emperor in AD 473 but died a year later

childhood pranks. Krishna's 'mother' is unaware of her child's divinity. One day, Krishna takes some food he shouldn't and eats it, whereupon his mother demands he opens his mouth so that she can see what it is. He does so and, looking in, his mother sees the entire universe in all its glory, all within her young child. He is, literally, the world and contained within him, as within every human child, is the power to change both the world and himself.

Another child deity within Hindu culture is Skanda Kumara, the son of Shiva and Parvati who is created through the intermingling of fire and water. He is said to be the god of war, male beauty and occult wisdom, is forever youthful, lithe and elegant with dark skin, ruby-coloured eyes, black curly hair and adorned with serpents and the moon. As a baby he is found by seven sisters (the Pleiades) who fight over who will nurse him. Unwilling to disappoint the sisters, it is said that Skanda either created for himself another six heads so that all the sisters could suckle him, or he divided his body into seven portions so that each could nurse a part of him. Representing youthful bliss, Skanda also had a hazardous and anti-social side. To him are credited many childhood trickeries and mischief; he is the patron saint of thieves and is often accompanied by a gang of rogues, ghosts, outlaws and magicians.

Ancient Egypt had several child deities, all of them male. Probably the best known is Horus the Child. This name was fairly commonly associated to a number of related forms of divine infant, most being the identified as the son of Osiris and Isis. There may also have been more specific names – for example, within the Pyramid Texts he is known as Harherywadj which means 'Horus upon his papyrus plants' and is depicted as a child sucking his finger. Horus the Child is most commonly called Harpocrates, the Greek version of the Egyptian Harpakhered. In this aspect, he was usually represented as a vulnerable child seated on the lap of his mother Isis and sucking his thumb. The similarities here with depictions of the Madonna and child are unmistakable.

The male child deity Ihy represented the transportive euphoria associated with the playing of the sistrum, a percussive musical instrument sacred to the Ancient Egyptian cow-headed goddess, Hathor, said to be Ihy's mother. As is the way with a pantheon of deities, though, Ihy was also regarded as the son of a few other deities such as Isis, Nephthys and Sekhmet, although Horus was most frequently considered to be his father. Although most commonly considered a deity associated with music, Ihy also had some responsibilities in the afterlife. He is called 'the lord of bread' in the Coffin Texts and the Book of the Dead and is also supposed to be in charge of the beer at offerings. Linking music and beer shows that Ihy can best be said to represent the youthful abandonment and intoxication that a combination of both can provoke!

Nefertem was the child god of the lotus blossom that, according to ancient Egyptian myth, emerged from the waters of the primeval ocean. Linked to Re, the pre-eminent solar deity, Nefertem is also recognised as a god of perfumes. During the period of the New Kingdom (from c.1550-1070 BC) at Memphis,

Nefertem became associated with the god Ptah and his lion-headed goddess consort Sekhmet, forming a very important triad in which he was commonly viewed as their son. They became a holy family. Anthropomorphically, Nefertem is depicted as a male god sporting a lotus blossom on his head. When shown as a child, he usually wears a short kilt and carries a sickle sword. Also as a child, and linking back to his connection to the creation myths, Nefertem is shown seated on a lotus blossom or as a head emerging from the flower. A particularly fine painted wooden example of this was found in Tutankhamun's tomb. Nefertem was not popularly worshipped as he was mainly a deity of divine and royal monuments and was, in fact, feared in his manifestation as the son of the fierce goddess Sekhmet; protective amulets promising to protect a new-born child from Nefertem have been found dating to the Third Intermediate Period (*c.* 1069 to 672 BC).

Dating from the New Kingdom period, Shed was known as 'he who rescues' or 'the enchanter' and was said to be the god of weapons of war as well as a provider of protection from wild animals in the desert and the river, black magic and illness. He is often depicted as a youth with a shaved head and sidelock, wearing a kilt with a broad collar and often wears a quiver on his back, possibly grasping some dangerous wild animal while standing on the back of a crocodile. It could be argued that Shed represented that aspect of youth that knows no fear.

Remaining in the Middle East, Damu was a Sumerian god popular in Mesopotamia and dates from around 2112 BC, the beginning of the Third Dynasty of Ur. A divine child, Damu was responsible for healing, abundance and vitality, and is closely linked to fruit harvests and the rising of tree sap, signifying regrowth, renewal and new life every year.

In the Far East, Li-Nezha (in China), Nou-jha (in Taiwan) or Nataku (in Japan) is the trickster boy god of childish pranks and tantrums as well as an accomplished demon fighter.

Evidence for female child deities, by comparison, is sparse. Some are the female counterparts of male child deities, such as Jyoti, the sister of Skanda (and occasionally the sister of the elephant-headed god Ganesha). Skanda represents fire and water, Jyoti air and space, and both require the presence of the other in order to exist. In depictions, Jyoti is usually dressed in brightly coloured clothing symbolising the darkness of ignorance being dispelled by the light of her knowledge.

Other female child deities exist in their own right, such as the Inuit child goddess Sedna. The story goes that Sedna's father wished to marry her off but she was stubborn and refused to obey. Her father finally lost patience and decided to kill her as punishment. He forced Sedna into his small fishing boat and rowed out into the Arctic ocean where he threw her overboard. Terrified and struggling, Sedna grabbed onto the boat to save herself but her father took out his sharp knife and sliced off her fingers one by one until she could no longer grip and sank into the icy waters. Miraculously, her severed finger joints were turned into sea creatures such as whales and seals who, considering Sedna to be their mother, escorted her safely to the sea bed where she was transformed into a powerful Arctic sea-goddess. Interestingly, in March 2004 astronomers discovered a new planet, the tenth, within our solar system and named it 'Sedna'.

It can be argued that male child deities seem to be closely linked with aspects of childhood playfulness and mischief, while female child deities are more closely aligned with creative aspects, which seems natural. Boys often seem to be more rowdy and playful than girls, while it is a fundamental aspect of the female gender to create new life through giving birth. Both genders of child gods seem to carry elements relating to fertility, liveliness and energy in one form or another, perhaps a useful balance or antidote to the more formal and severe adult pantheons.

In some respects, the existence of child deities may offer a way to engage young children in the study of religious ideas and associations, as is the case within Christianity. The modern Nativity play, with its lambs, donkeys and baby Jesus, is often the first introduction to the tenets of belief for the very young, offering them a level at which understanding of religion can begin to take root. This can pose problems for the archaeologist in interpretation of artefacts and symbols, as was noted in chapter 1 – separation of dolls from votive or sacred figures can be difficult. Crib figures of shepherds and kings have a clear context within a church at Christmas, but their meanings would be harder to detect outside that setting.

5

SUFFER THE LITTLE CHILDREN

Our own affections still at home to please
Is a disease:
To cross the sea to any foreign soil,
Perils and toil:
Wars with their noise affright us; when they cease,
We are worse in peace :-
What then remains, but that we still should cry
Not to be born, or, being born, to die?
(From 'Life' by Lord Bacon 1521-1626)

INTRODUCTION

Even the most cared for and cherished child is desperately vulnerable, and for those born without a silver spoon, life can be at best a lottery, and at worst a horror. Children's small size and lack of worldly knowledge and influence mean that they are particularly liable to suffer abuse and neglect, exploitation and accident. They are subject to abuses of conscious power, such as paedophilia, and to careless power in various forms of exploitation. Misuse may not even be primarily directed at the children themselves; threats towards children can be a tool used to control their parents and even their whole societies. A recent report[1] notes that:

> Children in Northern Ireland are being shot in paramilitary punishment attacks at a rate of one every three weeks....Children aged 16 or under were the victims of 12.5 per cent of republican 'punishment' shootings and 26 per cent of such beatings. The attacks often cause lifelong injury and involve weapons such as baseball bats, breeze-blocks, nail-studded sticks and sledgehammers'.

It is not easy to forget, either, the children used by Saddam Hussein as a 'human shield'. Children are often victims of abuse in employment; they are cheap labour, easily cowed and controlled, as the operators of sweat shops, carpet factories and brickfields in the Third World know well. Child slavery is still rife in certain parts of the globe, where schools are sometimes targetted by gangs of kidnappers, or parents are threatened into giving up their children to slavers. Despite huge efforts by governments and agencies, child prostitution, sexual abuse and pornography seem to be thriving in every country, made even more rife by use of the internet. Horrific tales of physical abuse and neglect still surface in the most wealthy and advanced societies, such as the two small children recently rescued from a life confined to cages in Arizona. For a certain type of personality, any smaller or weaker creature than themselves, animal or child, can be a target for the expression of their own anger or frustration. Such people, who often also have a history of cruelty to animals, seem to be able to divorce the notion of 'child' from the idea of 'person', and consequently do not recognise the existence or force of moral constraints about their treatment. The idea of the child as liminal, not yet part of society and the real world, that is met with in some cultures, can be used against children to excuse forms of abuse of them by some aberrant minds.

In times of disease or hunger, children are often the first victims too. Their small bodies are often less able to withstand the rigours of illness and starvation than those of adults, and so they die more quickly and in greater numbers. If their parents succumb, surviving orphans often stand little chance of life without someone to protect them and care for them. Even if they do survive, they are vulnerable to exploitation and abuse, like the street children of Brazil, or their life chances are severely curtailed by the need to care for siblings or earn their own living at a cruelly early age, as has been the experience of so many children in countries where AIDS is decimating the adult population.

Warfare, too, is particularly cruel to children in many ways; it affects them as victims of violence, as targets and tools of aggressors, and as survivors in a world of uncertainty and want.

With the odds so stacked against children, it is a miracle that so many do survive, and survive with their sanity and hope intact; in some ways children are remarkably strong and resilient. Many aid and charity workers have cited the determination and hope of the children they care for as the power that bolsters and maintains their own ability to go on helping them. Somehow, the children do survive, and with them goes the future of our species.

Archaeology can illustrate something of the suffering of those children in the past who did not make it through, even those of the very recent past. The pitiful remains that come to light can tell us much about the want, the abuse and the terror that can affect the lives of children and their families.

WAR

The bodies of children are frequently found as casualties of war. In 'primitive' war, children may be deliberately selected as victims; without children, the viability of the enemy's survival is severely compromised, and the killing of children also achieves demoralisation among their parents with minimum risk to the attackers. This sounds horribly callous, and indeed it is. It may be a defensible strategy at the level of combat where the survival of one group depends on the annihilation of another; it becomes completely indefensible when used as a tactic of modern politics.

History abounds with accounts of the massacre of children; it is a common charge to level at an enemy, and therefore one needs to treat the stories with some caution, but examples include Geoffrey of Tours' account of Thuringian atrocities against young boys and girls, the record left by Abbon of Saint-Germain of the siege of Paris by Normans in the late eleventh century when:

> Children of all ages, young people, white-haired old timers, and fathers and sons, and also
> mothers, they kill everyone. They massacre the husband before the eyes of his wife, the wife
> is the victim of slaughter; children perish in the presence of their fathers and mothers' and
> Bede recounts the torture and massacre of children by Cadwallon against the subjects of
> the Christian king Edwin in the year 633.

Among the better-known mass graves discovered by archaeologists is one near Talheim in Germany, where at least 34 people (nine men, seven women and sixteen children and adolescents) appear to have been massacred around 5000 BC. Eighteen of the skulls had indications of fatal injury, mostly damage to skulls by polished stone axes but also blunt force trauma and arrow wounds.[2] The arrow wounds would seem to indicate that the attack took place in daylight, and the absence of defence injuries suggest that the attackers met with little resistance. Many victims sustained wounds from behind.

At a Middle Bronze Age site at Velim, in the Czech Republic a series of large pits seem to contain the bodies of hundreds of people, some bodies complete, some disarticulated, scattered or incomplete; some pits contained groups of skulls, and a number of bones had evidence of cutmarks. Men, women and children were represented here.

One of the best-studied mass graves is the fourteenth-century AD Crow Creek site. At this prehistoric (before European discovery and recording) American village, 486 individuals, thought to represent some 50 per cent of the village population, were found in the remains of the fortification ditch. The paleopathological evidence includes numerous examples of mutilation (nearly 90 per cent of the skulls, including those of the children, showed evidence of scalping); it is also suggested that teeth and tongues may have been removed and noses cut off. Decapitation was fairly common and hands were often removed; cut marks were found on joints suggesting dismemberment. Many of the dead (around 40 per cent) had suffered blows to the skull and others died within burned houses. Canids had had time to gnaw bones before burial.

It is believed that the attack took place in the late autumn or early winter, based on analysis of the process of decomposition. The moment for the attack seems to have been chosen while the village's defences were undergoing refurbishment:

> ... six of the post holes of the inner ditch contained human skull fragments. This suggests that the inner ditch holes may have been open at the time of the massacre, the posts having been pulled, perhaps to place them along the newer, outer ditch. The outer ditch may well have been under construction at the time of the massacre to protect an expanding village and to replace an old ditch that had lost its effectiveness because filled with village debris.[3]

The problems of establishing the facts of the case, even in such apparently clear cases of massacre as those recorded in recent history, are largely due to the casual disposition of bodies, the length of time they remain exposed before burial, and the degree of mutilation and destruction incurred by the bodies at or near the time of death. At Kibuye Church, in Rwanda, during the conflict between the Tutsi and Hutu peoples, bodies were buried several days after death and exhumed by war graves investigators six months later. It was found that the remains of children and especially infants were so badly decomposed that their bodies were, in some cases, unrecognisable as such. Forty-four per cent of the identified dead were children under the age of 15; of the 460 skulls found, 65 per cent had suffered blunt force trauma, 10 per cent sharp force trauma, and there were gunshot and shrapnel wounds, although cause of death of 24.2 per cent was undetermined.[4]

At El Mozote, El Salvador, the remains of 143 individuals including 136 children and adolescents and seven adults were disinterred from a mass grave. The average age of the children was six years; the adults comprised six women aged 21–40 (one pregnant) and one man who was approximately 50.

> ... uncertainty regarding the number of skeletons is a resection of the extensive perimortem skeletal injuries, postmortem skeletal damage and associated commingling. Many young infants may have been entirely cremated; other children may not have been counted because of extensive fragmentation of body parts ....The specific cause of death could not be determined in all cases because of the absence of soft tissues, the extent of postmortem skeletal damage and the long postmortem interval.[5]

Minimal postmortem insect activity and scavenging of animals proved that the deaths were roughly contemporaneous with each other. The massacre took place on 12 December 1981, and the exhumations were undertaken between 13–17 November 1992. Similar difficulties have been reported from other such sites, including the dry well containing a minimum of 162 individuals (67 under 12 years old) at Dos Erres, El Petén, Guatemala, exhumed in 1994 (the massacre of this village having been carried out in December 1982).[6] In these and other massacres in the region, government and rebel troops have both been accused of atrocities; villages are attacked when the men are off working in the fields. The work of the forensic archaeologists who have been attempting to recover the bodies and the evidence has shown that these children were burned alive, mutilated with machetes, or clubbed to death with rifles and sticks. These attacks have various aims: to discourage villagers from co-operating with one side or the other, or to wipe out populations with different ethnic backgrounds. The children represent an easy target and their murder a way to achieve political ends with little risk of injury to the perpetrators.

Post-war ritual may be the cause of the curious deposits found at Ofnet in Bavaria – two pits containing carefully placed skulls of men, women and children. Frayer calls this 'the first clear evidence for a mass murder in prehistory'.[7] The skulls (about 31 in one pit, six in the other) were packed 'like eggs in a basket', most facing west, stained with red ochre and in the cases of the females accompanied by pierced red deer teeth and shells. This strange deposit was created in the late Mesolithic. Most of the skulls show evidence of blunt trauma, deemed not to be due to postmortem factors because of shape and position on the skull. Clear marks on many skulls also show that the victims were decapitated by first having their throats cut, then having their cervical columns cut through above the first thoracic.[8] Ofnet has a high proportion of children compared to other sites (59.5 per cent under age 15), a figure which compares interestingly with those of the modern massacres mentioned above. Comparable figures for Talheim and Crow Creek are, respectively, 44.1 per cent and 46.3 per cent.[9] Ofnet also has an extremely high proportion of women (66.7 per cent) compared to Talheim (43.7 per cent) and Crow Creek (45.3 per cent). It seems clear that the skulls were deposited in a single incident. It would seem odd, in view of contemporary burial practice, that the bodies were not recovered along with the skulls if these were buried by relatives or survivors. It is therefore possible that the skulls were placed in their pits by their killers, perhaps as part of a cleansing or propitiatory ritual.[10]

Interesting observations can be made about general health; it was noted that among several examples of graves of victims of violence in prehistoric communities, there was a high incidence of debilitating conditions pre-existing, perhaps making these people less able to fight or flee. In many cases, it would seem that work parties of women and children were particular targets. Over time, people would have been less and less able to reach their fields or hunting grounds for fear of attack, and so the general diet and health of the community would suffer.

The bodies from Crow Creek also showed signs of poor health including all the signs of repeated, prolonged malnutrition; Harris lines in the long bones were common, and among the skulls studied, 18 had orbital cribra, four had orbital cribra associated with other skull lesions and six had porotic hyperostosis. Harris lines are formed during childhood, while the bones are still growing; they are shadows visible on X-rays of the bones, each shadow representing a period of arrested growth due to malnutrition or disease. This kind of evidence allows us to determine something of the childhood biographies of the adults represented at the site, who had managed to survive their compromised upbringing only to die later as victims of war.

Even migration away from trouble can endanger children. Possible stress markers for displaced or endangered population groups include many that are specifically visible in the health of children such as dietary deficiency conditions such as scurvy and rickets, dental enamel hypoplasia, Harris lines, osteoporosis in young people and overall decrease in size and weight. Some of these conditions are visible on the skeleton; others may be identified through the analysis of trace elements and stable isotopes. Isotopic and trace mineral analysis (particularly of heavy metals) may also be used to demonstrate population movements; particular concentrations of these elements are sometimes restricted to quite specific locales. If we were to find communities where the children's pattern of these features is markedly different from that of their parents, we could suggest in some cases the kind of demographic movement that may result from warfare.

That warfare creates the conditions for general population distress is, of course, well known. Referring to ethnographic evidence from the Mae Enga of New Guinea, it has been observed that:

> We simply do not know how many infants and old people succumb to pneumonia in these flights, how many refugees are drowned when trying to cross boulder-strewn torrents, how many already sick and weak people die because food supplies are interrupted. These less obvious costs of war, I believe, accumulate significantly through time.[11]

Children in the modern world are sometimes kidnapped and/or coerced into becoming soldiers. One boy, Abdul Rahman, has recorded how he was recruited into Sierra Leone's Revolutionary United Front:

> I was in class, second grade. I was eight years old. They threatened to kill us. In front of us, they brought a grown-up man, going gray. They put his hand on a stump and amputated it. They gave me a gun and I refused it. They fired between my feet. I took the gun.[12]

Some adult commanders use child soldiers quite cynically as expendable forward troops, and as shock troops. It has been reported that:

> Rwandan backed rebels [in Congo] did not have enough arms for each soldier, so deployed children unarmed as a diversionary force. The children would be instructed to take sticks and beat on trees. They drew the fire of the opposition, allowing older, armed combatants to attack from a different direction.[13]

The amorality of children makes them perfect terrorists; they are less aware of the consequences and horror of their actions, and carry less in the way of social constraints. It is estimated by the United Nations that over 300,000 children are fighting as soldiers in more than 30 countries worldwide.

Children have been involved in conflicts throughout history as participants as well as victims – late into the nineteenth century, the British Army had its drummer boys, and the Royal Navy of Nelson's day recruited boys as young as eight or nine as cabin boys and 'powder monkeys' on its battleships. The career path of the officer class began at a similar age. Young midshipmen went to sea to learn not only their trade, but the basic essentials of schooling; one day they might be sat over their books and slates, the next they might be commanding a section of men many years their senior in action on the gundeck or in small boat actions. Bizarre as this might seem to modern sensibilities, at the time it was unquestioned, the assumption being that the social superiority of the boys' class made them suitable for command despite their young age. Institutions were created during the nineteenth century to house and train the orphaned children of lesser soldiers and sailors, to prepare them in their turn to enter the armed forces. One of these was the Royal Military Asylum, in King's Road, Chelsea. This institution annually supported 550 boys aged between nine and 14, orphaned sons of 'respectable' non-commissioned officers. Reveille was at six in the morning, and from then on throughout the day the children were divided into strictly organised ranks and platoons, and were provided with a basic education in scholastic and practical skills such as laundry and needlework. There was a well-run infirmary, a band, and opportunities for sports and games.

40 Scene in 'The Sewing Room' of the Royal Military Asylum. Reproduced from *The Strand Magazine*, 1892

A record in 1892 suggests that on the whole, the children were well cared for, although the diet was basic and the sermons they had to sit through were overlong and inappropriate for their age, leaving Mrs Frances Low, the visitor, envious of the apparent ability of the children to suppress their yawns better than she could herself. In 1892, some 1,368 boys had entered the army from the school, and 'only one has turned out badly, whilst one has risen to the rank of Lieut.-General' (reported in an article 'Boy Soldiers and Sailors' published in *The Strand Magazine*, Vol. IV).

A similar institution for the Royal Navy was the training-ship *Warspite*, moored off Woolwich Pier. Unlike the army school, *Warspite* was not supported with government funds. This institution accepted destitute boys between the ages of 13 and 16 for a period of nine months, after which they were drafted into either the merchant or Royal Navies. They received basic schooling and practical training in seamanship, navigation, swimming, physical training and the tying of

41 A parade on the deck of the training-ship *Warspite* in 1892

knots! Conditions were rather more basic than those provided by the Army, but sermons seemed to play a lesser part on board! Each boy was also provided with a good supply of clothing, necessities and comforts when he left the training-ship, with which to begin his life at sea as comfortably as possible. *Warspite* had been a three-decked capital warship in a previous incarnation, when she had been known as *Conqueror*.

Sometimes weapons are found in the graves of children, and it is often assumed that these are either toys or status symbols. In many cases these are probably reasonable assumptions, but it is perfectly possible, too, that these children could and did participate in battles. There is little proof of this, but it is an interpretation that cannot, in the light of modern experience, be dismissed out of hand. A number of classical sources and later historical documents support the identification of children as warriors, sometimes with specific forms of weaponry and particular tactical roles, such as light infantry armed with spears, in support of older and more experienced men armed with swords, or as adjuncts to mounted troops. The weaponry recorded in the graves of adolescent boys of the Saxon and Viking worlds seem to suggest such organisation.

HEALTH AND DIET, DISEASE AND MORTALITY

Children's bodies are particularly susceptible to certain physical and dietary stresses. Illnesses or lack of food during the period of growth frequently leave permanent marks upon the body such as Harris lines and enamel hypoplasia (ridges on permanent teeth). Each ridge or Harris line represents a separate period of stress. Because the long bones grow at their ends, the lines retain their relative position throughout life, and it is possible to make an assessment of the age at which the stress was experienced. To some extent this is also possible in the case of teeth alteration up to the age when the permanent tooth crowns are fully formed, around six years old. Dietary deficiencies are revealed by the changes that result in children's bones; a lack of Vitamin D can result in curvature in the leg bones, a condition known as rickets. A shortage of dietary iron (anaemia) is also often visible as porotic hyperostosis, lesions which form in the cranium and the upper bone of the eye sockets. Failure of bones to develop properly, or deformity of bones, may result from infections such as tubercular disease or poliomyelitis. Children of families regularly deprived of a good diet are likely to grow less tall and robust than those of wealthier or more favoured families. Modern studies have suggested that wealthier children aged seven-and-a-half years in India can be up to 9.75cm taller than poorer children of the same age.[14]

From the Late Upper Palaeolithic period in Britain (10500–8000 BC) we have very little in the way of human remains; however, the scanty evidence we have does include the remains of a child from Gough's Cave, Cheddar. This child's bones show evidence of disease, specifically anaemia. This may have been caused by a lack of iron in the diet, or due to an infection, possibly a parasitic infection of the gut. We have no way of knowing how many Palaeolithic children suffered from illness, but we must suppose that it was not uncommon. We cannot know, either, what percentage survived childhood, or how many suffered accidents during hunting and foraging expeditions. It must have been a hard life – children who did survive would have been hardy and strong, but perhaps many were at least partly affected by the struggle for life in their early years. Anaemia is also indicated in the bones of two Mesolithic (8000-4000 BC) juveniles found at Mackay and Distillery Caves, in Oban, and Harris lines in the bones also indicated that they had suffered from periods of hunger or disease in childhood.

During the Neolithic (4000-2500 BC), the size of the population seems to have begun to rise, increasing the likelihood that children would contract transmitted diseases, perhaps rare in the scattered and small human groups of the earlier stone ages. Other factors that might have contributed towards illness at this time derive from the change from a hunter-gatherer lifestyle to a more settled life, living at least part of the time within houses, and increasingly relying on agriculture for subsistence. Health would have been affected by smoky dwellings, much more intimate contact with farmed animals, and perhaps by periodic over-reliance on cereal, replacing the more varied and meat-rich diet suggested for earlier periods. Vitamin C deficiencies might also result in an inability to absorb iron from the diet; this is sometimes represented by a condition known as cribia orbitalia, which was noticed in the remains of five young people excavated at the causewayed enclosure site of Hambledon Hill.

The following Bronze Age in Britain saw, for the first time, an increase in dental diseases and enamel hypoplasia, again indicating childhood health stress. The incidence of cribia orbitalia increased from 2.3 per cent to 5.8 per cent.[15] In the Iron Age, we find the first evidence for scurvy – a lack of Vitamin C affected a three- to four-year-old child found at Beckford (Hereford & Worcs.), and the first child cancer victim. A five-year-old child found at Monkton-up-Wimbourne in Dorset was found to have had a malignant tumour in the skull. A recent find in France, during the construction of a new motorway, near Thiais, has been the bones of a two- or three-month-old baby. These bones were apparently thrown out amongst a heap of animal bones, pottery and food remains at some time between 700-500 BC, the Early Iron Age. Pathological examination of the tiny bones has revealed the presence of lesions which have been identified as the result of congenital syphilis, a disease which, at one time, was thought not to have occurred in Europe until it was brought from the New World in the sixteenth century AD.[16]

By the coming of the Romans, the population had grown vastly, and for the first time, people began to live in urban communities. Congenital diseases become more common in the archaeological evidence – conditions such as spina bifida, other spinal defects and congenital hip dislocation. There are also at least two known cases of hydrocephalus, one in Yorkshire and another in Dorset at

Poundbury, just outside the Roman town of Dorchester. The Poundbury burials include a number of other examples of childhood disease. Fifty-seven infants buried there had suffered from Caffey's disease (infantile cortical hyperostosis). The causes of this may include malnutrition or viral infection. It manifests itself in the first three months of life in the form of fever, swellings and paralysis, and skeletal change includes thick layers of new growth on the long bones. Another child from Poundbury suffered from deafness caused by bony growth blocking the ear canals. This child was buried face down, perhaps a reflection of the fear with which deformed or handicapped people were regarded.

While Roman advances in plumbing are well known, it is perhaps less often recognised that piped water offered its own dangers for health, particularly the use of lead to make the piping. Bodies in Cirencester showed very high levels of lead, and this can be another cause of anaemia and predisposition towards infection and even reduction in mental capacity; small children may have been at risk from lead poisoning, partly derived also from the use of pewter vessels for food preparation. Urban life carries its own risks, particularly pollution. Roman towns have produced evidence of infestations, lice and intestinal parasites. Piles of rotting organic matter have been found in second century AD towns: 'This included manure, human faeces, and butchery waste. Evidence at York has been found for pests and vermin such as the black rat, human, rat and dog fleas, human lice and house mice'.[17] Tooth disease was increasingly common, and a further rise in evidence of dietary stress in the form of cribia orbitalia, rising from 5.4 per cent in the Iron Age to 8.05 per cent in the Romano-British period. The people buried at Poundbury were often malnourished or anaemic – a quarter of the adults and over a third of the children showed signs of dietary hardship; other sites of the period have also provided evidence of scurvy and rickets, a condition caused by Vitamin D deficiency in childhood.

By the fourth century, child mortality in Dorchester was high, particularly among toddlers. This seems to have been due to the way food was prepared once the child had stopped breastfeeding. Fruit juices are particularly liable to dissolve the lead in pewter, and many people, as a result, suffered from long-term, low-grade malnutrition; symptoms of the condition include light bones, poor teeth, and a predisposition to catching other diseases such as tuberculosis and smallpox, and conditions manifesting in later life such as stomach ailments, osteoporosis and infertility. Development was slowed, children's growth levels being up to two years behind those of modern infants, and the onset of puberty is likely to have been quite late, about the age of 15. The end of the Roman urban life of Dorchester in the fifth century is marked by an unusual burial. In a pit lined with grass, a man and a woman were placed sitting surrounded by glass vessels, keys and silver and bronze jewellery. Across the man's lap were their two dogs, whilst the women held a young girl in her lap and another lay at her feet. One of the children seems to have died from a violent blow to the head, and perhaps the whole family had been victims of violence.[18]

The climatic downturn of the Saxon period may have been a contributory factor to the large number of chest diseases noted in the period. As the weather worsened, people would have been more likely to huddle in their warm but smoky houses in the harsh winters which saw wolves moving from the countryside to lurk near settlements as far south as Hampshire and Sussex. Lesions of the ribs of many skeletons may indicate tuberculosis or bronchitis, and sinusitis is also likely to have been common. Other conditions noted in the period include an increase in spina bifida (associated with folic acid deficiency in the diet of pregnant women), several cases of hydrocephaly and cleft palates, and two possible cases of Down's syndrome. Up to a quarter of the population may have suffered from childhood illness or malnutrition, judging from the incidence of Harris lines in the long bones. Two studies of East Anglian samples suggest that children betwen the ages of seven and eleven years were particularly liable to this sort of stress. The Anglo-Saxon Chronicle and other documents list many periods of disease of people or stock, and periods of at least localised starvation. In AD 695, for example, there was a terrible famine and pestilence 'so that men ate each other'; in 975 a great famine was seen as the 'Vengeance of God'; in 1012 the Chronicle reported that 'endless multitudes died of famine in England and on the continent'.[19]

The winter and spring could be very hard seasons, and at best, people would have suffered from vitamin deficiencies in those months. A lack of Vitamin A, found in butter, meat offal and eggs, usually unavailable for much of the winter except in preserved forms such as cheese, would have resulted in diseases of the skin, eyes and urinary tract. Without Vitamin C from fresh meat, vegetables and fruit, scurvy would have been commonplace; scurvy results in bleeding gums and loosening of teeth, ulcers and a form of bloody dysentry. There are many Anglo-Saxon charms and medicinal recipes for cures for loose teeth and sores which have survived. The evidence suggests that girls suffered more than boys, with more tooth loss, enamel hypoplasia and Harris lines; as adults, they died younger than men, often due to obstetric difficulties brought on by poor physical development. A study in Hampshire shows that the height of men increased proportionally more than that of women between the end of the Roman period and the sixth century AD. It seems clear that girls were not fed as well as boys, perhaps because the labour of boys was seen as more important for the family survival. There are stories, too, of parents selling their children into slavery during the period – not for selfish reasons, but because the owner of slaves was legally bound to feed and care for them, something the parents could not guarantee to be able to do.

At Winnall, Hampshire in a rural cemetery of the mid-seventh century 45 graves were studied. Seventeen were of males, 20 females and eight unidentified to gender. Of these, nine were under 15 years of age and six males and five females died aged between 15 and 30. So in this community, 20 per cent of the people died in childhood or early adolescence; only about 50 per cent outlived their twenties. Dietary deficiency may have been a major contributing factor. At a slightly earlier cemetery, dating to the late fifth and early sixth century at Alton in the same county, 14 graves were identified as belonging to children aged 15 or under (eight of which were under four years of age), and five graves belonged to young people aged between 16 and 19. A further eight people died in their twenties (mostly male), leaving just 14 graves of older adults, so here two thirds of the represented population died before the age of 30. We do not know how complete these samples are or how representative of the region and population they may be, but there were clearly many risks for the young to survive. Interestingly, at Alton, women who survived their twenties tended to reach greater ages than men, a pattern noted in some other regions.

A further threat to children in times of plague and famine is recorded by the chronicler Raoul Glaber; in Burgundy in 1033 there was a great famine, creating widespread distress. This led to dreadful practices:

> Alas, a thing rarely heard of through all the ages, raging hunger pushed men to devouring human flesh. Sometimes travellers were carried off by those more robust than they, their limbs severed, roasted over fires, and devoured. Even people going from one place to another to flee the famine, having found a place along the way to rest for the night, would have their throats slit, and be served as food to those who had received them. Many would present eggs or pieces of fruit to children to lure them to isolated spots, and then massacre and devour them.[20]

Conditions in later Saxon towns were sometimes also particularly dangerous for the health of young children, especially, it seems, at towns within the Danelaw occupied by Viking settlers. Environmental evidence from Jorvik (Viking York) showed that houseflies and their relatives were very common; pupae were found everywhere, sometimes in great numbers. Other insects include bees, earwigs, ants, parasitic wasps and human fleas. There were many variety of beetle, some which live in decaying wood or water, some associated with barns and stores such as weevils and mealworms, but the vast majority of the types that are associated with decaying organic matter. These were found in pits and middens, but were also abundant on house floors, suggesting that rubbish was just left on the floors and allowed to rot. Various forms of dung beetle were common even inside houses. There were also lots of weeds. Many areas would have been damp because of the regular flooding of the Ouse and Foss. The evidence also showed that food was often adulterated. Corncockle seeds were found in bran and bread made from this becomes poisonous. Corncockle was planted because it discouraged other weeds in the corn, but it should be carefully separated – clearly this was not happening. There was lots of evidence for parasitic worms, (coprolites – fossilised human faeces – were found everywhere in York), in cess pits, heaped in yards and even on internal building floors. Analysis of one sample found it contained the eggs of whipworms and maw worms. Untold millions more were found in the Coppergate material; the worms live in the small intestine and cause diarrhoea, indigestion and skin ulcers. Roundworms were found, too, potentially causing hepatitis and other severe gastrinal conditions. Botulism would have been likely in badly cured pork and lead poisoning would come from salt containers, with salt being used to preserve the meat that people relied on through the winters. There was clearly little notion of hygiene in Jorvik – not only was rotting organic matter left lying around in heaps, attracting many flies and beetles, but wells for drinking water were dug next to cess and rubbish pits in alluvial drainage, and must often have become contaminated. Mice and black rat bones were common.

Nevertheless, it is clear that great efforts were made to try to keep children alive in a number of cases. Children with cleft palates survived until six (at Burewell, Cambridgeshire) and nine (at Raunds, Northamptonshire). A two- or three-year-old child from Castledyke South, Barton-on-Humber, was buried with a breast-shaped pot, probably a feeding bottle; despite the best efforts of its carers, however, the baby had failed to prosper. Some adults show the kind of disease conditions that must have begun in childhood and through which they had been successfully nursed, such as the man aged between twenty and thirty buried at West Hendred, Oxfordshire who had suffered from severe deformities as a result of contracting poliomyelitis and tuberculous arthritis.

Post-Conquest Britain (after 1066) still has plenty of evidence for childhood disease and hunger. Conditions in many towns were still poor, and towns were particularly badly hit by the Black Death in the fourteenth century. The worst outbreak occurred in 1349, halving the population of London, but this was followed by others, including the so-called 'Children's Plague' of 1361 which took the lives of many born after 1349. At the medieval cemetery of St Nicholas Shambles in London, of 241 bodies examined, 20 were aged under three, 21 aged between four and 12, and 13 aged between 13 and 18; 26 per cent of the bodies were those of children and adolescents.[21] The first hospital designed especially for maternity care was opened at Blyth in Nottingham in 1446, although some charitable institutions had cared for mothers and children in earlier centuries, such as at St Mary of Bethlehem in London which was recorded as taking in pregnant women and, if the mother died, maintaining the children within its walls until the age of seven. Medieval populations have been recorded as having an average of 35 per cent incidence of tooth enamel hypoplasia, indicating childhood stress. Tooth decay was becoming more common; at Cuddington in Surrey 50 per cent of the children found had caries, similar to the percentage at Elcho, a Cistercian nunnery near Perth.

After the medieval period, the growth of towns led to severe health problems for children in many places. Even the highest levels of society may have suffered from diseases caused by dietary deficiencies, not because of starvation but because of cultural and economic choices and changes.

42 Leg pieces for the treatment of rickets (early eighteenth century). The design of these leg pieces, which were made for a child, is based on the armour of the period. *Courtesy Wellcome Library, London*

One component of Vitamin D deficiency (which can lead to rickets) may have been Puritan notions of decency which frowned upon nakedness even of small children – their bodies therefore had reduced opportunities to absorb sunlight and the vitamin. In the Royal Armouries collection is a tiny suit of armour, less than a metre high, and belonging to Charles I: 'some believe it was worn by him, as a child suffering from rickets, to encourage him to walk'.[22] The Industrial Revolution drew many families away from the countryside and sources of fresh and varied food, into the factory towns, with their smoke and grime. A great source of information about the diseases and other causes of death among children is the collection of annual Bills of Mortality produced in London from the mid-seventeenth century to the mid-nineteenth century. An example from 1775 contains a number of entries which could mainly (although not exclusively) relate to deaths of children. The cause of death and the number of cases of each is recorded:

Cause of death		
convulsions	5177	[mainly convulsions of teething infants]
abortive and stillborn	529	
consumption	4452	
cough, chin and whooping	206	
fever, scarlet, purple spotted	2244	
measles	283	
rickets	1	
smallpox	2699	

There was a great deal of contamination and sanitation was often very poor in towns. It was recorded in the 1850s that the town of Neath contained 500 dwellings which lacked even a shared cesspit, and 200 better quality houses shared just 40 privies between them, many unusable.[23] In many cases, town sanitation arrangements had not been updated since the medieval period. Water supplies were often prejudiced by the proximity of cesspits or even ground water seepage contaminated by badly maintained burial grounds. The Bills of Mortality show that in London before 1800 over 30 per cent of all deaths occurred before the age of two years, and half the population died before they reached 20. Rickets was rife, affecting a third of all children, and efforts to ameliorate their lot were less than successful – during its first year (1839) the London Foundling Hospital admitted 14,934 infants, of whom 10,389 died, and at a similar hospital in Dublin, all but 42 of the 10,272 children admitted, died.

> Urbanization and the later industrial revolution in the cities were the sources of such a danger; vitamin D deficiency has been termed a disease of civilization. The huddled, overhanging houses of the city would block out any sunlight that managed to penetrate the barrier of industrial smoke. The poor, often underfed children were compelled to work the daylight hours in the noise, danger and shelter of the factory. In such circumstances, rickets was prevalent.[24]

Other dangers to children's health derived from their employment – silicosis and other lung diseases were contracted from coal dust in the mines or cotton dust in the weaving mills; children lost life and limbs in machinery, or ruined their sight sewing by candlelight. Some of the worst suffering took place in pottery towns. Children were employed to carry rough biscuit-fired pottery to the glazing vats and dip the pieces ready for their second glaze firing. In cold and damp conditions, the skin of their hands split and chapped, and the toxic lead and copper in the glaze liquid entered their bloodstreams. Many children started this work aged between six and eight years old. By between 12 and 14, many were so disabled by the poison they were unable to work again. They were crippled, sometimes blind, sterile or dead.

43 Tokens left with children at the Foundling Hospital, London, as mementos of their parents, including a cap with a note pinned to it, a thimble, a padlock, a barrel label, and a filbert! After illustrations in *The Windsor Magazine*, 1895

There were frequent epidemics of smallpox, influenza, typhoid and typhus, diphtheria and cholera. It almost seems a wonder that any children survived to become adults at all. Much changed after the 1854 outbreak of cholera in Soho, traced to a water pump in Broad Street, and the realisation that urban sanitation was a priority.

In some periods, the feeding of children was, contrary to what might seem desirable, implicated in their poor health. Anglo-Saxon infants were commonly fed pap (a watery gruel) because it was thought that their systems could not deal with richer foods. In the medieval period, some people would not give fruit

44 A dormitory at the London Foundling Hospital, founded by Captain Thomas Coram, with cots laid out in 'prim regularity'

45 The schoolroom at the London Foundling Hospital, where maps 'very properly showed that we are the greatest nation upon earth'

or vegetables to children, believing that eating these foods produced colic or introduced worms into their bodies. It seems particularly odd that people would reject such healthy and useful food as wild blackberries, full of Vitamin C, but until recent years there was a belief in parts of Ireland that these fruits contained dangerous worms that would make you sick, and that only cultivated brambles were safe. Meat, when available, was often reserved for the adult males of the family, in order to support them in their labour. Women and children ate much more restricted and smaller meals as a result. These practices further endangered children whose diets were, in any case, often insufficiently supplied with essential vitamins and minerals.

The health and development of children in a society are important areas of study in a number of ways. The history and development of the diseases themselves are of great interest, not least in the battle to formulate cures. A number of important advances in medicine have already been made as a result of this type of research, particularly in the identification of diseases with a genetic susceptibility component. Because children are particularly vulnerable to diseases or health stress conditions which leave skeletal evidence in their adult bodies, study of these conditions can tell us much about subsistence strategies, episodes of stress, and social attitudes and reactions. Frequently, child morbidity in one sector of a population is likely to be higher than in others. Studies of the patterns of illness and death rates among children can help build a picture of levels of wealth and poverty, inclusion and exclusion, dietary preference and social practice in a community, sometimes in a way far less ambiguous than similar studies of adult mortality.

> Monitoring the health of infants and children can provide the prehistorian with a rich variety of information about the health of a community. As this segment of the population is very sensitive to environmentally and culturally produced insults, changes in morbidity in this segment of the population should provide one of the first signs of changes in environment and culture.[25]

One area that has received a great deal of research attention is the adoption of agriculture at various times around the world. How has the abandonment of a hunter-gatherer, nomadic lifestyle affected the human population? Has farming been a boon or a bane?

Between AD 950 and 1200, the people in the area of Lewiston, Illinois, gave up their foraging lifestyle and began to plant crops. At a site called Dickson Mounds, burials from both before and after this change were studied, and it became apparent that the health of the farmers was far worse than that of the foragers. Porotic hyperostosis (a sign of anaemia) increased four times in frequency. The incidence of infectious lesions increased from 6 to 40 per cent. The researchers studied the ages at which these conditions appeared in the bodies. Most infections and skeletal changes began in the first three years of life.

This was associated with decreased life expectancy levels. Bones also showed arrested or compromised development during childhood: 'there is evidence of delayed growth in the long bone length and circumference of Mississippian children between their fifth through fifteenth year...This delay may be a result of chronic stresses around 2 to 5 years of age'.[26] The level of dental hypoplasia rose from 45 per cent in the forager period to 80 per cent in the farming era. The worst stress was experienced during the period of weaning. The diet available to children of farmers was significantly less nutritious and healthy than that of their hunter-gatherer ancestors.

Another study has looked at variation in the bones of Ukrainian agricultural and pastoral peoples during the Bronze and Iron Ages.[27] The long bones of 79 children who had died between the ages of one and 13 were studied, and the results showed that the children from pastoral families had substantially longer femurs and tibias than contemporary children from settled agricultural groups. The different subsistence strategies of the two communities seem to have resulted in markedly different general physiques.

SLAVERY

Many children in the modern world are living in conditions of enslavement, as unpaid workers in a variety of industries, as domestic servants or as prostitutes. Children are particularly vulnerable to this form of exploitation; they often enter slavery either as a result of being sold by their parents for profit or as victims of kidnapping rings. Child slavery is endemic in many areas of the world, but particularly so in West Africa and parts of Asia. It has been reported that 200,000 children, mainly girls aged between four and 15, are trafficked each year in Benin alone. 'Parents do not believe it is a bad thing to give up their children; they believe they are doing the right thing', one Unicef representative said. 'For people who earn on average £20 a month, selling a child is the only way to survive'. The going rate for an eight-year-old girl in Benin is £8; they are told they will be taken to a school and have a better life, but they end up as domestic servants, physically and often sexually abused.[28]

Evidence for child slavery in ancient times comes particularly from the Roman world. Historical records suggest that children left abandoned on the streets of Rome – unwanted baby girls, illegitimate babies, or babies of the poor who were unable to raise them – were often picked up by 'slave farmers'. It was assumed that an abandoned child held slave status, and thus belonged to whoever wished to expend the time and effort to rear them. The slave farmers employed wet nurses to feed and care for the infants they picked up, and they trained them for service, selling them for a profit once they were old enough.

The wealthier class of citizen might prefer vernae ('home-born' slaves), children of selected slaves in their own households. These children came with the advantage of costing nothing except their keep, and could be raised and trained in the customs and preferences of their owners from the earliest age. As the household was also their home, they would also be supposed to have particular loyalties towards the family and staff. Slave children would grow up next to the children of the family and often formed close personal bonds with them. They could be deliberately chosen to become the child's particular servant – thus the daughter of the house might have a maid who would play with her as a child, and serve her as a woman, even accompanying her to her new home when she married. A boy's servant might become his valet, secretary or batman. The disadvantages of such a practice would include the costs of keeping the child, and the possibility that the mother might die in childbirth, thus depriving the owner of her value.

It has been suggested that wet nurses were used to allow the slave mother to return to her duties as soon as possible, and perhaps to speed up the end of lactation and allow her to become pregnant again. If the pregnancy resulted from non-consensual relations, wet nurses would ensure the survival of a child whose mother was unwilling to acknowledge it. There are some surviving tomb inscriptions to dead children which mention wet nurses; some of these tombstones are identified as those of slave children, such as the three children commemorated by the nurse Lucceia Donata, Sabina who was nursed by Caecilia Eupraesia and Victoria, nursed by Servea Marcellina, both at Puteoli. Very occasionally, the names of slave parents are known, such as the inscription naming Secundus and Successa, slave parents of Hylocharis Aemilianus, who recorded that their son had consoled them during their servitude.

Some masters encouraged slaves to marry and have children. Xenophon believed that slaves who were allowed to have children were better disposed towards their masters. Nevertheless, he advised that such liaisons must be approved by the master, and that otherwise male and female slaves should be strictly segregated. Such liaisons could form incentives for slaves to work well. Marcus Terentius Varro, in the first century BC, wrote:

> Overseers are to be encouraged with rewards to work more efficiently, and care must be taken that they have some property of their own and women slaves to live with them, by which they can have children; this makes them more reliable and more attached to the farm. It is because of these family ties that the slaves of Epirus are highly regarded and highly expensive.[29]

Columella, writing a century or so later, implied the existence of a slave farm when he recorded that he honoured those women who raised several children, allowing them to stop work after bearing three children and even occasionally giving them their freedom if they had more than three. An entry in Petronius' Satyricon demonstrates that such children could be counted as assets of the estate:

> July 26th. On Trimalchio's estate at Cumae: born – boys 30, girls 40. Taken from the
> threshing floor to the barn – 500,000 modii of wheat. Oxen broken in – 500.

This is a fictional account, intended to ridicule a certain type of rich man, but the implication that the practice was well known and understood cannot be denied. As well as wet nurses, owners such as Pliny would employ child-minders and even teachers to raise and train these children, to prepare them to lead useful lives in the service of their masters and their families.

Slaves lived at the whim of their owners – they could be moved from one estate to another, sold or even killed without legal impediment. It must have been partly due to this that some slave women were unhappy about getting pregnant, as recorded by Dio Chrysostom:

> ...free women often smuggle in children which aren't their own when they don't have any
> children themselves, because they can't become pregnant, since every woman wants to keep
> her husband and her home, and at the same time there is no shortage of money for bringing
> up children. But the opposite happens with slaves - some of them kill their children before
> they are born, and some afterwards if they can avoid detection; sometimes their husbands
> even connive at it – they don't want the additional problem of having to look after a child
> when things are difficult enough for slaves as it is.[30]

It was not until the fourth century AD, after the Emperor Constantine converted to Christianity, that a law was made which directed that when slaves were sold, families must be kept together.

Outside the Christian sphere, however, the experience of child slavery was sometimes extremely severe. The Visigoths of Spain in particular were noted for their lack of respect for the human feelings and frailty of their slaves, practising, according the contemporary accounts, a variety of cruelties, mutilations and castration on children who were sometimes captured and traded from far afield. Thuringians, Serbs, Bavarians, Angles, Saxons, Irish, Polish and Moorish victims were enslaved, and the children of prisoners were automatically unfree.

It was not unusual for parents to sell their own children into slavery. In the early sixth century peasants in southern Italy took their children to a large local fair:

> It is boys and girls who are put on display and categorized by age and sex; and if they are
> put up for sale, it is not a result of their captivity but of their freedom: their parents sell them,
> naturally, because they stand to profit by their servitude. And in truth, they are, without a
> doubt, better off as slaves, if they are transferred from work in the fields to domestic work
> in the city.

It is hard to be sure how many children were thus sold into bondage; the numerous statutes and laws forbidding or limiting the practice, however, suggest

46 A balsarium, or oil flask, depicting a weary slave boy waiting for his master. From the Roman town of Aldborough, Yorkshire

that it was a reasonably common occurrence. Some of these laws display less concern for the happiness of the children's lives than they do for their souls; the Third Lateran Council of 1179 was particularly distressed that Christian children were being sold as slaves to Jews and Saracens. It is probably the case that enslaved children did, indeed, have more chance of survival than their siblings back on the farm (who in turn had more chance once the size of the dependent family was thus reduced). Some slave children were extremely well treated, educated and valued by their owners, and could be as well treated as members of the family. They were, after all, often an expensive acquisition and mark of status.

PHYSICAL AND WORK ABUSE

Physical abuse of children by parents or guardians is often related to notions of discipline. The Bible advocates beating of children in order to bring them from evil into paths of righteousness. In *Proverbs* (13.24) parents are told 'He who spares the rod hates his son' and Talmudic literature offers a number of guidelines for suitable chastisement of young people, as a matter of course. Speaking against the practice, however, were such figures as Saint Benedict, who felt that beating a child for not learning was more likely to make him worse than better. Other medieval commentators saw the use of the whip as a symbol of a poor teacher, laying the blame for his incompetence on the pupil rather than questioning his own skill.

Roman parents in the Early Empire took an extremely robust attitude to child discipline, and children might expect to be beaten at home and at school, by teachers, mothers, fathers, and even grand-parents. Rods, whips, clubs and even hot irons were used. Literature of the period suggests that there was an assumption that children could not understand reason, and that a failure to beat the child would result in his being spoiled. Seneca, in *An Essay about Anger*, tells his readers: 'It is of the utmost importance that children be raised in the correct manner even if this means harsh discipline'.[31] It has been suggested that it was the conquest of Greece that led eventually to a more compassionate and loving attitude permeating Roman society. The Greeks, while capable of a certain degree of callousness towards children, were nevertheless disposed to be kind and loving within their own families, and the increased use of Greek slaves to raise Roman children began to soften Roman behaviour. Children who had been raised by Greek slaves in kindness (and in the absence of their own fathers who were often away on military or diplomatic service) were then more loving towards their own children in turn. By the time of the Emperor Augustus, Romans began to value the family and express much more sentiment towards their offspring.[32]

The plight of the medieval child sent off at an early age to work as a farmhand, in service or in an apprenticeship could be hard. Without the presence of families and friends, inevitably some became victims of abuse, like ten-year-old Perrotte Bidon, serving as a worker on her uncle's farm, who was raped by Jean Merlin, an adult farmhand, as she mucked out the byre, or 13-year-old orphan Marie Ribon who would became pregnant by her employer. In order to accustom working children to hardship, a Florentine writer in the fourteenth century advised parents to make their children walk barefoot, carry out hard work, sleep sitting up in their clothes with the windows open at least once a week, and get them used to going without food. He suggested that little attention should be given to caring for girls, beyond teaching them cooking, sewing and household skills; indeed, 'it doesn't matter how you feed a girl, as long as she stays alive. She doesn't need to be fat'.

Whilst most apprenticeship agreements were well maintained, there are records of ill-treatment of young people. Often, the abuse consisted of beatings, or a failure to provide sufficient food or clothing, or a failure to provide the agreed training. A particular problem could arise on occasions when a master sold on the apprentice's contract, perhaps because of his own financial or health difficulties. The new master might have less contact or association with the apprentice's family or background, and be less inclined to lenience or kindness.

In 1816 some 20 per cent of workers in the English cotton industry were under 13 years old. The poet Robert Southey recorded a visit to a Manchester cotton mill as resembling one of Dante's circles of hell, peopled with children. Other major employers of children were the pottery industries and the coal mines, and chimney sweeps. A major source of children for employment was the poorhouse or the orphanage; others were sold by their parents. In October 1794, records show that 50 pauper children were sent by the parishes of St Margaret and St John the Evangelist, Westminster, to a worsted mill in Nottinghamshire, and the parish of St Clement Danes resolved in 1782 that 'all those [children] above the age of six…be sent to the silk mills at Watford, or elsewhere as great savings might be made to the parish'.[33]

While some employers, like the Greys at Quarry Bank Mill, Styal, made provision for the care of these children, at other establishments, treatment was harsh. Children worked 12-14 hours a day, were poorly fed, and were exposed to a variety of dangers. Machine accidents happened frequently, and the dust of the processing of textiles entered the lungs and eyes, causing infections. Children were whipped or beaten to encourage them to stay alert and hard working. The lack of care is demonstrated by the nature of reforms introduced from time to time – it was necessary to insist that children should not work over 12 hours a day, that they be given a new set of clothes once a year, and that they be given a basic education during the first four years of employment. Ventilation and basic sanitation were also to be provided. Work in the mines also started at the age of five or six; boys and girls worked the ventilation traps or dragged the coal trucks from the face to the lifting gear. In some places, the workers stayed underground all week, only emerging for church on Sundays. Accidents, explosions and the effects of coal dust shortened the lives of many, and there were a number of reports of sexual exploitation of children in some mines.

Well-meaning liberal ladies and gentlemen eventually forced through a number of Acts of Parliament which limited the working hours of children and raised the age of employment in various industries little by little. Unfortunately, these philanthropic measures had unforeseen consequences; within a short period of time, people began to complain about the troops of unemployed youngsters roaming the streets of many towns and cities, making their living not in the factories and mines, but through crime and prostitution. The story is, of course, told by Charles Dickens in such works as *Oliver Twist*.

PROSTITUTION AND CRIME

The Greeks were no strangers to sexual use of young people, and relationships between young boys and older men were regarded as perfectly natural and part of the boy's social education. Many depictions on vases show homo-erotic scenes. Whether this can be seen as abuse of children is doubtful; the cultural norms of the society were accepting of these relationships, and there is no assumption that the boys were in any way forced into acts against their own desires and inclinations. We can argue that the children were too young to make such choices for themselves, but the liaisons were not regarded as in any way unnatural or perverted, and in such cases, it is doubtful that the children would experience the kind of psychological trauma associated with sexual relationships with adults in our own society.

In the Roman world, prostitution was a visible and normal aspect of society, as the less than subtle graffiti and images of Pompeii bear witness. Inevitably, children were part of that world. Slave children were particularly liable to use in this way, and indeed Horace advocates a sexual relationship with an available slave boy as a preferable alternative to the pursuit of married women. Slave boys were employed to give sexual gratification to clients of bath houses and young boys could be hired to entertain guests at feasts. There are a number of depictions and figurines showing sexual acts between over-endowed men and young girls, and we must suppose that many children were subjected against their wills to such treatment. It would appear that to the Roman mind, sexual acts with slave children or professional child prostitutes were regarded as unexceptionable; sexual crimes against the children of citizens or nobles, however, were seen to be appalling and worthy of extremely severe punishment. As in so many other aspects of their world view, Romans were quite capable to failing to equate the experience of one level of society with that of another in these instances.

The involvement of children in criminal acts lacks evidence in most past societies; it would be naïve, however, to assume that this was not the case. There is plenty of historical material to illustrate the range of crimes children commit, either on their own instigation or as minions of adult controllers like Dicken's Fagin. The laws of King Ine of Wessex, probably issued between 688 and 694, rule that a child of ten years can be regarded as an accessory to theft, and that the wife and children of a thief who knew of the crimes condemned themselves to slavery. The law code of King Athelstan excused from death only those thieves who were under 12 years of age and who stole goods worth less than eight pence. Athelstan attempted to introduce measures to protect underage criminals from the judiciary system, believing, it is recorded, that the death penalty for children under 15 was cruel. It is clear that this punishment was widely recognised although evidence does not suggest that it was always imposed, and we can therefore assume the existence of a good number of criminal children. Athelstan introduced a much more humane law, whereby criminals under the age of 15 would be imprisoned. If there was no available or suitable prison, his relatives would have to pay surety for his behaviour, and if no relatives were able or willing to do this, the child had to swear his own surety and become a slave until the amount of the surety had been paid off. Children who fought those who would arrest them, or ran off and refused to give themselves up, or who reoffended, were not offered any mercy, but could be hanged or killed as if they were an adult.

During the Middle Ages, a particular terror for parents was the practice of child abduction. Sometimes, kidnappings were simple attempts to extract ransom, but peasant children or lost children could become the victims of gangs who would mutilate or cripple the child for use by adult beggars as a tool to excite the pity and stimulate the generosity of almsgivers.

A number of cases where apprentices turned to crime against their masters have been recorded. Their presence in the homes of their masters sometimes gave them access to treasures that were easily stolen, stock that could be purloined, and customers who could be persuaded into under-the-counter deals. Apprentice boys were also notoriously unruly and given to excessive drinking and rowdy behaviour in the streets. The traditional Shrove Tuesday apprentice boy football matches in towns such at Kingston upon Thames and Dorking in Surrey led to appeals to the parish constables and the Guildford constabulary to control the games; these were generally unsuccessful, as the officers of the law were extremely unwilling to expose themselves to the wrath of the youths, and preferred to be elsewhere on match days.

For many children, born and living in the streets of European cities, crime was the only way to subsist, right up to the late Victorian period, as it is for children in many other places in the world today. Very young children could be involved – there is a record of a five-year-old thief, found with stolen wool in his hat, who died in 1324 as a result of too heavy a slap from the irate merchant victim. The prison records of Paris for the fourteenth and fifteenth centuries include incidents of the flogging and imprisonment of thieves as young as nine. However, generally, there seems to have been a recognition that young children could not be held completely responsible for their wrongdoings, and mercy was routinely shown. In later centuries, a number of children were hanged for crimes. The youngest on record was Michael Hammond, hanged at Lynn in 1808 at the age of seven alongside his 11-year-old sister, although details of their crime are unknown. Generally, however, death sentences passed on child criminals were commuted, often to transportation.

As well as young girls raped by their employers or co-workers, child prostitutes were numerous in some places. Mothers or other family members were often those who turned the children to such employment, sometimes by the age of eight or so, but more usually between ten and 14 years of age. Prostitution was often the only source of earnings for a girl who had been raped by her employer; in Victorian London many of the recorded prostitutes had started their careers after having been turned off from their posts as maids by their 'respectable' employers after suffering rape at the hands of the master, the son of the house or other male employees. Most of the thousands of 'working girls' recorded in late nineteenth-century London were between 15 and 22 years old. The girl, suffering from the 'sin of Eve', was automatically assumed to be the guilty party and thus her subsequent descent into streetwalking was regarded as only to be expected. There was even a belief in some quarters that such girls did pretty well out of their lack of morality, and deserved no sympathy.

O 'Melia, my dear, this does everything crown!
Who could have supposed I should meet you in Town?
And whence such fair garments, such prosperi-ty?' –
'O didn't you know I'd been ruined?' said she.
(From: *The Ruined Maid* by Thomas Hardy)

6

BECOMING HUMAN

Tempora mutantur, et nos mutamur in illis

FORMING ANCESTORS

Humans are not the only animals that care for and display affection and concern for their young; nor are they the only animals which maintain contact with their young for longer than a season. Most of the anthropoid apes seem to display extended nurturing behaviour towards their offspring, and youngsters remain connected to the matriarchal group for several years at least. But why have humans evolved differently? Did we become what we are because of our longer maturation periods, or did our longer maturation periods evolve because of what we are? This is a very difficult question to attempt to answer, because we have so little evidence and so few examples of early hominid skeletons and behaviour.

For most animals, the young have just one season in which they must grow, learn to hunt or forage, and become able to take care of themselves. In many species, the parents will actively drive the young out to fend for themselves at the end of that season, to free the mother for breeding again in the next. Few species allow their youngsters to remain dependent after the conception of the next siblings. Human children, however, would be unlikely to survive such treatment (at least in the absence of a handy she-wolf prepared to act as a surrogate). Growth is much slower, motor skills take much longer to acquire, the cognitive skills needed to stay alive seem to develop more gradually. What makes us so vulnerable?

Humans differ from the other apes in several important ways. We are fully bipedal – we stand upright all of the time. We are mostly hairless. We have relatively large brains. We have spoken language. Our babies are born with very large heads, and are born in effect prematurely – if they were to reach the level of development in the womb that other animals do, they would be too large to pass through the birth canal: 'When [the human baby] is unceremoniously evicted after nine months, it is only halfway through the usual primate prenatal programme'.[1] Thus we are more helpless at birth and for longer than the young of most other species. These factors are important in considering how the young are treated.

A female chimpanzee can carry her baby with her; the youngster clings instinctively to its mother's fur, leaving her hands free to assist her movement and to undertake tasks such as termite-fishing and fruit-gathering. If a human mother wishes to transport her child, she must either carry it, impeding her use of her hands and arms, or she must invent and make a carrying device. It has been suggested that one of the first technological advances made by humans was the invention of the baby sling, offsetting the disadvantage to the mother of the handicap of carrying her infant and thereby losing her ability to forage or defend herself successfully.[2] This means that an important cognitive hurdle had to be overcome; to invent a baby sling, the primitive hominid had to collect materials together, imagine them into a different form with a different purpose, and then create that different form. This process involves a number of mental steps that most animals do not possess the ability to take. Imagination, memory, manipulation of thoughts, relationship of those thoughts to concrete objects, and the creation of an artefact are vital parts of our ability to be human and were essential in our development; our talents in these fields are what make us fundamentally different from other primates. One perhaps controversial view is that 'In practice, the development of the baby-sling removed the crucial factor limiting the efficiency of postnatal care and allowed hominid females to bear underdeveloped babies that, with postnatal brain growth, could subsequently catch up and, crucially, overtake australopithecenes in brain development'.[3]

The human infant has a great deal to learn – not just motor and social skills and foraging knowledge, but language and all that language implies for such cognitive skills as prediction, memory and interrogation of experiences. Language allows us to live not just in the present and the observable, but in the past and future, and in the abstract or theoretical. So it simply takes longer to become fully functional; there is so much more data to input, organise and manipulate. Most of that learning takes place within the social group, from observation, experience and participation with other members of the family. Chimpanzees, being our closest relatives, have many similarities with us in their patterns of child-rearing. They tend to live in matriarchal groups in which the young feed with their mothers and grandmothers, and with their older and younger siblings. Their exposure, therefore, to the teaching that these members of the family group can offer is extended in the same way that human learning is assisted. Their learning is cumulative; each season adds a little more. But chimpanzee learning is observational; they learn what they can physically experience or see in others. Humans have the added dimension of speech and so they can pass on knowledge of things that they themselves have not personally experienced, through the medium of language.

What is hard to establish is whether this extended period of growth and learning is a cause or an effect of our being human. It is possible that because our maturation period is so extended, early hominids were forced to keep their young with them for longer periods, dealing with the offspring of several seasons at the same time. Clearly, even with fur, a mother could not carry all her children at the same time, another reason why she may have needed to invent the baby sling. Once that happened, thick body hair may have become less necessary. Once it was not imperative that the baby should cling on, and it could be carried by some other means, she would be able to alter her posture to a more upright one, giving her the advantages of a better view of danger, the ability to reach higher fruits and, as they would no longer be needed so much for locomotion, the opportunity to develop her skills in using her hands and fingers in different ways. The differences between the maturation rates of chimpanzees and humans can be briefly summarised:

	Chimpanzees	Humans
Age at which full height is achieved	11 yrs	20 yrs
Age of sexual maturity in females	6–7 yrs	13 yrs
Life expectancy	35 yrs	70 yrs

Thus the chimpanzee's rate of growth and aging is roughly twice as fast as ours. Other differences between our species are the gestation periods, on average 230 days for chimpanzees against 266 for humans; cranial capacity at birth differs only slightly, just 0.2 per cent of body size larger in humans, but a human pregnancy is 16.7 per cent longer than the chimpanzee's and produces an infant 92.2 per cent larger, though in many ways far less developed and much more helpless for a great deal longer.

The necessity to care for the young of several seasons at once would probably have required better communication abilities, assisting the development of language. Older siblings would help to care for younger ones, extending and making more complex intergroup social relationships, and this level of extra care would have protected the young, lowering the infant mortality rate and allowing the numerical expansion of the species to proceed more rapidly – a true baby boom.

Very early evidence of the tendency towards slow maturation in early humans has been found in a study of the remains of three young individuals discovered in a cave in the Atapuerca mountains of northern Spain. Assigned by their discoverers to a new species, homo antecessor, the bodies are believed to be 800,000 years old, and comprise one child and two adolescents. Studies of the tooth development, in particular the relative maturity of pairs of front and back teeth, compared to those of modern humans, apes, and fossil species, have shown that the Spanish youths shared many traits with ourselves. Many of the teeth developed quite late, compared to apes, with just the wisdom teeth erupting earlier than those of modern Europeans. The size of the brain cases was also almost as large as in modern populations. F. Clark Howell of the University of California, Berkeley, has commented that the 'Atapuerca individuals seem to have crossed some time of growth-related Rubicon'.[4] There is speculation that the Atapuerca people were ancestral to modern humans and possibly also to Neanderthals, whose remains have also been found in the region in deposits between 135,000 and 30,000 years old. Further studies have suggested that the change to a longer period of maturation occurred between 800,000 and 300,000 years ago, making the Atapuerca children amongst the first hominids to display this trait. Research into tooth development in the early form of human ancestor called Australopithecus anamensis, dating from 4.2-3.9 million years ago, as well as closer species including homo habilis, who lived between 2.3-1.8 million years ago, and homo erectus and homo ergaster, who lived between 1.9-0.8 million years ago, showed that their teeth matured at about the same rates as modern and fossil apes, more rapidly than humans. Homo antecessor may have been the first hominid species to display not only the physical, but also possibly the cognitive, traits of modern man, and to have reaped the rewards of an extended childhood, and to some extent passed these traits on to both homo sapiens and homo Neanderthalensis.

Other evidence, however, may suggest that the length of time required for maturation, and thus the length of time available for learning, and the relative effects of this on the development of the species, may have been the crucial differences between us and our close cousins the Neanderthals:

> Studies on the perikymata (incremental growth ridges) on the teeth of the Devil's Tower (Gibraltar) child have suggested that Neanderthal children matured skeletally somewhat faster than modern children do. This evidence has been more recently confirmed by demographic studies suggesting that in order to keep a viable gene pool, considering group size and age of death, Neanderthals would have needed to reach reproductive age much earlier than modern humans.[5]

In competition with modern human groups, therefore, Neanderthals would have been at a disadvantage in terms of communication skills and accumulated learning, and possibly more fundamentally in areas of cognitive and physical development and skills. Hawcroft and Dennell also point out that modern human children would have had the opportunity and time to challenge, reorder and assess their learning, while Neanderthal children would have been perhaps more constrained by time and would have been more inclined to be disposed against challenging their elders. Like chimpanzees, young Neanderthalers may have learned more by imitation and observation than by explanation, debate and cognitive assessment. At the same time, modern human children would have challenged, queried and affected the teaching and behaviour of their parents, while Neanderthal adolescents may have been less able to do so. These challenges, however annoying most parents find them, are nevertheless important in the social maturation of our species, forcing us to rationalise, explain and defend ideas that we want our children to accept, and this may have been partly instrumental in the development of our brain size and power, and our abilities to analyse and communicate abstractions. Perhaps this seems rather speculative, but it is not possible to dismiss such theories easily, any more than to accept without question that we developed our abilities through hunting activities. Earlier theories tended to assume that it was the co-operative nature of hunting in bands for food that led to the development of human cognitive abilities, without explaining why lionesses had failed to develop similar brain sizes. The notion that it was trying to argue with teenagers that stretched our brains may strike a more familiar chord with some parents!

Earlier maturation among Neanderthals may have other costs. It has been observed that in animals that mature early, there is a tendency towards smaller adult size:

> And small size can be a liability, as it is often associated with increased risk of mortality, reduced fecundity, and reduced offspring size and viability… moreover, early maturation frequently forecasts a short life, as both rapid growth and reproduction itself effectively wears animals out. On the other hand, animals that delay maturation risk loss of reproductive opportunity while their size passes the point after which further growth confers no significant advantage.[6]

Longer maturation can increase chances of survival of youngsters in adverse environments, as they waste no energy in reproductive activity. It is a complex equation – different hominid species probably adapted to varying environmental stresses by reducing or lengthening maturation. Ultimately, the survival and success of our own species depended on the ability of its children to survive long enough to reproduce, and our victory in the competition between the various forms of human antecedents is due to having the optimal length of childhood for the environments in which our ancestors found themselves.

Traditional views of primitive societies have tended to assume that the child was, although vital to the survival of the group, a hindrance and a possible source of danger. However, the casually accepted idea that the men went out hunting and the women and children stayed safely in the cave has been challenged by many modern writers.

Ethnographic studies have shown that the contribution of women's work (foraging for plant foods and the hunting and trapping of small prey species) often provides the major portion of the diet of 'gatherer-hunter' societies. It also seems to be true that it is this food providing behaviour that is most reliable and upon which the social group chiefly depends. Meat is often a rare luxury, involving greater risk and uncertainty for its collection. There may also be evidence that women were perfectly capable of joining in the hunt for big game too. The relatively small gut of the human means that they would have learned to concentrate on obtaining food with a high calorific value; meat provides fats and proteins, but humans also need a range of vitamins, fatty acids and minerals to maintain health. This is especially true of women during pregnancy. Many of these essential nutrients are only available in plant foods, so it seems unlikely that hunting alone would have been regarded as essential food procurement. Few cultures have developed the ability to survive without this range of foods – the Inuits, who typically used to rely on meat and fish with very little plant food, do not have a typical human dietary biology, and suffer when exposed to more extended modern food choice. In any case, it would make no sense for women to have been passive and non-contributory just because they had to care for children. In a very small social group, survival depends on the economic contribution of all its members. It has been shown that early Palaeolithic people assisted the growth of plant foods by selective weeding and irrigation, and the collection of seeds and their removal to preferred locations by the gatherers is thought to have been the origin of farming. It has even been suggested that the adoption of motherless young animals by children could have led to the domestication of farm animals. If that is the case, and if it was the women and younger children who were engaged in these activities, then it is possible to suggest that it was women and children who were responsible for the development of agriculture, and therefore settled and permanent communities, and therefore the social and technological world we live in today. This is a far cry from traditionalist perspectives!

The claim that the crying child would have posed a threat to the survival of early human groups has also been challenged. It has been pointed out that in fact in more traditional societies, babies cry far less than they seem to in the western world. This is because, it is claimed, babies cry when they are hungry, and more particularly to draw attention to themselves and to obtain contact. In more primitive or traditional societies, babies are rarely left unattended or unheld; they are not strapped into car seats or left in playpens or cots, but are constantly handled not only by the mother, but by other family members. When people travel, they walk, carrying the baby in their arms or in versions of a baby-sling, so the child has less need to attract attention. In addition, a 'newborn's crying would signal its abandonment, which itself would be a danger signal to the group: it would be signalling that in effect something had happened to itself or its mother or carer; and the older baby's crying could signal the presence of animals or 'strange' adult humans which might be dangerous in certain circumstances. Infant crying might therefore have acted as an early warning system for the rest of the group that there was danger'.[7] This might explain why the crying of the human infant is so particularly piercing.

47 A mother chimpanzee teaching her three-year-old daughter to fish for termites

Of course, all this is highly speculative and the evidence to confirm some of these ideas is so far lacking, but they suggest that the role of children in the development of our species may, far from being passive and a hindrance, have been dynamic and essential.

Recent research among chimpanzees at the Gombe National Park in Tanzania has suggested that we share other characteristics with our close ape cousins. It has been observed that chimpanzee mothers teach their young foraging skills such as fishing for termites with sticks. The female youngsters were seen to be more conscientious and patient in learning these skills, while the males were more likely to 'bunk off to play with other chimps swinging about in the trees'.[8] The researchers calculated that female chimps learned to extract termites for themselves by the age of 31 months, while it took males up to 58 months to achieve success. Boisterous male play, it was thought, gave the male chimpanzees the strength and agility to compete for dominance among other males and to be efficient hunters, while the females were obtaining essential protein and fat from the termites which compensated for their inability to hunt as frequently while pregnant or nursing infants. The behaviour of the juveniles was therefore closely related to their adult roles. This observation has obvious interest for a study of our own species. The inattention and poor school performance of boys have become major concerns in modern societies, and in most countries, girls tend to out-perform boys academically. If these are traits we share with our closest living relatives, the chimps, then they became entrenched in human behaviour before the species diverged into their present forms; perhaps more than six million years ago. Further study of these behaviours among other anthropoids and perhaps, in clues left behind by fossil humans, might illuminate this question, and help us to find mitigating strategies that would assist in helping boys to benefit more from formal education than many do at the present time.

FORMING ADULTS

Another form of evolution associated with maturation is the process of achieving stages of social integration on the road from babyhood to full adult status; each child attains varying levels of independence, acceptance, and recognition from their community as they age. The points at which changes in a child's social status occur vary from society to society, but are generally related to physiological and cognitive changes. In general terms, and following the analysis of Jean Piaget, there are four main stages to childhood:

Stage I: infancy	Birth to 18–24 months; in this stage behaviour is instinctive and reflexive, the baby acquires basic motor habits but lacks language and cognitive skills.
Stage II: early childhood	Age 2–7 years; the child displays intuitive intelligence and spontaneous inter-personal feelings.
Stage III: middle childhood	Age 7–11/12 years; the child is capable of concrete intellectual operations and displays a moral sense and the ability to engage in social and co-operative behaviour.
Stage IV: adolescence	Age 11–12 years; the child is capable of abstract intellectual operations, and the individual's personality is fully formed. The child approaches sexual and physical maturity during this stage and can act effectively in social and ritual behaviours alongside adults.

The observed or recorded customs of a number of ancient societies appear to mirror the Piagetian stages quite closely; communities were able to recognise the changes in a child's physical and mental competence de facto at perhaps surprisingly similar ages. It is a common belief that 'children grew up faster in the old days'. In fact, it seems they did not, at least physically or cognitively, although perhaps their emotional and social growth would have been accelerated due to their greater exposure to adult society. These aspects of development may be delayed in modern children because of their relative isolation from the adult world and their extended adolescence.

We have seen earlier, something of the rituals associated with childbirth, and have mentioned some other the customs attending other stages of children's maturation in passing. There are numerous further examples in archaeological and documentary records of the ways in which the developmental stages of children have been marked.

The second stage, that of early childhood, begins in most societies when the infant is weaned, and therefore not so directly dependent upon the mother for food and care. At this stage, other adults and siblings can take care of the child and provide for it, and its circle of interaction consequently widens. This stage may be marked by some sort of ceremonial, such as the presentation of the Athenian boy to his kinship group, or phatry, during the festival of the Apatouria. Greek depictions of such young children show them playing with toys and in domestic settings. Adulthood was, for boys, achieved by their formal entrance into society at 18 or so. The intermediate stages of childhood are nevertheless recognised through conventions of artistic depiction, particularly in the more naturalistic art styles developed from the later fifth century. Babies are usually shown naked and crawling or being held by an adult. Children between the age of about three and puberty are shown shorter than adults, the boys often naked and the girls wearing a dress. Children aged up to about seven are usually shown playing with toys or in the home, while those a little older are sometimes shown as school pupils. Pubescent children are harder to identify, but may be depicted a little shorter than adults, with the girls wearing their hair loose, and boys sometimes wearing cadet uniform.[9] Boys and youths are depicted as beardless and lacking pubic hair, and girls may be shown with long hair loose or in a braid, and never veiled. A ceremony associated with the transition to adulthood of girls may have been the Heraia festival at Olympia; this is suggested by an analysis of the representations of clothing and attitudes in associated iconography.[10]

There are iconographic indications that part of the transition to adulthood for both boys and girls was a ceremony in which they gave up their childhood toys, or replicas of them, such as ceramic discs representing yo-yos, in dedications to the gods. A number of these discs have been recovered from archaeological contexts, including a very fine example now in the Metropolitan Museum of Art. Funerary stelae associated with young people sometimes depict the offering-up of childhood symbols, part of a rite of passage into death.

Roman boys also achieved adult status in a number of stages. They gained their *toga virilis*, or manly costume, around the age of 15 or 16, and would begin military service around two years later, but would not normally marry until their early twenties, if they belonged to the upper classes. Upper-class girls would expect to marry as young as the early teens, while lower-class youngsters married rather later. The children of lower-class families who did not benefit from an extended education might be working for a living by the age of 10.

In Europe, small children from the later medieval period to the early twentieth century were often dressed identically, and the day on which a boy was 'breeched', or put into masculine attire, was an important step on his journey

48 A funerary stela from Pentelicos, Greece, depicting a deceased woman holding a doll, and a servant holding a pet duck; objects representing the surrender of childhood treasures. Marble, 0.49m high, from the first quarter of the fourth century BC. *Musée Calvert, Avignon*

to the next stage of development. The practicality of skirts for small children, particularly before toilet training was complete, has been mentioned earlier, but for some at least, there was another reason for dressing both sexes in similar clothing. In 1802 a Dr Struve published an instructional tome entitled 'Domestic Education of Children', in which he advocates a lack of gender distinction in clothes, lest 'the attention of children be excited to the differences of the sexes, a circumstance which would deprive them, at an early age, of their innocence and happy ignorance'. In periods before the division of housing into separate, designated rooms, people literally lived cheek by jowl, and children were not screened from the sexual appearance, and indeed activities, of the adults around them. By the seventeenth century, however, a combination of religious and social changes had begun to remove children from inclusion in the adult world before the age of puberty, at least in the middle and upper classes. Portraits of children under about six or seven years of age that were painted during the seventeenth to nineteenth centuries are often sexually ambivalent, underlining the separation of children from ordinary society and stressing the social recognition of this particular life stage.

Burial customs display something of the attitudes to stages of maturation in Anglo-Saxon society. Children below the age of two or three were not given specific forms of ceremony, but once they had been weaned, the burial rite is more closely related to that of adults. After weaning, 'age clearly exerts a bearing on the quantity of burial wealth; the number of grave goods, and the types of grave goods, both increase with age'.[11] As older children are encountered in cemeteries, the burial rite more nearly approaches the adult form. In the one to seven years age group, personal knives and jewellery become relatively common, and between seven and 15, spears (but rarely shields or swords) often accompany the bodies of boys, while the dress fittings and jewellery of girls increase in amount and elaboration. The value of items also increases with age. In the graves of girls, feminine characteristics in grave furniture become evident around the age of five, and this becomes particularly marked around the age of ten or 12. Items such as keys that might represent full adult female life do not generally appear in the graves of individuals before the later teens. This gives us some sort of clue as to the life stages of Anglo-Saxon children, and their progress towards full adult status.

The graves of young Anglo-Saxon children were often of a non-standardized form; infants were sometimes placed within adult graves, and their remains were uncoffined and resting places unmarked. The older the child, the more likely that they had an individual grave, that their body had been properly laid out and a full ceremonial had taken place. A study of Irish Bronze Age burials has indicated that the age at which a full adult-type burial might be expected to occur was around 14, although the evidence is not extensive.[12]

Documentary clues to the status of young people in Anglo-Saxon England include terminologies that appear to separate youths from adults; the words

49 A Saxon-period woman, girl and child wearing costume and ornaments associated with different life stages: the child has simple paired dress brooches, a string of beads and bangles; the girl wears a pendant, dress pin, finger-ring, more ornate brooches and beads; the adult woman has complex paired disc brooches and bead strings, a pin, a ring and a 'girdle-hanger' with a set of keys. After N. Stoodley, 2000, figs.1, 2 and 3

cnapa (the original version of the modern word knave) seems to refer to people of junior status and cniht (later knight) refers to a warrior, but several references show that a child may be a cniht. One text describes Hannibal thus at the age of nine, and Bede refers to Osred as a cniht at the age of eight when he became king of Northumbria. A ten-year-old thief is also a cniht in the laws of King Ine of Wessex. The finds of spears in the graves of boys may represent not only a symbol of their gender, but also a reflection of the possibility that boys had a recognised role in warfare, despite their youth. Military training in the medieval period started from the age of about six, and the example of modern child soldiers reminds us that they are often a potent and effective fighting force. 'The presence of shields and spears in the graves of Anglo-Saxon teenagers cannot be taken as an empty token in the burial ritual, nor as a sign of adult imposition of non-child-related symbols, nor may these burials be taken as proof that weapons were not necessarily buried with warriors'.[13] In Merovingian France, ceremony attended the presentation of manly arms to a young man; the change from boyhood to adulthood was also marked by cutting of the hair (worn long in childhood) or the first shave, often carried out in front of other family members and neighbours. This rite generally occurred somewhere between the ages of 12 and 15. That the hair was considered an important feature of childhood is borne out by an article of Salic law, which provided that anyone who cut a boy's hair without his parents' permission was to be fined 45 gold sous.

Less ceremony attended the maturation of girls, who generally did not achieve adult status until their marriage. However, this could be at a very young age, both in France and England. Records include those of Vilithute, married in the late sixth century at the age of 13, and dying in childbed at 16, Segolène, later abbess of Troclar, married at 12 in the mid-seventh century, and 13-year-old Judith who married Edilvulf of Wessex in 856. These early marriages were favoured because it was believed that they prevented the risk of 'corruption' of the girls – the chance that they might lose their virginity before marriage if they were allowed to remain unattached beyond puberty. This attitude reflects the interest in dynastic alliances of the period. A girl's role was to bring a suitable dowry to her husband, and to provide him with heirs; a prospective husband wished to be certain that those heirs were really his own, and the safest way to do that was to marry a pubescent virgin. It is also the case that the age of maximal fertility for females is considered to be between 13 and 18 years.

By the medieval period, the boundaries between different stages of life seem to have become much more blurred. The age of responsibility under criminal law was regarded to be twelve, whilst under canon law and tax laws, it varied between 12 and 14, and a boy could not be called up into the army until he was 16. The age of majority for inheritance purposes varied but was generally older, being 21 for males and unmarried females in London, and younger for girls who married before that age, but this could be set aside for various reasons, such as the need to support other family members. Young people deemed incapable or unready to take on responsibility for their inheritance could find themselves waiting for a considerably longer time. Parents and guardians could make pleas to restrict access to inheritances if they considered their children insufficiently mature and sensible. The only ceremonials attending adulthood were the guild ceremonies at the completion of apprenticeships (for boys only), or marriage.

In Aztec society, the first major ceremony after birth took place at around four years of age. In fact, because the rituals were held every four years, children younger or older than four would be included. The ceremony marked the beginning of the child's process of education. Brought to the temple, rituals included the piercing of the children's ears, followed by a feast for the sponsors of the children, who would normally be unrelated adults, and then a further visit to the temple followed by more drinking and eating. For the first time in their lives, children participated in adult activities such as singing and dancing, the drinking of pulque and the ritual shedding of blood. Following the ceremony, the children would begin their training in the crafts and occupations for which they were destined. Specific costumes and hairstyles were ascribed to each stage of childhood. Children were given a set of adult clothes when they were born, to be set aside until they grew enough to wear them. Toddlers were dressed in just the blouse or shirt appropriate to their gender and status, with a skirt for girls being worn from about four years, and a loincloth for boys by about seven years old. Hair was worn cropped until the age of eleven, after which both sexes wore their hair long until the boys had proved themselves as warriors, when their hairstyles changed according to the number of captives they had taken. The earlobe piercings were extended and increasingly elaborate ear ornaments were worn. These changes are observable in figurines, and in the nature and form of objects accompanying graves.[14]

Inca society also recognised clear stages in the lives of individuals, particularly in the elite classes. One record of this was compiled by Guaman Poma, and was based on Incan census methodology. Perhaps for the sake of symmetry, he divided life into ten stages, illustrated separately for males and females. These stages are listed below (various versions of the list given different age limits to some of the stages):[15]

Stage 1: *awqa-kamayoq* – the warrior *awque-kamayoqpa warmin* – the warrior's wife	Age: 25 (or 33) to 50 Age: 33
Stage 2: *pureq-machu* – the old man who can walk *payakuna* – the old woman	Age: 60 or 70 Age: 50
Stage 3: *roqt'u-machu* – deaf old man *puñoq-paya* – the old woman who sleeps	Age: 80, 100 or 150 Age: 80

Stage 4: people suffering from various disabilities or infirmities	
Stage 5: *sayapayaq* – the helper or companion '*allin zumaq sipaskuna* – beautiful girls of marriageable age	Age: 18 or 20 Age: 13
Stage 6: *maqt'akuna* – adolescent boys *qhoru thazkikuna* – girls with short cut hair	Age: 12, 18 Age: 12, 18
Stage 7: *toqliakoq warmakuna* – children who set snares *pauau pallac* – female gatherer	Age: 9, 12 Age: 9, 12
Stage 8: *pukllakoq warmakuna* – boys who play *pukllakoq warmi wamra* – girls who play	Age: 5, 9 Age: 5, 9
Stage 9: *llullu lloqhaq warmakuna* – crawling boys *lloqhaq warmi wawa* – crawling girls	Age: 1 to 5 Age: 1, 2
Stage 10: *wawa or k'irawpi-kaq* – boy baby in a cradle *llullu wawa warmi k'irkawpi-kaq* – girl baby in a cradle	Age: newborn, 1 month Age: 1–5 months

50 Life stages among the Incas

At about two years old, in stage 9 of Poma's classification, babies were weaned and given their names at a ceremony which also involved cutting of their hair and fingernails, and drinking and dancing by their friends and relatives. After the age of about nine, children began to carry out chores or learn trades. Transition to adulthood was marked by sometimes elaborate ceremony. For girls, the crucial moment was the onset of menstruation, apparently around 13 or 14 years of age. After three days of seclusion and fasting, her mother would wash the girl and dress her in special new clothes. These she would wear whilst serving visiting relatives for several days. Her most important uncle would deliver an address exhorting her to behave well in her future life and then he would bestow her adult name on her, such as Cuyllor (Star), or Ocllo (Pure), names often signifying purity and beauty. One source claimed that girls remained virgins until they were 18, under pain of death, and that for both sexes, poverty and abstinence marked the years from age 18-20 from when they could begin to do chores unaccompanied. It is not until the ripe old age of 25 that they were considered subjects of the empire and registered as such in official records.

Boys' ceremonies took place annually, for those who had reached the age of 14 or so. They would wear a breechclout which their mothers had woven for them, and for sons of the nobility there would be a range of pilgrimages, sacrifices, dances and races. The whole ritual lasted a month, during which time the boys were whipped to encourage them to be brave. They would also receive their adult names. Records list names such as Kusi (Happy), Uturunku (Jaguar) and Yupanki (Honoured) amongst royalty, and Amaru (Snake), Kuntur (Condor) and Waman (Hawk) amongst other Inca youths. At the close of the ceremonies, the boys would receive gifts from their male relatives, who each gave them a swipe with a whip at the same time. Noble boys would then have their ears pierced to wear the earspools that marked their rank.[16] Some sources suggest that boys would not normally marry for some years to come, often not until their mid-twenties, whereas girls tended to be married in their middle teens. The variation in details results from conflicting accounts accredited to various Jesuit annalists and historians, some of whom obtained their data from converted members of their flock, some from general hearsay, and some from interviews with people identified as officials of various types within the Inca administration.

Evidence for recognition of the entry into puberty in ancient Egypt may include some suggestions that male circumcision was part of the process. A scene depicting this event, involving a boy possibly aged around ten or 12, was found in the mastaba (or tomb) of a state official named Ankhmahor at Saqqara. While there are contradictions in records and statues, 'it is evident that in early ages circumcision was possibly general, obligatory for every youth in order to attain social adulthood. That the phallus hieroglyph is depicted as circumcised constitutes an additional indication. In later periods it became voluntary, compulsory only for particular groups such as boys who were to become priests'.[17] Other indications of adulthood in Egypt were the shaving off of the childish sidelock, and possibly the adoption of different forms of dress.

Artefacts associated with initiation rites and ceremonies have been collected by ethnographers from many different historical societies. The stories accompanying these artefacts give some clues to the complexities and forms of ways in which young people have become part of adult society. In Botswana, tswana dolls, which were being made into the early twentieth century, were created by men specially initiated into the craft; heavily decorated with beads in amuletic patterns, these dolls had a number of meanings. They were played with as dolls, the designs protecting the child from evil spirits, and they were also used symbolically by women in a variety of rituals concerned with childbirth, education and initiation of young girls into adult female societies. The Kikuyu people carved small shields from solid wood for the use of boys in initiation ceremonies that involved mock battles. From Zambia come Chokwe Akishi masks, which represent Cikunza, the 'father of masks' or 'father of initiation'. These masks were used in circumcision ceremonies through which boys were separated from the world of women and led into the world of man. The boys, when they approach the age for the ceremony, are taunted with promises that unless they go through the rite, they will be unable to have sex with women or be able to father children. Then Cikunza and other masked 'spirits' come to 'abduct' the boys from their homes and take them to an initiation camp, where they are circumcised and, over the period of a year, are taught the secrets of the men's society. The initiation camp is called 'the place of dying' and represents the location for the death of boyhood and rebirth as a man. Thus in order to become an adult, the boy has to die; childhood is another existence, not part of the experience of being fully human. Without the ethnographic records, the artefacts associated with these ceremonies would be hard to recognise or interpret in their true terms, and this fact poses a challenge for the archaeological recognition of similar items. It is possible that the miniature weapons found in some Anglo-Saxon and other graves might have been used in a similar manner to the Kikuyu initiation shields; the problems of differentiating dolls from cult figurines may disappear if we can regard them in the same manner as the Botswana tswana dolls, serving both purposes at different stages in a child's life.

The presence in caves containing prehistoric art of the footprints of children, and children's handprints amongst other forms of painting, has led some writers to suggest that we are seeing evidence of Palaeolithic rites of passage for young people about to enter adult society. If the cave art found as such sites as Altamira and Lascaux was produced by shamans conducting hunting magic rituals and other sacred activities, it may have been the case that the caves were normally out of bounds for children, and indeed for most adults except on particular ritualistic occasions. Somewhat lurid speculations have been made about the form of the initiation rites that could have taken place – the child being sent through the darkness to find his way to the sacred chamber, the flickering torch light throwing the painting of bulls and horses into sudden life, the beating of drums, and the use of hallucinogenic plants and fungi to create an atmosphere of terror and awe. Of course, it is perfectly possible that this sort of thing did happen in a few times and places, but perhaps rather less spectacularly than some cavern guide-books would like to suggest! Certainly, children did make their way into caves, and sometimes these were very young children. At a number of French Palaeolithic art sites, children's footprints have been seen in the soft sand floors; they are recorded at Chauvet, Pech-Merle, Le Tuc d'Audoubert, Niaux, Le Reseau-Clastres (where three children walking side by side left their footprints in a heap of glacial sand) and elsewhere.[18] Handprints, a common feature of rock art of this period, were made by placing a hand against the rock wall, and then blowing or spitting pigments around the hand, leaving a negative imprint on the surface. Some of these handprints are quite small, and are likely to be those of children, but whether or not their inclusion in the rock art was part of an initiation or rite of passage ceremony is impossible to say.

Much of the possible evidence for recognition of stages of childhood comes from children's graves, and is based on the mortuary treatment, the clothing and the grave goods present in them. We must beware, however, of reading these clues wrongly. Differences between the treatment of children may result from the social status, wealth or aspirations of the parents of the child. Many graves contain no clues whatsoever, but was this due to the social and age status of the child, or to the poverty or beliefs of the parents? Children of richer or more important families would probably have received fuller and more ornate rites when they died. The children of different social groups may have achieved levels of status at varying ages and this may be demonstrated in unrelated ways. We can recognise that poorer children are likely to have 'grown up' faster than their more privileged counterparts, receiving less education and entering the workforce at an earlier stage. In some societies, adulthood was achieved very young; thus in the early Anglo-Saxon period, a ten-year-old was considered to be legally responsible for their own actions, and therefore to some extent at least already adult. On the other hand, a Roman male did not achieve full autonomy until after the death of his father, no matter how old he was. Children are often fully capable of participating in most areas of adult life, given the chance or if necessity forces them to do so, and it is wrong to suppose that modern assumptions about the capabilities and status of children can be used without qualification to try to understand the roles and status of ancient children. At the same time, we must also recognise that the definition of 'child' can vary with the attitudes of each society; we have a modern tendency to pigeonhole young people according to their age, or the level of schooling they have achieved, but:

> … some communities did not regard the rigid adult-child distinction as a valid one to emphasise....It may, in fact, have been more likely that the treatment of individuals was based more on features such as personality or ability, rather than fixed conceptions of biological age groups. The idea of what a 'child' was may have been a far more flexible (possibly even non-existent) concept than we can imagine.[19]

Similarly, the concept of 'adulthood' may have been equally fluid; as we have seen, becoming an adult may be associated with the onset of puberty, but it could be delayed until marriage, or the achievement of parenthood, or the reaching of occupational or economic independence. Full entry into the adult world might depend on gender or status; black slaves in the United States were regarded, and treated, as immature no matter what their age until after the Civil War in the 1860s, and the word 'boy' has remained a pejorative term for a black man among racial bigots until recent times. In the bizarre mindset of such people, black people do not achieve full adult independence and therefore respect. They remain as children, and therefore, as not quite fully human. We rightly regard such attitudes as appalling when applied to racial differences, but it is still not unusual to find children similarly set aside from the human race on the grounds of their age and immaturity, their achievements belittled, their abilities ignored. Of course children lack the knowledge and experience of their elders, but they often exceed adults in certain cognitive realms – the ability to learn, the capacity to remember and order new experiences, and the willingness to think and act in adventurous and innovative ways (often because they do not yet know why they should not do so, but equally often because their view of the constraints accepted by adults is not so fixed). It is dangerous to assume that because children in our society are rather marginalised and thus not quite 'human' in a full sense, they were marginalised in all societies in the past. We need to search actively for evidence of the degree to which children participated in past societies and communities, and overcome modern assumptions about their abilities and agency.

CONCLUSION

Our modern world places a great deal of significance on the health, rights, education and happiness of children. Rightly, we recognise the importance of raising children to become knowledgeable, effective actors in the future. We are concerned with their protection and their development, and we are concerned that each child has the chance to achieve their full potential. In this, we are surely no different, emotionally or rationally, from people in past societies. Why, then, has archaeology so studiously ignored the roles or treatment of children in those societies?

It is generally assumed that the parental bond is one of the most powerful forces in nature; the lioness will defend her cubs, and the cat will always teach her kittens to hunt. We are fascinated by the behaviour of the animal kingdom towards the young, witnessed by the popularity of natural history films and picture books. But oddly, we seem to ignore the natural ancient history of our own species. 'Children remain peripheral and difficult to assimilate into archaeological discussion'.[1] Why should this be the case?

Kathryn Kamp[2] believes that it is our 'ethnocentric construction of childhood as a time of little economic, political or social importance that has blinded us to the need to use it as an analytic category' and she rejects the excuse that evidence of childhood is too ephemeral to be recovered by archaeology, on the grounds that once upon a time, exactly the same rationale was produced for ignoring the presence of women at archaeological sites. We have now managed to produce research agenda that have added vast amounts of data to our understanding of the lives and work of ancient women, simply because we have started to look for it; surely the same is possible for children. It seems somewhat strange at first glance that few of the feminist archaeologists have embraced the notion of the archaeology of childhood. Perhaps, however, it is possible to speculate that it is precisely because of now outmoded and androcentric perceptions of the role of women that this has occurred. When women were considered by previous generations of researchers (and this could be relatively rarely), it was often within a cultural model derived from Victorian ideals of womanhood: women as weak,

51 Children at work – members of the Surrey Young Archaeologists Club excavating at a Roman villa in 1995

women whose primary role was as producers and nurturers of children, but not as powerful actors or producers in the social or economic spheres. Of course, these notions were illusory even in the world of the nineteenth century about women of all but the wealthiest classes, but these ideas seem to be dying hard even now. The 'glass ceiling' is still a reality in many professional spheres, and we are aware that on the whole, women hold fewer positions of power and earn on average less than their male counterparts, despite their higher levels of educational achievement and their greater longevity.

Feminist academics have, perhaps, been unwilling to consider the equivalence of the failure to recognise children in archaeological research with the past lack of attention to female roles, simply because to be seen to be concerned with children would undermine their claims to be recognised as fully equal with their male counterparts. It would, as it were, lump them back together with the little women whose proper place was in the home, rather than at the cutting edge of scientific development. I think, if the reader will forgive the pun, that this is a case of throwing the baby out with the bath water. Fortunately, there is a growing number of male archaeologists who are coming to realise that learning about how children were regarded and treated in the past is an important part of understanding the cultures they study, and there are female archaeologists who have the courage to allow their interest in the way children have contributed to ancient societies to be voiced, without the fear that this will destroy their own credibility as academics. One of archaeology's greatest enemies has always been the present; we have to fight through our own socialisation, education and culture before we can start to understand the past, and that can be surprisingly hard to do. Archaeologists have to unlearn a great deal before they are in a position to start learning properly from their discipline; the profession is aware of this, but every day it has to face a new battle as new finds challenge our beliefs and understanding of people and the world. It is a truism that every site we excavate produces more questions and problems than it does answers, and we often feel, at the end of a dig, that we actually know less than we did before. Bizarrely, it is this very confusion and uncertainty that grips the archaeologist, that turns a normal person into the type of idiot who actually enjoys getting covered with mud, freezing cold and physically exhausted time after time! We are given the opportunity to come to grips with the great questions of human development and change, and to wrestle with a complexity of ideas that few other professions can provide.

In this struggle to come to an understanding of our own history, the lives of children must be an important topic for research. The ways in which this can be achieved are, basically, the same as for any other topic of archaeological interest. 'Direct evidence for children is found in contexts with human remains, skeletons or other organic material intentionally or unintentionally deposited in graves, dwellings, buildings, middens, bogs, lakes or sea. Indirect evidence can be found in archaeological data associated with the time, space and place of daily life, inside and around settlements, habitation camps and work places. Children can be found in every locale in the environment in which they live and die'.[3]

It is in the interpretation of this evidence that the potential for knowledge lies. In this volume, I have attempted a very incomplete and partial collation of the evidence for children's lives in a number of domestic, productive and cultural spheres. In each case, the artefacts and remains, the depictions and documentary details, offer potential for different theories and observations not only about the children themselves, but about their whole societies and environments. For example, it is easy to dismiss playthings at face value – ways to amuse and entertain children. But there is much more to the topic than that. 'Toys and children-specific artefacts (such as cups, clothing, mugs, medicines, school paraphernalia, etc.), when purchased or made for children, represent attempts, made by adults, to suggest and enforce certain norms of behaviour for children based upon their gender, age, socio-economic class and even socio-cultural ideals of beauty'.[4]

What we give children to play with reflects our own interests and values. Many parents object to toy guns and weapons, recognising that their use can reinforce more general violence in adult society. There are concerns among some people about boys playing with dolls because this might affect their adult masculinity, and conversely about girls doing the same because this might restrict their perceptions and aspirations when they grow up. We have ideas about safety and toys undergo strict testing before they can be sold. These ideas might have seemed very foreign to those Tudor parents who allowed their children to play with working models of cannons, complete with real gunpowder! Some parents will choose 'improving' educational toys, while others are happy to indulge their children in anything that keeps them quiet for an hour or two. Some toys are chosen in order to demonstrate the wealth of the parents; many are designed to introduce children to skills and activities that are considered valuable in adult society. So there are toy tool kits and cooking sets, Bob the Builder and nurse outfits, and the like. Other toys are related to physical education and development, another activity highly regarded in our society. We have seen that many past societies have encouraged sports and games – balls, hoops, skipping ropes and yo-yos from ancient Egypt, Greece, Rome and elsewhere have been mentioned. But many toys are made by children themselves, and can reflect their own views and interests. These are often harder to interpret than toys chosen by adults for children – we all know how much more interesting the cardboard box can be than its expensive contents. It can be spaceship or fort, car or house, its possibilities unlimited. So the simple mud toys made by Egyptian children may appear to be simply hippopotamuses or lions, or just lumps of dried clay, but may have represented many other things that only the maker's mind could encompass.

Starting with care of small babies, a study of the archaeology of childhood can lead us into many avenues. Which children were welcomed into the world and which were not suggests interpretations of the stresses faced by societies and demographic balances. We can discern something about gender relationships and values in patterns of selection and care for male and female children respectively, and judge something about a society's ability and willingness to support non-productive members in their treatment of handicapped children. The values attached to children of different sexes and classes can be discerned by the variations in treatment and care meted out to them, and by patterns of infanticide and abandonment. Rituals associated with birth illuminate attitudes to future gender roles within society, and also about the relationship between society and its notions of spirituality. In some societies, the future roles of children are heavily underlined by the way in which they are welcomed into the world, while in others, no assumptions seem to be made during a child's early life. The way children have been fed reflects social organisation in the case of wet nurses, issues about work and fertility when we consider weaning ages, and the way societies have understood or believed in the role of food types. Feeding practices can affect the spacing of births and the availability of the mother for labour, and tell us a great deal about the degree of contact and association between parents and children.

Studies of children's bones and burial offer information about disease and nutrition; children and the elderly are often the first victims of stress in a society, and their bones can aid in mapping the patterns of subsistence success and failure experienced by communities. Children are also frequently particularly selected as victims of warfare or unrest; evidence of violent death of children is a good indicator of hostilities, especially invasion, while long term attritional aggression will tend to affect the general health levels of children particularly strongly.

The forms of burial afforded the bodies of children are particularly informative. Their study can illuminate the degree to which children were accepted as part of their communities, the emotional attachment of their grieving parents, ideas about religion, and demonstrations of wealth and status. Often, the bodies of small children are buried according to a different ritual than that used for older children and adults. They are buried close to or within dwellings rather than in outside cemeteries, perhaps as a desire to continue to offer care and proximity, perhaps in order to retain the fertile power of the baby, or to avoid the costs of repeated rituals when infant mortality levels are high. The forms of burial and the grave goods accompanying the child display affection, or status, or wealth, or demonstrations of social norms, in ways that cannot result from the attainment or power of the individual. Child burials can demonstrate the existence of inheritance systems and class hierarchies in a more unequivocal manner than those of adults. They can also signal changes in cultural or religious attitudes, such as the gradual effect of Christianity on the population of late Roman Britain revealed in the inclusion of child burials in general cemeteries.

The use of children for sacrifice demonstrates more information about human values and social stresses. In most societies where this has been practised, the sacrifice of the child is the ultimate expression of need, fear or devotion within the community, demonstrated by the use of substitute victims when available.

The need to care for, educate and raise children has had a fundamental effect on the development of our species. The premature birth of the human infant has been instrumental not only in the physiological form of both women and children, but in our patterns of emotional and rational thought. Language, bipedalism and social behaviour have all been modified as a result of our need to protect and teach our young for far longer than other mammalian species. The infant child may also have been the cause of important forms of practical invention, from which much of the rest of our technologies have developed.

The forms of education, formal or informal, given to children demonstrate the perceived needs of their societies and sectors within them. Practical, cognitive and artistic skills have been differentially stressed at different times and in different places, reflecting the values and expectations of cultures. It is worth remembering that children tend to learn as much from each other as they do from adults in many situations, as ethnographic evidence has shown, and these observed behaviours may help to reinterpret some forms of archaeological data to reflect the activities of youngsters otherwise invisible in the material evidence recovered from sites.

The role of children as economic actors is of particular significance. Modern views of children tend to stress their roles as recipients of production, but even today millions of children are regular participants in subsistence, craft and industrial production. In the vast majority of incidences, the labour of children in simply an accepted part of family or community activities. They start by carrying out simple chores, and progress through stages of responsibility and skill until almost seamlessly they become part of the adult world. When we speak of prehistoric hunting and gathering, or early farming, we must recognise that the contribution of children to the labour was integral and probably essential. Reconstructions of these societies must include children not as carefree attendants, but as equal partners in the general effort. Where other forms of subsistence are required, involving absence from the home for the adults, the labour of children in domestic chores and the care of younger siblings may be essential to enable their parents to earn enough to support the family, as it is in much of the Third World today. Children may also be employed precisely because they are children in more formal labour – because of their size, their dexterity, their cheapness, their tractability or their expendability. The economic role of children is often vital to the survival of a people today. How much more so is this likely to have been the case in the past?

In so many ways, the study of an archaeology of childhood can be as vital as that of the archaeology of women, or indeed archaeology in general, for an understanding of the development of the human species, its cultures, societies and technologies. It is surely time to call for the development of research agendas that recognise this fact, and that actively seek to remedy the exclusion or invisibility of children from so much of the archaeological record.

NOTES

INTRODUCTION

1 Sofaer Deverenski, J., 1994 'Where are the children? Accessing children in the past', *Archaeological Review from Cambridge*, 13(2), 7-18; Kamp, K.A., 2001 'Where have all the children gone? The archaeology of childhood', *Journal of Archaeological Method and Theory* **8**(1), 1-34

2 Kamp, 2001:2

3 Ehrenberg, M., 1989 *Women in Prehistory*, London: British Museum Press

4 Sofaer Deverenski, J., 1997 'Engendering children, engendering archeology' in Moore, J. & Scott, E. (eds), *Invisible People and Processes: Writing Gender and Childhood into European Archaeology*, London and New York: Leicester University Press, 192-202

5 Kamp, 2001:27

CHAPTER ONE: LITTLE DARLINGS — THE CHERISHED CHILD IN THE PAST

1 Scott, E., 1999 *The Archaeology of Infancy and Infant Death*, British Archaeological Reports International Series 819, p.2

2 Scott, 1999:62

3 Shahar, S.,1990 *Childhood in the Middle Ages*, London and New York: Routledge, p.45

4 Sanctii Augustini Confessionum Libri XIII, L. Verheijen (ed.) (Corpus Christianorum Series Latina, Turnhout, 1981) Vol.27:6

5 Scott, 1999:63-4

6 Rawcliffe, C., 2003 'Women, childbirth and Religion in Late Medieval England' in Wood, D. (ed.) *Women and Religion in Late Medieval England*, Oxford: Oxbow, 90-117, p.92

7 Rawcliffe, 2003:103

8 Rawcliffe, 2003:95

9 CIL.4.294, 8149, tr. J-A Shelton

10 Scott, 1999:1

11 Crawford, S. 1991 *Childhood in Anglo-Saxon England*, Stroud: Sutton

12 Gies, F. & Gies, J., 1987 *Marriage and the Family in the Middle Ages*, London: Harper & Row, p.198

13 Scott, 1999:63

14 Coe, M.D., 1993 (5th edn.) *The Maya*, London: Thames & Hudson

15 The Lewis and Clark Journey of Discovery website, http://www.upos.gov/jeff/LewisClark2/Timelines/1805/1805Timeline.htm (accessed 12.04.04)

16 Burch, C., 1956 'The Indigenous Indians of the Lower Trinity Area', *Southwestern Historical Quarterly*, p.42

17 Burch, E.S., 1988 *The Eskimos*, Norman, Oklahoma: University of Oklahoma Press, p.90

18 Hillman, G.C., 1989 'Late Paleolithic plant foods from Wadi Kubbaniya in Upper Egypt: dietary diversity, infant weaning and seasonality in a riverine environment' in Harris, D.R. & Hillman, G.C. (eds) *Foraging and Farming*, London: Unwin Hyman, 207-239

19 Jay, M., 2004 quoted in Binns, A., 'Why breast may not have been best for Iron Age babies', *Yorkshire Post*

20 Dettwyler, K.A., 1995 'A time to wean: the hominid blueprint for the natural age of weaning in modern human populations' in Stuart-Macadam, P. & Dettwyler, K.A., (eds) *Breastfeeding: biocultural perspectives*, New York: Aldina de Gruyter, 39-73

21 Mays, S.A., Richards, M.P. & Fuller, B.T., 2002 'Bone stable isotope evidence for infant feeding in Medieval England' *Antiquity* **76**: 654-6

22 Orme, 2003:60

23 Janssen, R.M. & Janssen, J.J., 1990 *Growing Up in Ancient Egypt*, London: Rubicon Press, p.26

24 Janssen & Janssen, 1990:34

25 Carter, H., (Walker, P.J., 1954) *The Tomb of Tutankhamen*, London: BCA, pp.76-7

26 Bonnichsen, R., 1973 'Millie's Camp: an experiment in archaeology', *World Archaeology* **4**(3), 277-306

27 Wilkie, L., 2000 'Not merely child's play: Creating a historical archaeology of children and childhood' in Deverenski, (ed.), 100-113, p.102

28 Turek, J., 'Being a Beaker child: The position of children in Late Eneolithic society', http://www.kar.zcu.cz/texty/Deti/deti.hym (accessed 19/05/03)

29 Park, R.W., 1998 'Size counts: the miniature archaeology of childhood in Inuit societies', *Antiquity* **72**, 269-281

30 Rasmussen, K., 1931 *The Netsilik Eskimos: social life and spiritual culture. Report of the Fifth Thule Expedition 1921-24*, 8, 1-2, Copenhagen: Gyldendalske Boghandel, Nordisk Forlag, p.507

31 Park, 1998:276

32 Bellessort, M-N., 1992 'Le Jeu de Serpent' *Les Dossiers d'Archéologie* **168**: 8-9

33 CIL VI. 10078; Durand, A., 1992, 'Jeux et Jouets de l'enfance en Grèce et à Rome' *Les Dossiers d'Archéologie* **168**: 10-17

34 Manson, M., 1992 'Les Poupées Antiques', *Les Dossiers d'Archéologie* **168**: 48-57

35 Wilkie, L., 2000 'Not merely child's play: Creating a historical archaeology of children and childhood' in Deverenski, (ed.), 100-113, p.101

36 MS Bodley 264/fol. 112, Bodleian Library, Oxford

37 Egan, G., 1998 'Miniature toys of medieval childhood', *British Archaeology* **35**, 10-11

CHAPTER TWO: EDUCATION AND WORK

1 Janssen, R.M. & Janssen, J.J., 1990 *Growing up in Ancient Egypt*, London: Rubicon Press, p.76

2 Herring, A., 2002 'Coming of Age in Ancient Greece – Topic: Education', Hood Museum

3 Werner, P. 1986 (tr. D, Macrae) *Life in Greece in Ancient Times*, Minerva

4 Horace, *Satires* I.6.xi.70-90

5 Martial, *Epigrams*, X.62

6 Orme, 2003:242

7 Leyser, H., 'Women and the Word of God', in Wood, D., (ed.) 2003 *Women and Religion in Medieval England*, Oxford: Oxbow, (32-45) p.36

8 Orme, 2003: 244-5

9 Orme, 2003:144

10 Orme, 2003:270

11 Quoted in Alexandre-Bidon, D. & Lett, D., (tr. J. Gladding), 1999 *Children in the Middle Ages*, Notre Dame, Indiana: University of Notre Dame Press, p.119

12 Alexandre-Bidon & Lett, 1999: 127

13 Blurton-Jones, N., 1993 'The lives of hunter-gatherer children: Effects of parental behaviour and parental reproductive strategy' in Pereira, M.A. & Fairbanks, L.A. (eds) *Juvenile Primates: Life History, Development and Behaviour*, New York & Oxford: Oxford University Press, 309-326, pp.316-7

14 Blurton-Jones, 1993: 315

15 Heywood, C., 2001 *A History of Childhood: Children and Childhood in the West from Medieval to Modern Times*, Cambridge: Polity, p.123

16 Heywood, 2001:124
17 Kamp K.A., 2001 'Where have all the children gone?: The Archaeology of Childhood' *Journal of Archaeological Method and Theory* **8**(1):1-34, pp.16-17, citing United Nations Development Programme 1995 *Human Development Report 1995*, New York, Oxford University Press; Rivera, R.L.K., 1986 'Children at work: The labor scene through the eyes of Filipino children', *International Sociology* **33**:11-17; Sancho-Liao, N., 1994 'Child labour in the Philippines: Exploitation in the process of globalisation of the economy, *Labour, Capital and Society* **27**(2):270-281; Gulranjani, M., 1994 'Child labour and the export sector in the third world: A case of the Indian carpet industry', *Labour, Capital and Society* **27**(2):192-214; Mehra-Kerpelman, K., 1996 'Children at work: How many and where?' *World at Work: The Magazine of the ILO*, 15:8-9
18 Bird, D. & Bird, R.B., 2000 'The Ethnoarchaeology of Juvenile Foragers: Shellfishing Strategies among Meriam Children', *Journal of Anthropological Archaeology* **19**, 461-476, p.464
19 Grimm, L., 'Apprentice flintknapping: relating material culture and social practice in the Upper Paleolithic', in Sofaer Deverenski, (ed.) 2000, *Children and Material Culture*, 53-71
20 Quoted in Finlay, N., 1997 'Kid knapping: the missing child in lithic analysis' in Moore, J. & Scott, E. (eds) *Invisible People and Processes: Writing Gender and Childhood into European Archaeology*, London and New York: Leicester University Press, 203-12
21 Kamp, K.A., Timmerman, N., Lind, G., Graybill, J. & Natowsky, I., 1999 *Discovering Childhood: Using fingerprints to find children in the archaeological record*, *American Antiquity* **64**(2): 309-315, p.314
22 Quoted by Davis, M.L., 1998 'Ideology and Reality: A clash between society's perceptions of childhood in Ancient Rome and Ancient Athens': http://www.edu/CAS/classical_studies.html (accessed 4/25/02)
23 Booth, C., 1886 'On Occupations of the People of the United Kingdom, 1801-81', *Journal of the Royal Statistical Society* 49

CHAPTER THREE: PARENTS, CHILDREN AND DEATH

1 Bahn, P., 1996 *Tombs, Graves and Mummies*, London: Weidenfeld & Nicolson
2 Harrington, S.P.M., 1999 'Early Portuguese Burial' *Archaeology* **52** (2) March/April
3 Gambier, D., 1995 'Pratiques Funeraires au Paleolithique Superieur – l'Exemple de la Sepulture des Enfants de la Grotte des Enfants (Site de Grimaldi-Italie) in Otté, M. (ed.), *Nature et Culture, Colloque de Liège (13-17 Decembre, 1993)*, Liège E.R.A.U.L. **86**:811-831, p.813
4 Gopher, A., 1995 'Infant Burials in the Neolithic Period in the Southern Levant – Israel: a Social View' in Otte, M., (ed.) *Nature et Cultures, Colloque de Liège (13-17 décembre 1993)*, Liège, E.R.A.U.L 68, 913-918
5 After Richards, J., 1991 *Stonehenge*, London: EH/Batsford, pp.116-7
6 *British Archaeology*, **10**, December 1995
7 Richards, J., 1991, pp.116-7
8 Thomas, J. & Whittle, A., 1986 'Anatomy of a tomb – West Kennet revisited', *Oxford Journal of Archaeology* **5**(2):133
9 Thorpe, I.J., 1996 *The Origins of Agriculture in Europe London*: Routledge, p.80
10 Scott., 1999:100
11 Hodder, I., 1990 *The Domestication of Europe*, Oxford: Blackwell, p.37
12 Whittle A., 1996 *Europe in the Neolithic. The creation of new worlds.* Cambridge World Archaeology. Cambridge: CUP, p.167
13 Becker, M.J., 1995 'Infanticide, child sacrifice and infant mortality rates: direct archaeological evidence as interpreted by human skeletal analysis' *Old World Archaeology Newsletter* **XVIII**(2), 24-31; 1997 'Perinatal burial patterns as cultural markers in peninsular Italy' unpublished paper abstract, p.24
14 Meskell, L., 1994 'Dying Young: the Experience of Death at Deir el-Medina', *Archaeological Review from Cambridge* **13**(2), 35-45
15 Dabrowski, J., 1989 'The social structures of the Lusatian culture population at the transition of the Bronze and Iron Ages', in Stig Sørensen, M.L. & Thomas, R. (eds) *The Bronze Age-Iron Age Transition in Europe – Aspects of continuity and change in European societies c 1200-500BC*, Oxford: British Archaeological Report International Series 483 (ii), 408-429, p.411

16 Collis, J., 1977 'Owslebury (Hants) and the problem of burials on rural settlement' in Reece, R. (ed.) *Burial in the Roman world*, CBA ResRep 22, London: CBA, pp.26-35

17 Scott, 1999:116

18 Tertullian, *De Anima* 57

19 Soren, D., 1996 'Malaria, witchcraft and a late Roman infant cemetery near Lugnano in Teverina, Italy' *Journal of Osteo-Archaeology*, London: University of London

20 Evison, V.I, 1987 *Dover: The Buckland Anglo-Saxon Cemetery* HBMC Report 3, London: HBMC, 146, cited by Crawford, S, 1991 'When do Anglo-Saxon children count?' *Journal of Theoretical Archaeology* **2**, Oxford: Oxbow:20-1

21 Crawford, S., 1993 'Children, Death and the After-life' In: Filmer-Sankey, W. (ed.) *Anglo-Saxon Studies in Archaeology and History* **6**:83-91; Molleson, T., 1991 'Demographic implications of age structure of Early English cemetery samples', *Actes des Journees Anthropologiques* **5**:113-121

22 Buckberry, Jo, accessed 2003 'Missing, Presumed Buried? Bone Diagenesis and the Under-Representation of Anglo-Saxon Children': http://www.shef.ac.uk/assem/5/buckberr.html

23 Crawford, 1999:28

24 Crawford, 1999:143

25 Knol, E., 1987 'Knucklebones in Urns: Playful Grave-goods in Early Medieval Friesland', *Helinium* **XXVII**, 280-28

26 Halsall, G 1992 'Social change around AD 600: an Austrasian perceptive' in Carver, M (ed.) *The Age of Sutton Hoo*, Woodbridge: Boydell Press, 265-78

27 Binski, P., 1996 *Medieval Death: Ritual and Representation*, London: British Museum Press, p.106

28 Ibid.

29 Oxyrhynchus Papyrii 744n(Select Papyri 105), tr. J-A Shelton, 1988

30 Gunnlaugs Saga, chap.5; cited by Wicker, N. 1998 'Selective female infanticide as partial explanation for the dearth of women in Viking Age Scandinavia' in Halsall, G. (ed.), *Violence and Society in the Early Medieval West. Private, public and ritual*, Woodbridge, Boydell Press, 205-222, p.205

31 Rega, E., 1997 'Age, gender and biological reality in the Early Bronze Age cemetery at Mokrin' in Moore, J. & Scott, E. (eds) *Invisible People and Processes: writing gender and childhood into European archaeology*, London: Cassell/Leicester UP, 229-247

32 Smith, P & Kahila, G., 1992 'Identification of infanticide in archaeological sites: a case study from the Late Roman-Early Byzantine periods at Ashkelon, Israel' *Journal of Archaeological Science* **19**, 667-75

33 Heneage Cocks, A., 1921 'A Romano-British homestead in the Hambleden Valley, Bucks' *Archaeologia* **71**:150

34 Johnston, D.E., 1983 (2nd ed) *Roman Villas*, Princes Risborough: Shire, 11; Mays S 1993, 'Infanticide in Roman Britain' *Antiquity* **67**:883-888, p.887

35 Scott, E., 1991 'Animal and infant burials in Romano-British villas: a revitaliation movement' in Garwood, P. *et al* (eds), *Sacred and Profane*, OUCA Monograph 32, Oxford: Oxbow, 117-118,; Scott, E. 1988 'Aspects of the Roman Villa as a Form of British settlement', PhD Thesis, University of Newcastle upon Tyne:192-286

36 Scott, 1991

37 Alvarez-Sanchez, J., 2000 'The Iron Age in Western Spain (800 BC-AD 50); an overview' *Oxford Journal of Archaeology* **19**(1): 65-89

38 Pearce, J., 1997 'Constructions of infancy – aspects of the mortuary rituals for infants and children in late Iron Age and Roman Britain' Paper presented to TAG Conference, University of Bournemouth

39 Crawford, S., 1991 'Age Differentiation and related social status – a study of Anglo-Saxon childhood', PhD Thesis, University of Oxford

40 Lee, K.A., 1994 'Attitudes and prejudices towards infanticide: Carthage, Rome and today' *Archaeological Review from Cambridge* **13**:2, published in 1996 for 1994

CHAPTER FOUR: THE DIVINE CHILD

1 Taylor, T., 2002 *The Buried Soul: How Humans Invented Death*, London: Fourth Estate especially pp.8-10

2 The Times, 3 March 2004 'Witch doctors cause rise in child sacrifices' by C. Philp

3 Barber, J., Halstead, P., James, H. & Lee, F., 1989 'An unusual Iron Age burial at Hornish Point, South Uist' *Antiquity* **63**: 773-778

4 Hartley, B.R., 1957 'The Wandlebury Iron Age Hill-Fort: Excavations of 1955-56' *Proceedings of the Cambridgeshire Antiquarian Society* **50**:1-27, p.15

5 Cunliffe, B., 1991 *Iron Age Communities in Britain*, 2nd ed., London, Routledge, p.572

6 Woodward, A., 1992 *Shrines and sacrifices*, London: Batsford pp.18 and 85

7 Merrifield, R., 1987 *The Archaeology of Ritual and Magic*, London: Batsford, pp.51-2

8 Niblett, R., 1999 *The Excavation of a Ceremonial Site at Folly Lane, Verulamium*, London: Britannia Monograph Series No. 14/Society for the Promotion of Roman Studies

9 Isserlin, R.M.T., 1997 'Thinking the unthinkable: Human sacrifice in Roman Britain' *Proceedings of the Sixth Annual Theoretical Roman Archaeology Conference*, Oxford: Oxbow

10 Penn, W.S., 1960 'Springhead: Temples III and IV' *Archaeologia Cantiaca* **74**, pp.121-2

11 Watts, D.J., 1989 'Infant Burials and Romano-British Christianity', *Archaeological Journal*, **146**: 373-383

12 Scott, E., 1991 'Animal and Infant Burials in Romano-British Villas: A revitalization movement' in Garwood, P., Jennings, D., Skeates, R. & Toms, J., (eds) *Sacred and Profane: Proceedings of a Conference on Archaeology, Ritual and Religion*, Oxford, 1989, Oxford University Committee for Archaeology, 115-121, p.118

13 Benson, E.P., 2001 'Why Sacrifice?' in Benson, E.P. & Cook, A.G. (eds), *Ritual Sacrifice in Ancient Peru*, Austin: University of Texas Press, 1-20

14 Bourget, S., 2001 'Children and ancestors: Ritual practices at the Moche site of Huaca de le Luna, North Coast of Peru' in Benson, E.P. & Cook, A.G., (eds) *Ritual Sacrifice in Ancient Peru*, Austin: University of Texas Press, 93-118

15 de Vaux, R., 1964 *Studies in Old Testament Sacrifice*, Cardiff: University of Wales Press, p.60

16 Dio Cassius *Roman History* XXXVII.30.3, tr. Cary, 1914:149

17 Brown, S., 1991 *Late Carthaginian Child Sacrifice and Sacrificial Monuments in their Mediterranean Context*, Sheffield: Sheffield Academic Press/JSOT Press

18 Diodorus Siculus *Library of History* XX, xiv, 4-6

19 Plutarch, *De Superstitione* Xiii, 171d

20 Terullan, *Apologeticus* IX, 2-4

21 Stager, L.E. 1980 'The rite of child sacrifice at Carthage' in Pedley, J.G. (ed.) *New Light on Ancient Carthage*, Ann Arbor: University of Michigan Press, 1-11

22 Lee, A., 1994 'Attitudes and prejudices towards infanticide: Carthage, Rome and today' *Archaeological Review from Cambridge* **13**(2): 65-79, p.75

23 Brown, S., 1991 *Late Carthaginian Child Sacrifice and Sacrificial Monuments in their Mediterranean Context*, Sheffield: Sheffield Academic Press, p.171

24 Pausanius, *Description of Greece*, X.22.3

25 Sillar, B., 1974 'Playing with God: cultural perceptions of children, play and miniatures in the Andes', *Archaeological Review from Cambridge* **13**(2): 47-64

26 Skeates, R., 1991 'Caves, Cults and Children in Neolithic Abruzzo, Central Italy' in Garwood, P., Jennings, D., Skeates, R. & Toms, J. (eds) *Sacred and Profance: Proceedings of a Conference on Archaeology, Ritual and Religion*, Oxford, 1989, Oxford University Committee for Archaeology, 122-134, p.127

27 Ó Flóinn, R., 1995 'Recent Research into Irish Bog Bodies' in Turner, R.C. & Scaife, R.G., (eds) *Bog Bodies: New Discoveries and New Perspectives*, London: British Museum Press

28 See Glob, P.V., 1969, *The Bog People*, London: Faber & Faber, pp.114-6; van der Sanden, W.A.B., 1996 *Through Nature to Eternity: the Bog Bodies of Northwest Europe*, Amsterdam: Batavian Lion International, p.98

29 Vitebsky, P., 1995 *The Shaman*, London: Macmillan, p.146

30 Information on relics available at http://members.lycos.co.uk/jloughlan/sec1_012.htm

31 *The Times*, 2004 'Living goddess on strike over fees' by M. Browne

31 Quirke, S. & Spencer, J., (eds) 1992 *The British Museum Book of Ancient Egypt*, London: British Museum Press, p.25

CHAPTER FIVE: SUFFER THE LITTLE CHILDREN

1 *The Times*, Tuesday 8 July, 2003

2 Makkay, J., 2000 *An early war: The Late Neolithic mass grave from Esztetrgályhorváti*, Budapest: Makkay

3 Zimmerman, L.J. 1997 'The Crow Creek Massacre: Archaeology and Prehistoric Plains Warfare in Contemporary Contexts' pp.75-94

4 Schmidt, S. 1998 *The Rwandan Genocide – Statistics of a Mass Grave – The Kibuye Case*, http://garnet.acns.fsu.edu/~sss4407/Rwanda/RWStats.htm (accessed 23 May 2002)

5 UN Truth Commission, 1992 *Report of Forensic Investigation, El Mozote, El Salvador 10 December 1992 to the Members of the United Nations Truth Commission.* http://www.parascope.com/articles/0197/el_mozdocb.htm (accessed 23 May 2002)

6 Van Lier, P., *Excavation of Mass Grave, Dos Erres, El Petén, June 1995*, http://www.peacebrigades.org/guatemala/cap-piet05.html (accessed 23 May 2002)

7 Frayer, D.W., 1997 'Ofnet: Evidence for a Mesolithic Massacre' in Martin, D.L. & Frayer, D.W. (eds) *Troubled Times: Violence and Warfare in the Past*, Amsterdam: Gordon & Breach

8 Frayer, 1997:205

9 Frayer, 1997:207

10 As suggested by Thorpe, I.J., 2000 *Fighting and Feuding in Neolithic and Bronze Age Britain*, Paper – War and Society Group Meeting 29/4/2000, Winchester: King Alfred's College

11 Meggitt, M., 1977 Blood is their argument, Palo Alto, California: Mayfield, p.12

12 T. Masland, 2002 'Voices of the children – 'We beat and killed people....' *Newsweek*, May 2002 (quoted in Stohl, 2002)

13 Becker, J., Presentation at 20 March 2001 Workshop, quoted by R.J. Stohl, 2002 'Under the Gun – Children and Small Arms', *African Security Review*, 11(3)

14 Stinson, S., 2003 *Diet and Child Nutritional Status*, CUNY, www.cast.uark.edu/local/icaes/ conferences /wburg/ posters/sara_stinson/stinson.html (accessed 03/12/03)

15 Roberts, C. & Cox, M., 2003 *Health and Disease in Britain from Prehistory to the Present Day*, Stroud: Sutton, p.75

16 Hadjouis, D., 2003 'Traces de Maladies Protohistoriques', *Archeologia* **406**, 42-49

17 Roberts & Cox, 2003:130

18 Fleming, R., 2003 'Mute witness: Ancient Britons took the story of Rome's rise and fall to the grave', *Boston College Magazine*, Spring Issue, www.bc.edu/publications/bcm/spring_2003/ ft_mute.html (accessed 26/11/03)

19 Hagen, A., 1998 edn., *A Handbook of Anglo-Saxon Food Processing and Consumption*, Hockwold-cum-Wilton: Anglo-Saxon Books, who cites Bonser, W., 1963 *The Medical Background of Anglo-Saxon England*, Wellcome Historical Medical Library, p.86, Whitelock, D., 1955 *The Will of Aethelgyfu*, New Collection Roxburghe Clun, p.209 and Walford, C., 1879 *The Famines of the World Past and Present*, Statistical Society of London, p.6 among many others

20 Alexandre-Bidon, D. & Lett, D., (tr. J. Gladding), 1999 *Children in the Middle Ages*, Notre-Dame, Indiana: University of Notre Dame Press, p.35

21 Werner, A., 1998 *London Bodies*, London: Museum of London, p.17

22 *The Times*, September 2002

23 Roberts & Cox, 2003:298

24 Roberts, C. & Manchester, K., 1997 *The Archaeology of Disease*, Stroud: Sutton, p.174

25 Goodman, A.H. & Armelagos, G.J., 1989 'Infant and childhood morbidity and mortality risks in archaeological populations' *World Archaeology* **21**(2): 225-243

26 Goodman & Armelagos, 1989:233

27 Piontek, J., Jerszynska, B. & Segeda, S., 2001 'Long Bones Growth Variation among Prehistoric Agricultural and Pastoral Populations from Ukraine (Bronze Era to Iron Age)', *Variability and Evolution* **9**, 61-73

28 *The Times*, 17 September 2003 'Land where a child is a commodity, not a gift', by Janine di Giovanni

29 Marcus Terentius Varro, *Agriculture*, 1, 17

30 Dio Chrysostom 'On Freedom 2 – 15.8: Slavery and Freedom' tr. J.W. Cohoon & H.L. Crosby (5 vols., Loeb, 1932-51)

31 Seneca, *An Essay About Anger*, 2.21.1-6

32 Davis, M.L., 1998 'Ideology and Reality – A clash between society's perceptions of childhood in Ancient Rome and Ancient Athens', www.wm.edu/CAS/classical_studies/wehutt/150Wp/MLDAVI.HTML (accessed 25 April 2002)

33 Horn, P., 1994 *Children's Work and Welfare, 1780-1880s*, London: Macmillan, p.31

CHAPTER SIX: BECOMING HUMAN

1 Morgan, E., 1994 *The Descent of the Child: Human Evolution from a New Perspective*, London: Souvenir Press, p.23

2 Ehrenberg, M., 1989 *Women in Prehistory*, London: British Museum; Taylor, T., 1996 *The Prehistory of Sex: Four million years of human sexual culture*, London: Fourth Estate

3 Taylor, T., 1996 *The Prehistory of Sex: Four million years of human sexual culture*, London: Fourth Estate, p.46

4 Bower, B., 1999 'Human Growth Displays Ancient Roots', *Science News Online*, 155(14) (3 April), www.sciencemews.org/sn_arc99 (accessed 25 April 2002)

5 Hawcroft, J. & Dennell, R., 2000 'Neanderthal cognitive life history and its implications for material culture', in Sofaer Deverenski (ed.), pp.89-99, p.92

6 Pereira, M.A., 1993 'Juvenility in Animals' in Pereira, M.A. & Fairbanks, L.A., (eds) *Juvenile Primates: Life History, Development and Behaviour*, New York & London: Oxford University Press, 17-27, p.21

7 Scott, E., 1999 *The Archaeology of Infancy and Infant Death*, Oxford: British Archaeological Reports International Series 819, p.46

8 Henderson, M., 2004 'Why boys ape about and girls learn lessons', *The Times*, 15 April 2004

9 Beaumont, L.A., 1994, 'Constructing a Methodology for the Interpretation of Childhood Age in Classical Athenian Iconography', *Archaeological Review from Cambridge*, 13(2): 81-96

10 Serwint, N., 1993 'Female athletic costume at the Heraia and prenuptial initiation rites', *American Journal of Archaeology*, 97(3): 403-422

11 Stoodley, N., 2000 'From the cradle to the grave: age organization and the early Anglo-Saxon burial rite', *World Archaeology*, 31(3), 456-472, p.459

12 Ó Donnabháin, B. & Brindley, A.L., 1989/90 'The Status of Children in a Sample of Bronze Age Burials containing Pygmy Cups', *The Journal of Irish Archaeology*, V, 19-24

13 Crawford, S., 1999 *Childhood in Anglo-Saxon England*, Stroud: Sutton, p.163

14 Joyce, R.A., 2000 'Girling the girl and boying the boy: the production of adulthood in ancient Mesoamerica', *World Archaeology* 31(3): 473-83

15 Based on D'Altroy, T.N., 2002 *The Incas*, Malden, Mass. & Oxford: Blackwell, Table 8.2, pp.184-5).

16 D'Altroy, 2002

17 Janssen, R.M. & Janssen, J.J., 1990 *Growing Up in Ancient Egypt*, London: Rubicon Press, p.97

18 Clottes, J. 2002 'Paleolithic Art in France', *Adorant Magazine*, www.bradshawfoundation.com/clottes, (accessed 24 Februrary 2004)

19 Lucy, S., 1994, 'Children in Early Medieval Cemeteries', *Archaeological Review from Cambridge*, 13(2): 21-34, p.29

CONCLUSION

1 Lillehammer, G., 2000 'The world of children' in Sofaer Deverenski, (ed.) 1-26, p.17

2 Kamp, K.A., 2001 'Where have all the children gone?: The Archaeology of Childhood', *Journal of Archaeological Method and Theory*, 8(1), 1-34, p.2

3 Lillehammer, G., 2000, p.21

4 Wilkie, L., 2000 'Not merely child's play: Creating a historical archaeology of children and childhood' in Sofaer Deverenski (ed.), 100-113, p.100

INDEX

If you are interested in purchasing other books published by Tempus,
or in case you have difficulty finding any Tempus books in your local bookshop,
you can also place orders directly through our website

www.tempus-publishing.com